330.956102

SALE 1996

Com

The definition of a peripheral economy: Turkey 1923–1929

Studies in modern capitalism · Etudes sur le capitalisme moderne

This series is devoted to an attempt to comprehend capitalism as a world-system.
It will include monographs, collections of essays and colloquia around specific
themes, written by historians and social scientists united by a common concern for
the study of large-scale long-term social structure and social change.
    The series is a joint enterprise of the Maison des Sciences de l'Homme in Paris
and the Fernand Braudel Center for the Study of Economies, Historical Systems,
and Civilizations at the State University of New York at Binghamton.

Other books in the series
Immanuel Wallerstein: *The capitalist world-economy*
Pierre Bourdieu: *Algeria 1960*
Andre Gunder Frank: *Mexican agriculture 1521–1630*
Folker Fröbel, Jürgen Heinrichs, Otto Kreye: *The new international division of labour*
Henri H. Stahl: *Traditional Romanian village communities*

This book is published as part of the joint publishing agreement established in
1977 between the Fondation de la Maison des Sciences de l'Homme and the Press
Syndicate of the University of Cambridge. Titles published under this arrangement may appear in any European language or, in the case of volumes of collected
essays, in several languages.
    New books will appear either as individual titles or in one of the series which the
Maison des Sciences de l'Homme and the Cambridge University Press have
jointly agreed to publish. All books published jointly by the Maison des Sciences
de l'Homme and the Cambridge University Press will be distributed by the Press
throughout the world.

The definition of
a peripheral economy:
Turkey 1923–1929

CAGLAR KEYDER

Cambridge University Press

Cambridge
London New York New Rochelle Melbourne Sydney

& Editions de la Maison des Sciences de l'Homme

Paris

Published by the Press Syndicate of the University of Cambridge
The Pitt Building, Trumpington Street, Cambridge CB2 1RP
32 East 57th Street, New York, NY 10022, USA
296 Beaconsfield Parade, Middle Park, Melbourne 3206, Australia
and Editions de la Maison des Sciences de l'Homme
54 Boulevard Raspail, 75270 Paris Cedex 06

British Library Cataloguing in Publication Data

Keyder, Caglar
The definition of a peripheral economy.
– (Studies in modern capitalism).
1. Turkey – Economic conditions – 1918–1960
I. Title   II. Series
330.9561′024   HC492   80–41829

ISBN 0 521 23699 1

Contents

vi   Contents

Preface and acknowledgements

This book, as will be evident to the reader, was originally a dissertation. When I first started working on Turkey, I wanted to study the etatist period of the 1930s. This period with its autarkic economic policy seemed attractive especially from the third-worldist perspectives of the 1960s. As I worked my way up from the Ottoman period to the 1930s though, I was detracted both by ideological estrangement from 'non-capitalist', nationalist models of development, and by the concerns of a different paradigm leading to a new set of research objectives. The 1920s seemed propitious from the point of view of these interests: it was a period of full integration into the world economy despite the constitution of an independent nation-state, and it exhibited an almost exemplary structure of a dependent economy. By establishing that political independence in itself did not imply an 'independent' path of economic development, my interpretation of the 1920s would constitute a revision of the dominant view on a little studied period. On the other hand, it was important to demonstrate that dependence consisted of a set of hierarchical relations within the world economy and rather than stagnation it engendered a particular kind of growth. Thus, my attention shifted to capture the structure of this growth and the nature of the mechanisms through which it was conditioned. This emphasis allowed me to illustrate some debated propositions about peripheral economic structures while describing the Turkish case.

In adopting this emphasis the economic reductionist perspective was reluctantly accepted, and a discussion of both internal and inter-state political relations was omitted. Such a position is obviously inadequate even for a conjuncture where the dominant fraction of the bourgeoisie did not face any contenders. I felt, however, that it allowed me to focus on determinations acting upon the economic structure without falling into politicist−voluntarist perspectives common to studies on the periphery. The gains, I hope, will outweigh the losses.

I am indebted to colleagues who helped in various ways: V. Brown, S. Ilkin, A. Kudat, O. Kurmus, Y. Tezel and Z. Toprak all read parts of the draft and offered their comments. F. Birtek was the ideal friend with the encouragement and the critical eye. The institutional set-up within which a dissertation is

viii   Preface and acknowledgements

written may often be constricting. In my case R. Roehl and S. Cohen proved
to be the liberators. B. Ward made a very valuable suggestion which led to an
important revision. I am grateful to I. Wallerstein in too many ways to
mention. The usual disclaimer applies: all the remaining faults are my own.

1 Introductory remarks

1.1 Theoretical introduction

The theory of peripheral capitalist development in its Marxist version has received a new impetus in the past decade. The study of pre-capitalist modes of production, historical research on specific social formations transforming under the impact of capitalism, and theoretical attempts to formulate a unified framework of world capitalist development have increased our ability to approach the problems posed by non-autonomous developments of capitalism.[1] Such an approach derives directly from Rosa Luxemburg's problematic. Accordingly, the principal attention is focussed on the expansion of capitalism and the ensuing transformation of previously non-capitalist areas. Questions concentrate on the modes of integration of pre-capitalist formations into the capitalist system; and on the resulting patterns of development.[2]

Capital expands its area of operation in its search for higher profits. In the process it penetrates and transforms previously traditional economies, and it fosters the development of commodity production. The result is the expansion of the world market and the imposition of new patterns of specialisation on the new areas. By entering the world division of labour such areas lose their internal articulation to constitute part of the larger unit of the world market. Therefore, the unit of analysis relevant for the understanding of capital accumulation becomes the entire capitalist market, including the new periphery. This growing capitalist economy, however, is not homogeneous: various sub-units are assigned differentiated and hierarchical positions. Accumulation on the world scale implies the extraction of maximum profits by capital within this hierarchical framework.[3]

The position of the periphery in this totality is initially determined by the requirements of merchant capital which introduces world market determinations into the pre-capitalist economy.[4] Merchant capital creates an export sector that produces commodities for the world market, and simultaneously a pocket of consumers demanding imports. It endeavours to expand its area of operations within existing social relations and depending on the specific conditions of natural and other resources. This expansion might be through the installation of petty commodity production or through one or more of the

1

various forms of local exploitation such as plantations, haciendas, on enclave economies employing wage-labour. In its later stages, this expansion involves infrastructural investments such as in railways and ports which carry market incentives to a greater number of producers and allow the expansion of commodity production from the export outlets to the interior.

The principal claim in the approach summarised here is that a given level of integration into the world market results in the periphery's incorporation into the world economy as a subordinate component of that unit. This hierarchical ordering in the world economy begins to condition the history of the periphery: the internal dynamic of the peripheral formation is no longer sufficient to account for its structure.

The systemic position of the periphery does not remain fixed: it is subject to changes depending on the development of the world economy and its particular conjuncture; therefore a specific, historical analysis requires more than a structural identification. It becomes necessary to determine the impact of the conjuncture on the relationship between the periphery and the core areas of the world economy as well as to gauge the changing degree of autonomy that peripheral areas enjoy, depending on the strength of their ties with the world economy.

I have sketched the outlines of the paradigm within which I propose to study a particular example of peripheral structure, Turkey between 1923 and 1929. My purpose in this study of a particular case is to contribute to the elaboration of the theory, especially regarding the description of those mechanisms which act to ensure the integration of the periphery into the world market. As empirical correlative I have chosen to analyse a short period in the history of Turkey's peripheralisation which leads me to describe a certain stage during the peripheralisation process, and not the process itself. For most purposes in the analysis, the entire period will be taken as a single configuration in order to be able to consider together observations from adjoining years. The analysis of the changes during the period is intended to illustrate the process whereby the described patterns are reinforced. In other words, developments during the period show that, since the patterns are reinforced, there is justification in treating our observations as belonging to a structure of longer duration rather than as contingent to a particular conjuncture.

1.2 Remarks on the choice of the period

Similar to other areas in the Mediterranean basin, Turkey had always been inside the immediate penumbra of European capitalism. Yet it was in the nineteenth century that the industrial economies of Europe began to fully exploit the production and market potentialities of the territories inside the Ottoman Empire. As long as the Empire survived with its strongly centralised state tradition, penetration of foreign merchant capital was mediated by bureaucratic authority. Hence, the redistributive pre-capitalist concerns of the Porte conditioned and influenced the pattern of installation of commodity production inside the Empire.

Proper units of the capitalist system are nation states, and not redistributive empires which attempt to create economies with their own internal division of labour.[5] The dismantling of the Ottoman Empire following the First World War was followed by five more years of war which resulted in the foundation of the Turkish Republic in 1923, repudiating all imperial concerns and functions. Thus Turkey was the first peripheral area to become an independent nation state after a long history of capitalist penetration. Because of this political independence, coexisting with economic domination, Turkey's historical experience in the 1920s prefigured the later histories of many a peripheral country.

The main advantage in treating the period at hand, however, lies in the exceptional 'openness' of the Turkish economy between 1923 and 1929. For, five years after the treaty of Lausanne, with which Western powers recognised the existence of the Turkish state, the government was bound by the international agreement to maintain the pre-war level of tariffs. In addition to this imposed inability, the government legislated no restrictions on the movement of foreign capital either as direct investment or in the form of credit. The absence of a central bank, on the other hand, allowed the rate of exchange between the Turkish lira and foreign currencies to be established in the market. In effect, government policy, potentially effective in influencing the degree and pattern of world economic integration, was notably absent. This absence, of course, is an advantage if the purpose is to identify the structuring of the periphery according to forces and information emanating from the more developed centres of Western Europe. The minimal and uninhibitive nature of state activity, therefore, makes of Turkey a particularly attractive laboratory of peripheral integration.

Perhaps the most important factor underlying the behaviour of the state was the international economic conjuncture. The world economy as a whole continued to expand in the 1920s, although with a slackened momentum compared to the pre-war era. Opportunities in the periphery thereby made available to merchant capital were best tapped in an environment least encumbered by political authority. In as much as merchants constituted the dominant and politically effective fraction of the bourgeoisie, the ease of penetration of the Turkish economy was desirable both to the developed economies of the centre and to the dominant economic interests within the country. Once, however, the boom came to an end and trade ceased to be as lucrative as before, political authority found itself in a relatively autonomous position and began to implement the etatist policies of the 1930s. This option, of course, could only be taken together with strict controls over the movement of goods, capital, and currency into and out of Turkey.

While, in one sense, the boom of the 1920s renders our study a general character, it would be wrong to ignore the specificity of the mode of accumulation characterising the period ending with the depression of 1929. In order to analyse the mechanisms of world economic integration, it is necessary to focus on an expansionary phase since expansion itself is the structural necessity of capitalism underlying peripheral incorporation. Peripheral incorporation is a corollary of expanded reproduction, or continual accumulation of capital. In other words, the 'normal' functioning of the capitalist system is ideally reflected in the continual accumulation of a boom period, and the consequent intensification of capital's attempts to structure peripheral areas according to its needs. Yet, within the general parameters of expansion, each stage of capitalist development will exhibit peculiarities. The history of capitalism may be read as a succession of discrete modes of accumulation terminating with general crises. Each mode of accumulation is distinguished by a specific organisation of the forces of production and a world division of labour corresponding to this organisation. Accordingly the mechanisms of world economic integration will also be peculiar to a given stage.[6] An unprecedented expansion of trade through large scale infrastructural investments to constitute a primary accumulation in the periphery was characteristic of the pre First World War period. These projects aimed at expanding the sphere of commodity production in order to allow merchant capital a greater domain of activity. As opposed to the post Second World War period, it was not productive capital whose internationalisation constituted the principal mechanism effecting a world-wide division of labour. Merchant capital remained to be the privileged moment of total capital which performed this function.

By the end of the war, the expansionary momentum of the 1896–1914 period had largely exhausted itself. The decade of the 1920s may be seen as the tail end of the boom starting in 1896, or alternatively as a period of uncertain reconstruction, already signalling the crisis. In either case, the expansion of the world economy continued in the 1920s, albeit uncertainly; and this expansion was conditioned by the mode of accumulation of the previous stage of the world economy. When we analyse the case of Turkey, our findings will reflect this specificity. In other words, we shall be defining a peripheral economy of the 1896–1929 period.

1.3 Methodological remarks

In this study I did not attempt to give a complete description of the peripheral formation of Turkey. That would require a more in-depth treatment of agriculture and industry at the level of actual economic practices. It would also require a discussion of the economic role and the degree of autonomy of the state, which would imply a discussion of its class character. I have instead attempted to draw the main contours of the appearing patterns of economic activity, and have dealt with the state only in so far as its policies influenced the establishment of these patterns. A lengthier discussion of the state would require a different theoretical approach necessitating the determination of the nature of the political instance in the periphery. Hence the treatment here is selective: agriculture and industry provide the abstractions which define and delimit certain areas of activity in the peripheral economy. These areas are then investigated to reveal the basic patterns of integration with the world economy. In agriculture, commodity production for the market provides the principal perspective, because we are concerned with the transformation of a largely subsistence farming agriculture under the impact of commercialisation. The genesis of the new structure is determined by the transformatory impact of markets. Consequently, the morphological change in subsistence agriculture, during the period of its transition to commodity producing agriculture, may be traced through the marketisation of its various components and through the differential impact of other factors – such as land tenure, transportation, prices – on potential marketisation.

In the case of industry, which is the subject of Chapter 3, products were traded in markets to a much higher degree than in the case of agriculture. Here, therefore, instead of the degree of commoditisation, the impact of capitalist penetration may be gauged in the increasing scale of production and changing technology of manufacturing firms. Older manufactures which were oriented to local markets employed few workers, were of small scale and dependent on local sources for inputs. Manufactures which were set up as a result of the economy's opening up to the world economy were of a different nature. They employed greater numbers of wage workers, catered to larger markets, produced new commodities, used imported technology and imported raw materials, and were frequently funded by foreign capital. These differences are discussed on the basis of indices setting traditional and modern manufactures apart. Through this perspective we attempt to evaluate the respective importances of traditional crafts and modern manufacturing and we discuss the pattern of implantation of non-autonomous industry.

While agriculture and industry are the receiving media upon which the patterns of integration are imposed, the discussions of trade, and money and banking seek to describe the structuring forces. In other words, trade and credit are the mechanisms which transmit and implement the requirements of the world economy to the peripheral formation. It should, therefore, be remarked that there is a qualitative difference between agriculture and industry on the one hand, and trade and credit on the other. In a more classical framework this difference might be formulated as production vs. circulation of wealth. In Marxist terms, while agriculture and industry employ productive capital and create surplus value, trade and banks, which respectively represent merchant and interest-bearing capital, receive a part of this surplus value during the process of circulation. My claim, however, extends further in arguing that merchant and interest-bearing capital are forces which ensure the peripheral structuring of the productive forces employed in agriculture and industry.

The justification for this argument is not difficult to establish. Both merchant capital and money capital (or usurer's capital in its primitive form) may co-exist and articulate with pre-capitalist forms of production. This articulation, however, does not entail a potential to transform the prevalent social organisation of production. Both of these forms of capital remain subordinate to the pattern of reproduction of social relations prefigured by the dominant mode of production within the social formation. This same adaptability becomes important during the period of transformation of the pre-capitalist economy through its articulation with capitalism. Merchant and interest-bearing capital act as intermediaries between the systems because they can function in both capitalist and pre-capitalist environments. After the establishment of capitalism proper, they become subordinate to the interests of productive capital in the capitalist country. Since articulation of capitalist and pre-capitalist systems takes place in the sphere of circulation, primarily through trade, it is by means of merchant capital that the capitalist system taps the value created in pre-capitalist economies.[7] It is during this process that already existing native and newly introduced foreign merchant capital begin to penetrate the traditional, untransformed economies. Gradually, the expanding sphere of commodity production comes under the dominance of merchant capital, and the peripheral structure begins to be established.

The role of interest-bearing capital in the peripheralisation process is more complex: on the one hand foreign capital in the form of money seeks a simple valorisation through loans to the colonial state, while at the same time direct lending and bank credit contribute to the shaping of the peripheral economy. In the last half century of the history of the Ottoman Empire, loans by European capital played an important role in its political economy. During the period studied below, however, interest-bearing capital took on a more active role in the instigation of commodity production. As an adjunct to merchant capital, its peripheral function figured predominantly in the designation of areas of economic activity which developed in response to signals from the world market.

Merchant and interest-bearing capital act as the instigators of commodity production during the process whereby a pre-capitalist economy is transformed through its contact with the world capitalist system. An analysis of the workings of these linkages supplies the crucial information regarding both the direction and the modality of the transformation. Only through such an analysis is it possible to justify A. G. Frank's critique of the duality model, or to illustrate the 'world economy' concretely through a specification of the network which binds various levels of the peripheral economy with the metropoles.[8]

Interest-bearing and merchant capital share the additional advantage of international fluidity. Especially when controls on exchanges are weak, foreign funds may easily cross borders as credit or for trade dealings. Since the native counterparts of foreign merchants and bankers are the best placed recipients of such funds, a fusion of foreign and native capital, and a consequent division of labour between the two ensue. This division of labour creates a structure with an unequal relationship where foreign capital, commanding larger resources, more concentrated, with greater information, and enjoying a higher rate of profit as a result of these advantages, plays the dominant role. This dominance enables foreign capital not only to decide about the deployment of its own funds, but also to influence the total flow of funds in the economy. Hence circulating capital, because it plays the crucial role in the articulation between capitalist and pre-capitalist economies, and because it provides the appropriate medium for the cooperation of foreign and native capital, should be the privileged object of analysis in a study attempting to identify the forces structuring the peripheral economy. In as much as these forces emanate from the capitalist world economy, the analysis of circulating capital will provide conceptual reformulations regarding the direction and manner of the influence of central economies on the periphery.

I have summarised the theory underlying the mode of exposition of this study. Since, however, the research is historical, and does not attempt to cover the entirety of a historical process, it is necessary briefly to review the chronological background of the period under study. It is to this historical setting that we now turn.

1.4 Historical background

Beginning in the sixteenth century, various areas within the Ottoman Empire had entered into trade relations with Europe. Until the end of the eighteenth century, however, the central authority could keep movements of commodities under control, although an important volume of contraband trade existed. It was mostly by means of contraband trade that the Balkans came to be integrated into the expanding division of labour of the European economy. As a result of this incorporation, the eighteenth century witnessed extensive changes in crop patterns, and the 'feudalisation' of the Balkan economy. The intensification of trade relations of the entire Empire with Europe began during the third decade of the nineteenth century. From then till the end of the 1830s, Turkey's imports from Britain and France more than doubled, a trend which received further impetus from the series of trade treaties that the Porte concluded first with Britain (in 1838) and then with other European powers.[9] In addition to regulating trade and fixing low duties on both imports and exports, these treaties robbed the Ottoman government of one of its prerogatives which had allowed it to control trade. After these treaties it was no longer possible for the government to grant monopoly rights to appointed merchants; trade was freed from the political control of the central authority, and foreign merchants gained the right to operate freely on Ottoman soil. A further privilege granted to foreign nationals was that foreign merchants were taxed less heavily because natives were subject to the internal octroi in addition to import duties.[10] One result of this capitulatory regime was the almost complete disappearance of native merchants to be replaced by Christian minorities carrying the passports of signatory powers. Escaping Ottoman taxation and jurisdiction, merchants of minority origin became middlemen for foreign trading firms which dealt with Turkey. The impact of the growth of trade was felt especially in the Aegean and the Black Sea regions. As Turkey began to export tobacco, wheat, and fruits, these regions were integrated into a circuit of commodity production, and became part of the world division of labour.[11]

Turkey's imports had increased to a greater extent than her exports. This development, together with the Porte's revenue crisis, led to heavy borrowings beginning in the 1850s. Thus the domination of the market by foreign merchant capital was followed by the implantation of European money capital. After only twenty years, however, the Porte was no longer able to service the growing volume of debt. Its bankruptcy in the 1870s resulted in the establishment of the Public Debt Administration (PDA) which began to collect some of the taxes, monopolised the lucrative tobacco trade, and even made expenditures in the name of the state; in a role similar to the *fermiers généraux* of the Ancien Régime.[12]

A parallel development during this period was the construction of railways by foreign concessionary companies. Railways extended the domain of the market and increased the output – and therefore the taxes – in the areas within their reach. They were constructed in order to tap the productive potential of the Anatolian interior and to mobilise the potentially marketable agricultural surplus. The railway provided subsistence-farming peasants with access to new technologies and larger markets, and the price incentive to produce surpluses.[13]

During the period of the P. D. A. (1881–1914) net debt inflow no longer offset the servicing outflow, but the Empire began to receive private foreign investments.[14] Following the earlier merchants, and the banks, which had arrived in the 1860s, direct foreign investment gained importance after the 1880s. Two thirds of this investment was placed in railways, the rest in mines, utilities and a few productive concerns. Thus, in addition to commodity-producing sectors dominated by merchant capital, there began the development of a capitalist enclave employing wage labour. It may be argued that foreign investment of this period constituted a 'primitive accumulation' for the Ottoman economy.[15] Between 1881 and 1913, the economy experienced a growth rate of 1.5% p.a., despite the near-bankruptcy of the state.[16] Between 1897 and 1913, cotton cultivation increased fourfold, tobacco by 3.2 times, raisins, hazelnuts, and figs each doubled. In other agricultural products which did not benefit from the incentives offered by foreign markets, increases of output were between 20 and 30%. Of the former group approximately 40% of the output was exported; by contrast only 1.4% of the grain output was exported in 1913.[17]

When the Young Turks came to power (1909) there had been a sufficient development of a native merchant bourgeoisie to prompt them to introduce measures encouraging commercial and industrial undertakings by the Moslem population. However, since the trade regime and capitulatory privileges could not be unilaterally abrogated, Young Turk 'etatism' remained limited. Their crowning economic policy achievement was the law for the Encouragement of Industry (1913). When the war began and the Ottoman Empire sided with Germany, the Capitulations – the Porte's trade concessions to foreign merchants – were renounced, the P. D. A. lost its powers, and the government simultaneously gained both the power of legislating a new tariff and the right of printing paper money – a privilege which until then had been conceded to the Franco-British-owned Banque Ottomane.[18] The four war years witnessed a frenetic pace of economic activity by Turkish capital, which gained new advantages through encouragement by the government and government-supported banks.

Another significant development ushered in by the Young Turks was a shift through which Germany began to gain a dominant position among the contending economic powers in the Empire. Germany and her financiers expected the Istanbul government to provide a crucial bridgehead for Germany's commercial expansion to the Near East. When the war was lost, however, the Near Eastern provinces were divided among French and British spheres of influence. The area which later became Turkey escaped such an assignation due to the clash of major and minor interested parties, and to the success of the independence movement led by Mustafa Kemal. As a result of the Greek war, Turkey established its politically independent stature, but opened its economy equally to capitalists of all nationalities, and thus became one of the few countries where 'Open Door' conditions actually held.

In the history of Turkey's growing integration into the world capitalist system, the Young Turk episode was a short-lived attempt at attaining a new status in the world division of labour. The Young Turk policy, which was aided by a major disruption of the world economy because of the war, aimed to reconsolidate the Ottoman Empire under the domination of the central authority. Germany, whose interests coincided with the Young Turks' intention to prevent a British–French partition of the provinces, became their willing ally. This temporary and incomplete 'revolt' against the world hierarchy was forcefully terminated at the end of the war. In fact, the period we shall be studying was a continuation of the trends which were established prior to the Young Turk period.

The 1923–29 period ended with a general crisis of the world economy. When the depression and later the war upset the mechanisms which integrated the world capitalist system, the Turkish economy attained a relative independence, and state-directed policies once again sought to establish an autarkic alternative to peripheral development.

We will now turn to analysing the 1923–29 period, which constitutes the subject of this study.

2 Integration into the world economy through agriculture

2.1 Introduction

We shall now offer an analysis of the agricultural sector during the period starting with the foundation of the Republic in 1923 and ending with the onset of the world depression. Our objective is to identify and describe the structure of a peripheral agricultural sector and to discover its role in the process of integration into the world economy. This perspective requires a discussion of the degree and modes of commercialisation in agriculture and the structure imposed through commercialisation. Of the factors which influence the pace and the manner of commercialisation, the most important is land tenure. Land tenure, however, itself is modified under the impact of the market to better accommodate commercialisation. We shall argue that commodity production increased in small peasant farms as well as in larger farms. This hypothesis will be discussed through an analysis of production patterns and the distribution of cultivable land under different crops.

After this treatment of agriculture as a sector of economic activity, we shall discuss the role of the state in effecting developments inside the agricultural sector. We will treat specific policies of the state relating to the availability and pricing of inputs; transportation policy as a means of facilitating commercialisation; tax-policy as a means of influencing the structure of agricultural production. The chapter concludes with an evaluation of the development of agricultural output, and the degree of agriculture's integration into the world market.

2.2 Role of agriculture in the integration process

In the historical context under discussion, agriculture constituted the main economic channel of integration into the world economy; the economic surplus was produced mainly in the agricultural sector, and it was through the selling of this surplus in exchange for manufactured goods that the relationship with the world economy materialised. This particular relationship, however, does not imply a permanence, and it should be considered as historically specific. In the literature this relationship has been treated as if it were a permanent category of the integration of the periphery with the core, and the unequal nature of the integration has been mistakenly derived from the specificity of agricultural exports from the periphery versus manufactured exports from the core.[1]

At a certain historical stage during the internationalisation of capital, the periphery specialises in agriculture in the world division of labour, because the technology of agriculture together with the level of remuneration of labour require the periphery to fulfil the function of an agricultural exporter. Technology and (through the level of remuneration) costs of production ensure the profitability of trade with the world system. The integration of an economy into the world system is equivalent to the expansion of the world economy towards new peripheral areas, and the logic of this expansion requires the profitability of exchange with the periphery. Profitability of the unit exchange, however, while necessary, is not a sufficient condition for this expansion. The absolute volume of exchange has also to be of a degree to warrant an integration.[2] In other words a certain level of commodity production is required. In the historical context of Turkey in the 1920s, this necessary level of surplus production was attainable in the agricultural sector alone. Merchant capital dealing in Turkey could obtain both higher rates and larger absolute volumes of profit in agriculture than it could in other sectors.

An analysis of the role of the agricultural sector in the process of peripheral integration requires an investigation of its internal differentiation. In other words, we have to investigate the conditions of ownership and production, data which are translated into the crucial relationship of the appropriation of the surplus. For, certainly, in an agricultural sector characterised by small peasant holdings, the process of integration through the trading of agricultural surplus would follow a particular development, unlike, for example, the case of commercialised agriculture with coerced labour. These two differing situations would also imply dissimilar deployments of merchant capital. It may, for example, be necessary to deal with local merchants in the case of a large number of peasant proprietors each producing a small portion of the total marketed surplus. With a few large landowners, however, foreign merchant capital may find it possible to deal directly. For this reason, it is necessary to describe the specific nature of land tenure before we begin to analyse the position of the agricultural sector in the peripheral context.

2.3 Land tenure

In order to discuss land distribution in the 1920s, we need to engage in a brief historical excursus. The smooth functioning of the Ottoman socio-economic structure required the existence of small peasant family holdings where formal ownership rights were vested in the state. Actual producers who held the possession of the land were bound to the central authority in their responsibility as tax payers. This relationship, as long as it survived, was protective of the rights of the small holders as well as of the central authority: if the central authority remained powerful, would-be landlords would be stymied in their efforts to subjugate the peasantry, and the tax-collection mechanism of the central authority could survive unrivalled. This equation, however, was frequently disturbed as various external factors mobilised the internal potential toward the rise of landlord regimes. This secular tendency culminated towards the end of the eighteenth century in the virtual partitioning of Western Anatolia by *ayans* (local potentates). The *ayan* domination of the peasantry mostly remained at the level of tax collection, with share-cropping arrangements confined to the more commercialised areas. During the first half of the nineteenth century the central authority re-asserted its primacy yet could not effectively curb the landlords, with the result of increasing the exploitation of the peasantry. A land code in 1858, however, aimed at consolidating the rights of possession of the actual producers by establishing a cadastral system which precluded the registration of 'the whole of the land of a village or town . . . in its entirety' in the name of a single inhabitant. Although the law was less than fully reinforced during the second half of the nineteenth century, the dominant tendency in the structure of land distribution was fragmentation through inheritance.

The relative importance of different types of tenure during the 1920s is impossible to determine other than impressionistically. There is no doubt that small peasant farming was predominant although large properties operated under share-cropping continued to exist and there was a scattering of capitalist farms employing wage labour. Most of the cultivable land in the grain areas of the interior, and an even greater proportion of the Black Sea region, belonged to the category of peasant farming. While the interior was subsistence production oriented, the Black Sea peasants were highly commercialised. Share-cropping survived as a quasi-feudal tenancy arrangement in the sparsely populated Eastern highlands and the South-eastern settlements, but also more as a form of contract labour in the fertile plains of the Aegean and the Mediterranean, especially in the cultivation of labour-intensive commercial crops. The incidence of proper capitalist relations with year-round employment of wage-labour was extremely rare, although in the cotton-growing Adana region wage-labour through seasonal migration provided the greater part of the labour requirement.

According to the findings of a land survey conducted in the late 1930s, out of 1.1 million holdings 99.7% were of less than 500 donums (1 donum = 0.25 acres), and 88.7% less than 100 donums.[3] 5.5% of the rural households were landless and 36.7% owned less than 20 donums.[4] The 99.7% of households who owned less than 500 donums held 86.3% of the land while the remaining 3000 owners (out of 1.1 million) controlled 14% of the cultivable area.[5] According to the incomplete findings of another census which was conducted in 1927 over all of Turkey, the average *cultivated* area per family was found to be 25 donums.[6]

Yet regional variations around the average were considerable: the largest average area was in the Southern region with a predominance of cotton cultivation (40.5 donums), while the Black Sea area, with mainly labour intensive crops, was characterised by an average cultivation of 14.9 donums. This regional variation indicates that the visible unevenness in land distribution was partly mitigated through regional differences in crop technology and land fertility. However, the quantity distribution of land, in itself, was relatively even, especially if the comparison is made with former colonies characterised by landlord regimes. A more apt comparison would be with France, which also was characterised by the small peasant – strong state equation. On the other hand, the figures we have discussed refer to ownership and not exploitation; operation size was distributed much more evenly due to share-cropping arrangements and only a very small proportion of the large owners operated large units of exploitation.

Another survey dating from the mid 1930s indicates that the largest units of exploitation were in the Aegean and the Southern regions, and not in the Eastern or South-eastern where we would expect the concentration of ownership to be more pronounced. 'Maximum size of family farms' was 3000 donums in the Aegean and 2300 donums in the South.[7] In fact, a land survey conducted in 1912 had also yielded similar results. It was found then that 46% of the farms in both the Adana and the Aydin provinces were larger than 50 donums, (these 2 vilayets in the Ottoman administrative division corresponded to the Southern and the Aegean regions) while in the rest of Anatolia this figure was around 25%.[8] An administrative questionnaire conducted in 1934–35 and followed up in 1938 indicated that in terms of actual exploitation of land, large farms of over 5000 donums were predominantly in the commercialised regions. This statistic excludes large properties cultivated in small parcels through share-cropping. The result is summed up as follows: 'large agricultural exploitations are found in all coastal provinces, and the highest number of large farms are to be found on the Western coast of Marmara Sea (Thrace) and the Southern Aegean region'.[9] Following these two concentrations came the Adana region. As the reporter of the census remarks, the incidence of large agricultural operations parallels the availability of transportation, an indication that commercialisation is the most important factor in explaining the size of the units of cultivation.

The emerging picture is one of a vast number of small peasant holdings and a geographically specific incidence of larger farms. The latter were mostly found in the commercialised regions growing marketed crops, while large properties cultivated in tenancy arrangements, i.e. in small units, fell into the category of non-commercial quasi-feudal tenure in Eastern and South-eastern Anatolia.[10] Commercialised share-cropping existed alongside larger farms predominantly when the crop technology implied a year-round labour demand rather than a peak seasonal demand such as in cotton. Thus proletarianisation within agriculture was non-existent and actual labourers could be divided into four corresponding categories: semi-proletarian seasonal labourers, servile tenants in the most backward regions, share-croppers who mostly held their own plots as well, and – by far the largest category – self-employed peasant proprietors.

2.4 Land tenure and commercialisation

In the perspective of the integration of agriculture into the world economy and commercialisation resulting out of this integration, we are especially concerned with capitalist farming, share-cropping in the Western areas and peasant farming. In the Aegean region, capitalist farming producing for the export market developed during the latter part of the nineteenth century. Especially after the 1866 decree which had allowed foreigners to own land, former merchants of foreign nationalities purchased land in large quantities and proceeded to grow export crops employing wage-labour. Some farms in the area owned by British nationals employed as many as 135 workers.[11] These farmers also effected a transformation of the techniques of production. They imported agricultural machinery, which Turkish farmers also began to adopt.[12] At the same time, the traditional share-cropping relationship was altered. Landless peasants continued as tenants, but now they had to cultivate the crops indicated by the landlord. The new relationship represented a system where traditional techniques and crops were replaced by new ones.[13] Similar developments occurred in the Cilician region where cotton grown on large farms was rapidly turning the area into one of monoculture.[14] Wage-labour, however, despite British, and later German, colonists' hopes, failed to become an important category. This was due in part to the favourable land–labour ratio, but principally to the absence of legal and political arrangements which would have accommodated a capitalist relation. The 1858 Land Code had affirmed the state's rights to ownership and every subject's to possession of land. In fact, excepting Eastern Anatolia, all peasant families held *some* land. Within such a balance local notables could only impose additional taxation on the Sultan's subjects through share-cropping arrangements. When they could do that, they were loath to see scarce labour lured to work on foreign owners' plots. Nor would the peasants leave their own land and rented plots, where they could manage their own time, to be employed, especially during periods of coincident peak demand. As a result of these factors, wage rates in the Aegean area proved to be too high and would-be colonists left in disappointment.

Where wage-labour thrived, it was in the form of seasonal employment supplementing income from the peasant's own land. Usually crops were differentiated so as to allow the peasant to work on his own land and still to offer his labour during harvesting – most usually of cotton. Of course, the employment of seasonal labour always implied commercial agriculture. Commodity production was also a feature of large properties cultivated by share-cropping:

most of the grain surplus was produced in this manner. Out of the 428 large units of exploitation in the country (above 5000 donums) 40 were found in the Ankara administrative region, which specialised in grain production.[15] There was a certain degree of marketisation in peasant plots as well. Both on family-owned peasant farms and on the tenant plots of share-croppers production was to some degree market-oriented. There is no doubt that the subsistence component of their output outweighed commodity production. Yet the importance of peasant production in the agricultural sector as a whole necessitates a discussion of commercialisation within this balance of subsistence and petty commodity production.

Commercialisation accelerated the tendency toward larger capitalist farms, but peasant farms did not remain impervious to the market. In 1927, total consumption of grain in Turkey was 2.3 million tons.[16] Assuming that a person in the farming sector consumed twice as much grain as a non-farmer, an average peasant family consisting of 5.2 persons is calculated to require 1.07 tons.[17] If we add a third of this amount as seed requirement, an average family would have had to cultivate enough land to produce 1.4 tons of grain. Using the average yields calculated for 1927 we can come up with rough estimates for minimum land requirement for a peasant family to supply for their grain consumption needs.[18] In the Anatolian interior, this figure comes to between 25 and 35 donums. It is lowest in Thrace and in the Adana region at 20 donums. It is highest in Eastern Anatolia at 40 to 45 donums. In fact, even in the 1960s, 40 donums was considered as the lower bound of the size of operations required to produce for the market.[19] Following the usage developed elsewhere, we shall call the holders of family farms larger than 40 donums 'middle peasants'.[20] The distinguishing feature of the middle peasant was his marginal position in the market. While farmers who held more than 200 donums were definitely marketised, and had no other choice than realising their surplus on the market the middle peasant was dependent on external factors in his decision to bring his surplus to the market. Weather conditions determined whether he would have any surplus at all. Prices, on the other hand, constituted the most important variable influencing his marketisation of the surplus. The 1920s, up to 1928, were characterised by propitious weather conditions which allowed for good harvests. In addition, the world terms-of-trade for agriculture progressed favourably until the Depression. Hence the two conditions for the middle peasant to make use of the market were fulfilled. The abolition of the tithe also meant an increment of at least 12% in his disposable output which served to increase his marketable surplus. We should, then expect a marketisation of the holders of medium-sized properties as well as the already commercialised large farmers.[21]

According to the 1927 Agricultural Census, only in the Adana region does the average farm rank as a surplus-producing middle farm. In 1952, 32% of the peasant families in all of Turkey could be considered as middle peasants.[22] This figure, however, is much too high to apply to our period, because in the intervening years reclamation of land almost doubled the total cultivated area. According to the 1938 figures, middle peasants accounted for 25% of the families.[23] Considering that medium size farms were promoted in the 1930s through government-encouraged wheat-farming, a reasonable guess would put the number of middle peasants at between 15 and 20% for the 1920s. Therefore, in addition to the large farmers, who represented less than 3% of the total, middle peasants could also be considered as marketised. These two categories accounted for a fifth of all agricultural families. Of the remaining 80%, only about 5% of agricultural families were totally landless.[24] This leaves three quarters of the total number of families who owned some land but not sufficient to produce a grain surplus. Among these are found farmers engaged in more intensive cultivation, such as the tobacco-growers of the Black Sea Coast, Izmir and Manisa. Families in the regions in which such intensive cultivation was practised amounted to 20% of the total number of farming families. This means that around 60% of the peasant families who owned some land did not produce a marketable surplus. According to the 1952 census, families with less than 50 donums to cultivate owned 18.6% of the land.[25] We can safely assert that this figure remained below 20% for the earlier decades. On 80% of the land, then, *some* surplus was produced by 40% of the peasant families.

2.5 Distribution of output and commercialisation

We shall look briefly at the allocation of this land among different crops, and the composition of marketed agricultural output.

In 1927, 6.4% of the cultivated land was allocated to cash crops.[26] These included cotton (2.1%), tobacco (1.8%), and sesame (1.1%) which were entirely marketed, but also potatoes and onions. Pulses (beans, lentils, etc.) occupied 4% of the arable area. In some regions (around the city of Ankara and Bursa, for example) beans and lentils were cash crops, with entire villages specialising in their production. We may argue that a large proportion of pulses cultivation was market-oriented. The remaining 89.6% of the cultivated land in 1927 was under grains. Here we have no choice other than to follow the most educated guesses which put the ratio of marketed grain output at between one quarter and one third. In fact, using the same assumptions as before, we can estimate that the average non-farmer consumed slightly over 100 kg of grains a year, amounting to roughly 450,000 tons of grain that must have been purchased domestically by non-farmers.[27] Adding to this figure the 90,000 tons of net grain exports, we get 540,000 tons, representing 23% of the total output which had to be marketed. If it is considered that there were grain exchanges among the farmers as well, this 23% will have to be increased to a higher figure. Hence we may conclude that more than a quarter of the grain output, most of the beans crop, and almost all of the cash crops were marketed. In grains, large and middle farmers produced the surplus brought to the market; in beans and cash crops, there was specialisation and all farms produced for the market.

Commercialisation of the peasant household was also a function of raising animals for the purpose of marketing their products. In this activity, too, larger farms were more market-oriented, and were geographically concentrated. Yet, the average peasant household earned more cash marketing animal products than it did through grains. In fact, the beginnings of peasant commercialisation were through the marketing of animal and garden products rather than the principal crops. It was calculated in 1934 that a nuclear peasant family could provide sufficient labour to cultivate 60 donums of land in the grain producing area.[28] Since families who actually cultivated less than 60 donums were by far the majority, most families could dispose of labour to engage in side activities such as vegetable gardening, stock breeding, and processing of animal products.

The land-use pattern of the typical Turkish village consisted of three concentric areas around the central settlement. The immediate surroundings of the houses were confined to gardening and vegetable farming, and processing of animal products. The area farthest from the village settlement was the grazing land ordinarily held in common by the village-dwellers.[29] In between were the cultivated plots. In 1927, an average of 1.9 draught animals were owned by each peasant family, in addition to 6 sheep, and 5 goats.[30] In fact, those peasant families owning less land than the required area for subsistence had recourse to animal products to supplement their revenue. Stock grazing was on land held in common immediately outside the village settlement, while market-oriented activities such as cheese making, wool-clipping and spinning were carried out near the houses inside the settlement.[31] Wool production was an entirely commercialised activity whose output increased by 100% between 1923 and 1927,[32] mostly in response to export opportunities. At the same time, sheep were raised to be sold for slaughtering in nearby cities. In 1923, for example, total imports of meat supplied only 5% of the meat consumed in Istanbul.[33] Throughout the decade, Turkey remained a net exporter of livestock, with much of it originating from Eastern Anatolia.

It probably was not the poor peasant owning less than 50 donums who could bring live animals to the market. However, in certain non-perishable animal products, primarily wool and eggs, marketing was done by all strata of the peasantry. During summer months, 'egg-merchants' riding donkeys would visit villages collecting eggs, mainly through a barter mechanism. They would bring manufactures to villages and exchange them against eggs. Eggs were thus collected and packed in a central village of the area and were brought to the nearest port or railway station where they were exported.[34] Through this method of collection Turkey's egg exports increased from 1.4m TL in 1923 to 10.4m TL in 1931.[35]

Marketing of animals and animal products was the most common manner of obtaining cash for purposes of tax payments in money.[36] Especially after the abolition of the tithe (see below) the monetised new taxes required that the peasant realise some of his output in the market. The products which could be most easily converted to money without endangering the basic subsistence of the peasant were animals and animal products. Thus, peasant families, ordinarily engaged in subsistence grain-farming, also brought sheep and goats to the market to provide cash for outside purchases and money taxes.

It has been calculated that in the 1920s the animal sector accounted for one third of the value added in agriculture. Vegetable gardening, on the other hand, contributed only around 3% of the total agricultural income.[37] This later activity, however, was marketised to a greater proportion. Around the larger cities there was a belt of entirely commercial vegetable gardens. These gardens also supplied a growing canned vegetables industry. In 1923–24 this industry's output was 500,000 cans; by 1929 it had risen to 4m cans.[38] During the period we are treating, commercial vegetable gardening did not greatly increase in importance, because urban population remained stable.

2.6 Regional differences

The regional diversity of Turkish agriculture is apparent from the discussion above. From the point of view of crop distribution and of differential commercialisation, regions exhibited wide fluctuations. Above, we had oc-casion to stress the following points. (1) The Aegean and the Adana (Cilicia) regions were the first areas to fully integrate into the world market. In these regions land tenure varied according to crops. Cotton was characterised by large holdings employing seasonal wage-labour,[39] while figs, raisins, tobacco, opium, were cultivated on small-scale family plots. (2) The Black Sea coast with its intensive cultivation of export crops – in particular tobacco and hazelnuts – was also characterised by family gardens. Here the intensive labour requirements were met by family labour, and there were no landless peasants. (3) Of the remaining regions, the Eastern Anatolian plateau was the least commercialised, dominated by traditional tenancy arrangements, and large-scale ownership of land. The only exportable merchandise originating in this region was live animals, sold to Syria and Iran. (4) The interior of the country exhibited a diversity of tenure arrangements. Dominated by small-scale grain farming, ownership varied between large properties let out on share-cropping, and peasant property. Exceptional were the large owner-managed properties specialising in wheat farming. These were found along the path of the Anatolian railroad. (5) The Thracian region appeared to be a more developed version of the interior, because here proximity to the great urban market of Istanbul had provided the opportunity of earlier commercialisation. Thrace and the Marmara sea coast also supplied meat to Istanbul. The greatest concentrations of animal stock were found in the provinces adjoining the

Marmara sea, with a transportation advantage for the Istanbul market.[40]

The reasons for this regional diversity were manifold. We can only cite the two principal – and general – factors at this juncture. These are the agronomic capacity of the land – soil type, rain, climate conditions, etc. – and proximity to markets. Of course, the nature of the proximate market also influences the type of production. Export markets in nearby ports constitute incentives to produce for the world market, while a location in the interior may imply the development of commodity production oriented to domestic markets.

2.7 Concentration of land ownership

The period we are studying immediately succeeded the upheaval of the war years. As was mentioned above, the economic importance of the Christian minorities in the Ottoman Empire had been considerable. During the wars both Armenians and Greeks were forced to leave the country, and the remaining Greeks were the subject of a forced exchange of populations immediately after the formation of the Republic. We will argue that the appropriation of properties and economic opportunities left behind by the Greek and Armenian populations was a principal factor in the enrichment of a native capitalist class during the 1920s. In agriculture this appropriation contributed to a complex dynamic of concentration–fragmentation which had been in operation since the beginnings of commercialisation.

The tendency toward concentration of land dates from the transition of traditional agriculture to commercial agriculture. As private exploitation became more profitable than mediating the tax collection between the producer and the central authority, the landlord not only attempted to switch to an export crop and change the pattern of his surplus flows, but also to exploit the land directly.[41] However, not all of the land in commercialised regions was appropriated in large-scale farms. Small owners remained as peasant pro-prietors either on the outskirts of large commercial farms or because they were in direct contact with exporting merchants. Merchant capital attempted to enlarge the domain of commercial production, but not necessarily in the form of large farms. The persistence of peasant property gave merchant capital the advantage of dealing with small producers, and, therefore, a better bargaining position. More importantly, in the case of small owners, merchants had the opportunity to finance the entire production process by advancing capital at the beginning of the cultivation period and collecting their due after the harvest.[42] This seasonal indebtedness yielding high profit (i.e. 'interest') rates to merchant capital was preferable to a single transaction in which the merchant only financed the marketing of commodities for which producer's capital had been supplied by the capitalist grower himself. It was, therefore, in the interest of merchant capital to create and conserve a situation characterised by small, independent producers of the export crop. During the process of dissolution of

traditional agriculture, the ability of large farmers (old landlords) to concentrate their holdings depends on the balance of power between them and the
merchants who advance commercial capital. When the latter weaken, the
forces leading to large-scale farming re-assert themselves and concentration of
land gains a new momentum. When merchants hold sway, the survival of small
producers who are completely dependent on commercial capital becomes more
likely.[43]

Agricultural land in the areas of commercial production had long been under
this double influence. One factor which had an impact on the situation was the
fact that some small-holdings, especially in the Izmir region but also in Adana
and the Black Sea coast, were held by Greek and Armenian peasants who found
natural allies within the ranks of merchant capitalists, mostly of the same ethnic
origins. If not themselves the actual owners of capital, Greeks and Armenians
were often the agents who actually contracted the growers on behalf of French
and English trading companies.[44] One wave of nationalism which sought to
destroy this 'ethnic division of labour'[45] came during the Young Turk regime, in
the form of economic boycotts and more direct means, such as expulsion,
directed against Greeks. During the war, this 'nationalism' continued with the
Armenian deportation. Thus, between 1914 and 1916, large landlords had
ample opportunity to concentrate their holdings through expropriation of
smaller properties belonging to departing minorities.[46] The indirect impact of
these deportations, through the severance of the natural link between merchant
capital and the small producer, was to strengthen the large commercial
producer in his endeavour to enlarge his land.

A much more direct impact of the departure of minorities was observed in the
appropriation of their abandoned properties by the local population. Since the
beginning of the Young Turk period in 1909, there had been several waves of
mass deportations. The first incident occurring in Cilicia had involved
Armenians: 'Armenian land-owners, already in possession of the richest areas
of the Cilician plain were rapidly increasing their holdings; and the Armenian
population prospered and multiplied while the Moslem population declined',
wrote the *Encyclopaedia Britannica*.[47] Growing animosity between the two
populations developed into full-fledged fighting when the Armenian community attempted to interpret the Young Turk accession to power as a signal
for greater autonomy. In 1915 Armenians were removed from strategic areas in
a forced march, and in 1920 the Turkish nationalist army began operations
against Armenians who had immigrated to French-occupied Cilicia in great
numbers and had fought under the French flag, 'relying upon French
protection for the future'.[48] After killings, deaths, and emigrations, the 1927
census showed 77,433 Armenians in Turkey, and only 120 in Adana, the
principal city of Cilicia.[49]

According to the Turkish population statistics of 1910, Greeks in Turkey had
numbered 2.4 million.[50] Greek emigration out of Turkey started in 1912 and

continued during the war. When the Greek army occupied Western Anatolia in 1919, Greeks participated in the hostilities against the Turkish population, eliciting retaliation as the Turkish army advanced toward the Aegean coast in 1922. The Greek population, thus uprooted, fled to the coast and on to the islands and to Greece. Between 1912 and 1923, an estimated one million Greeks had emigrated from Turkey into Greece.[51] In January 1923, as part of the peace treaty, a convention was signed between Turkey and Greece, prescribing a compulsory exchange of the minorities of the two countries, excepting those Greeks living in Istanbul and Turks in Western Thrace. It was as a result of this convention that 1,200,000 Greeks and 400,000 Moslems were exchanged between 1923 and 1926.[52]

Merely in terms of numbers, Turkey had suffered a depopulation of around four million in the ten years preceding 1923. It should not be forgotten that this loss had more than a proportionate economic impact because war deaths – numbering about two million – were suffered mostly by the male population between the ages of 18 and 50. In order to gauge the social impact of the loss of population we should also look at the privileged status of the minorities in the economic life of Turkey prior to the Republic. It was mentioned in Chapter 1 that the terms of the nineteenth-century trade treaties had granted tax privileges and the rights of free trade in the Empire to foreigners. Christian minorities who could obtain passports of one of the signatory powers were considered foreigners and could benefit from the Capitulations. In addition to this protection, the growing commercial activity in the Empire had elevated Greeks and Armenians to mediating roles between foreign capital and Ottoman producers, which they were well-placed to perform. Before the Young Turk period, Greeks and Armenians virtually monopolised commerce, industry and urban professions. By the end of the war out of 391 manufacturing establishments in Izmir, 344 were owned and run by Greeks;[53] of more than one million Greeks emigrating out of Turkey more than half were of non-agricultural origin.[54] 'Among the Asia Minor refugees, there was a large percentage of merchants, doctors, and lawyers, as well as of retail traders, craftsmen and workers of all categories . . . . There were many more professional and artisan people than farmers, the latter coming mainly from Thrace and Bulgaria.'[55]

Despite the preponderance of non-agricultural occupations, the amount of land abandoned by the emigrants must have been considerable. In Thrace, for example, which was one of the most highly commercialised agricultural areas, catering for the Istanbul market, more than 250,000 Greek farmers became the subject of the compulsory exchange of populations.[56] In their place the government located 160,000 Moslem immigrants from Greece.[57] It is difficult to determine the impact of this exchange on the existing population of Thrace except to say that the resulting situation must have been characterised by a larger average holding size. In any case the Thracian settlements seem to have been carried out in a relatively orderly fashion. In the Aegean littoral, however, the land was abandoned during flight in a period when the Ankara government had not yet established state authority over the main theatre of war. The same was true for Armenians leaving various regions of the interior, especially Cilicia. We may reasonably guess that the abandoned land was either acquired at much below cost in hasty deals, or forcefully appropriated – in both cases by the locally powerful landlords. During the exchange of populations the Turkish government officially appropriated the property left behind by Greeks. That part of the property on which there was no official settlement was immediately sold to local bidders. Once again these sales must have contributed to the concentration of land in the hands of a few rich landlords.

A rough estimate might be made of the amount of land liberated in Anatolia by movements of population. We will do the exercise for Western Anatolia. Assuming that there were 500,000 Greeks of agricultural origin, at least 300,000 of them were in Western Anatolia. With five persons to a family this number is equivalent to 60,000 families or as many farms. Considering that the average size of farms in the Aydin vilayet before the War was 4.5 hectares,[58] we get 270,000 hectares, or approximately 2.7m donums as the size of the Greek-owned land. The total cultivated land in the Western Anatolian region in 1927 was 8.2m donums.[59] At an average land owned to land cultivated ratio of 2 : 1, total holding size must have amounted to 16.4m donums. Thus, about one sixth of the cultivable area in Western Anatolia had been abandoned by the departing Greeks, even under the conservative assumption that their holdings were, on the average, the same size as Turkish farmers' holdings. It must also be remembered that this sixth was found in the more fertile and commercialised areas growing the main export crops of raisins and tobacco.

In addition to Western Anatolia, the Trabzon area on the Black Sea with its concentration of Greek farmers, and the Cilician plains where rich Armenian farmers had been driven out, must have presented similar pictures. There is, however, no data on the later distribution of abandoned land, except for accounts about powerful local notables obtaining deeds on the empty land in order to enlarge and consolidate their holdings.[60] Since we know that most of this land was found in the most highly commercialised regions of Anatolia where agricultural exploitation could be expected to be lucrative, despite the accounts claiming the total destruction and ruination of Greek villages and property,[61] it is more plausible that the land was in a short time put under cultivation by its new owners. Under the conditions of a high land/labour ratio which characterised post-war Anatolia, it is probable that no pressure was exerted for an equitable distribution of the land, and the abandoned and reclaimed territory was a major factor in accelerating the concentration of holdings.

Tractor imports, which we will discuss below, also aided the commercial farmers in expanding their holdings. Those farmers of the interior who already commanded large domains and depended on share-cropping for the internal organisation of their production for the market were reluctant to adopt the newly available technology, which could not be put to direct use without altering the mode of exploitation.[62] Under conditions of share-cropping, where the grip of the landlord on the small tenant is through a perpetual indebtedness, any technology raising the productivity of the share-cropper threatens to break the cycle of usury. Thus the landlords have to control the level of technology for the perpetuation of their political and economic domination over share-cropping peasants.[63] For the commercial capitalist farmer, however, who employed wage labour, new technology was not only cost-reducing, but also land-expanding. Tractors enabled him to adapt to new forces of production without falling into a contradiction with the prevailing relations of production on his farm. The concentration of land within the framework of capitalist farming progressed through the introduction of approximately 2000 tractors, especially in the commercial agricultural regions of Izmir and Adana.[64]

The growing concentration of land implied the expansion of wage-labour relations to a larger group of producers. Although achieved in part through technological change introduced with new tractor imports, it did not lead to a 'seigneurial reaction' with peasants being driven out of the rural sector, mainly because there was always less fertile land available. In fact, the balance of population in the 1920s shifted slightly in favour of rural settlements due to a higher rural birth rate, and an almost total absence of migration to urban areas.[65]

The concentration of capital is a tendency resulting from competition among individual capitalists. However, the concentration of capital in a certain sector of economic activity requires explanation. Thus the opening of new land, the adoption of new forces of production, and the general expansion in commercial agriculture indicate that investment in agriculture at the margin was considered to be profitable. No doubt the low price of land was a crucial factor: as was mentioned above, land could be had at zero price by certain people. In general, the fact that only 5% of the land was actually under cultivation, and that a decade of wars had decimated the population causing a scarcity of labour, implied a low price for land.[66]

Another important factor making agricultural investments attractive was the considerable direct or implicit subsidy by the government for tractors and other agricultural machinery purchases.[67] Aside from this advantageous configuration of input prices the terms-of-trade also progressed in the farmer's favour.[68] Thus it was preferable to plough back agricultural profits into expanding cultivation, which helped increase the area under commercial agriculture (especially producing export crops) during our period.

2.8 State and agriculture

The policy of the state vis-à-vis agriculture is important not only because it influences the manner of development of production and production relations within the sector, but also because it is indicative of the global role of the state in the process of world economic integration. To the extent that agriculture is the primary channel of integration into the world economy, the policy of the state with respect to agriculture gains particular importance. Therefore, while analysing the impact of state policy on agriculture, we will also attempt a determination of the class character of the state, as this acts upon the process of peripheralisation. During this discussion, we have to assess not only the intentions of the state, to be derived from its class representation, but also the objective results of its intentions. The first inquiry concerns the politically specific class configuration in Turkish society, while the second necessitates an investigation of the historical development of the agricultural sector in response to the economic policies of the state.

State policies have differential impacts on various segments of the agricultural sector. Our descriptive account of the agricultural sector in terms of its division into wage-labour employing, rich, middle, and poor peasant farming, and share-cropping should provide a basis for gauging this differential impact. It is necessary then to assess government policy in terms not only of its global impact but also of its favouring or privileging certain strata of the peasantry to the detriment of others. We shall first concentrate on the actual policy instruments employed by the state in its attentions toward the agricultural sector.

Four categories of policies stand out in forming a possible strategy in the state's relationship with agriculture. (1) The state's influence on the real availability of the inputs that enter the production function of agriculture. For example, a military mobilisation that decreases labour availability, a policy of land distribution or reclamation, a decision to subsidise imports of tractors, or to levy forbiddingly high import duties. (2) State policies affecting marketability: transportation, road and railway construction, and transport tariffs and subsidies. (3) State regulation of, or influence on, market prices which concern the agricultural sector: the prices of output and inputs, e.g. land, machinery, fertilisers. (4) Taxes which directly appropriate a part of the agricultural output, either in levies in kind or money. (In the latter case price policy may be used in conjunction with taxation policy.)[69]

2.8.1 Labour, machinery, and credits

Immediately after the war, the government sought to effect a speedy recovery of pre-war output levels. In addition to the market disturbances caused by the war, the entire economy, and in particular the agricultural sector, had come to suffer from a scarcity of labour. War had continued for more than a decade with military conscription falling mainly on the peasants. The population of Turkey (within the 1923 borders) was 15.8 million in 1913, and by 1927 it had only recovered to 13.6 million.[70] As was mentioned above, the decline in population was due both to war deaths and to mass emigration and massacre of minorities. The decline in population caused an even greater proportional decline in the labour force.

According to the Greek census of 1928, 250,000 (out of the 880,000 interviewed) Greeks who had immigrated from Turkey were employed in agriculture.[71] They were mostly growers of cereals, with tobacco growing as the second most important branch of cultivation. In 1926, two thirds of the total production of tobacco in Greece was due to the refugees.[72] Vine-growing had assumed 'great importance with the arrival of the refugees' who had brought new varieties of grapes and currants with them.[73] If we remember that tobacco and raisins jointly accounted for close to 40% of Turkey's exports between 1923 and 1929, the loss of a specialised population creating rival export sectors in a neighbouring country becomes a salient datum.

The loss of the labour force was partly countered by a shift in the demographic trend. Impressionistic accounts by travellers mention a falling birth rate among the Moslem population of Anatolia during the nineteenth century. In 1927, however, 23% of the population was in the age group of six years-old or younger,[74] indicating that the trend had reversed in a post-war 'baby-boom'. Of course, the effects of this reversal on the labour force would not immediately be felt. On the other hand, the already mentioned exchange of population had brought to Turkey close to 400,000 immigrants from Greece. All but 10% of the immigrant families were skilled growers, especially of tobacco.[75] There was, however, no systematic effort to settle the refugees according to their skills. Although most of them were relocated into the vilayets out of which the Greek population had moved,[76] it was often the case that tobacco-growers were settled in vine districts, or professional and commercial people in villages.[77]

The government was aware of the scarcity of labour in agriculture, and took action to alleviate the situation. A law which was passed in 1924 stipulated that (a) farmers owning a pair of oxen were obligated to cultivate a minimum area of 100 donums, (b) every peasant was obliged to work one day a week on land owned by war orphans, widows, and cripples, (c) state-owned enterprises were to cultivate 250 donums of land for the first 5000 TL of their capital, and 25 donums for each 1000 TL thereafter, and (d) municipal councils were obliged to assist farmers in securing agricultural machinery and implements through the Agricultural Bank.[78]

Together with attempts to supply labour to agriculture, it was necessary to restore the area of land under cultivation. The devastation during the war had left many villages, especially in Western Anatolia, destroyed and abandoned. In addition, it was observed during the negotiations on the exchange of populations that 'as soon as the Greek army was pushed out of Smyrna, Turkish revenge . . . turned into ruins many flourishing Greek sections of cities and countryside'.[79] The destruction had also taken its toll on the main capital good of the peasant: draught animals. With a greatly diminished number of cattle (6.9m in 1913, 4.1m in 1920),[80] it was likely that less land could be ploughed. A law in 1923 responded to the situation, abolishing all import taxes on livestock with the intention of increasing the numbers of both draught and farm animals. More importantly, and with greater success, the government took measures to facilitate and subsidise the imports of agricultural machinery. The same law which had aimed at increasing the labour supply also urged farmers to appeal to the Agricultural Bank for credit to buy machinery. In 1923, this semi-official bank had been given authority to import agricultural machinery free of duties and was induced to increase its credits to farmer-producers to enable them to purchase the imported machinery.[81] As we shall discuss below, the Agricultural Bank's loans to agriculture increased during the first years of the Republic, although not all the credit served the government's original purpose of funding agricultural reconstruction.

The government's more direct contribution to the development of the forces of production was its pecuniary encouragement of tractor purchases. In addition to voting 1m TL as credits for the purchase of tractors and liberalising the import of machines, fuel and parts for agriculture, after 1926 a fund was set aside to grant 'indemnity' to tractor purchasers, to work as a subsidy against the purchase price. Between 1926 and 1930, 6.6m TL was distributed in this fashion which suggests that the subsidy amounted to close to the full price of the tractor. (It is estimated that 2000 'Fordson' tractors were imported in these years.) In 1930, when this subsidy was discontinued, a sum of 2.7m TL was distributed to tractor owners as lump sum indemnity.[82] Other laws dealing with agriculture included a law stipulating the instruction of military conscripts in agricultural techniques (1924), and one for improving agricultural schools (1927). The government also initiated the establishment of agricultural research stations, experimental farms, advisory boards; it also distributed seed, and encouraged the cultivation of certain crops.[83]

While agriculture was thus recovering with the aid of the state, measures were also taken to transform the (legal) property relations. To this end private ownership of land was reestablished; new deeds were issued to establish claims which had until then stood on traditional possession agreements among the farmers. In 1926 the new civil law reinforced the legality of private property by replacing the Ottoman categories, which varied between usufruct right and *de facto* ownership, with *de jure* private ownership, in words and concepts borrowed from Swiss jurisprudence.[84] These legal innovations led to large farmers' claiming ownership over large plots of land. Especially with the aid of new farm machinery to substitute for scarce labour, the incentives offered by the export market, and the government's encouragement, from 1924 to 1928 there was an expansion of cultivated land and recovery of pre-war levels of production.[85]

2.8.2 Transportation

In addition to already mentioned factors influencing the expansion of agriculture, two more have to be analysed, both originating from government policy and exercising a relatively greater effect on the marketisation of traditional agriculture. The first of these was the growing availability of a transportation network, which established the connection of many outlying areas with already existing markets. The second was the abolition of the tithe in 1925 and the attempt to substitute it with new monetary taxes on land and livestock as revenue sources. We shall first look at the contribution of transportation to the growth of the capitalist market.

In 1923, during the Izmir Economic Congress, one of the foremost demands of the farmers' group concerned the construction of new roads and a decrease in the price of railway transportation.[86] The justification which accompanied this demand was that these measures would allow the farmer to compete with imports. If we remember that in the economic structure of the empire the main consuming centre of Istanbul had been more closely integrated into Western and Balkan economies, with which it had sea-route connections, than with the inner parts of Anatolia, this demand seems to fit in with the development of a national economy generating new lines of integration. In fact, the entire railways policy in particular and transportation in general should be analysed from the two perspectives of strengthening the already existing lines of external integration and attempting to construct an internal integration.[87]

Every railway (or transportation) project during the period of participation in the world division of labour has a dual effect. It increases the mobility of commodities, i.e. diminishes the resistance to the further extension of the division of labour; at the same time, it alters the specific modality of integration. An exporting capital city, for example, when it is more efficiently connected with its hinterland, will be collecting a larger proportion of the surplus produced in the interior and the exporting merchants will therefore increase the volume of trade. In conjunction with this, however, the primary materials and food that it might have hitherto obtained from abroad due to more favorable prices, now can more readily be obtained from its own hinterland. This is by no means a small quantity. In Turkey, for example, in 1923, the share of non-manufactured food imports in total imports was 16%. This figure, which excludes 'colonial' produce, declined to between 6 and 9% after 1925.[88] In this category of the changing modality we may also include the effect of lower transportation costs on the development of food manufacturing industry, usually the largest manufacturing sector during the beginning periods of industrialisation.

In 1923, Turkey possessed (excluding the Syrian line) 3126 kilometres of single-track, standard-gauge rail line, and 323 kms of narrow-gauge line.[89] All of the first category and 70 kms of the narrow-gauge had been built by foreign concessionnaires, either under a system where the government guaranteed an acceptable financial return proportional to the length of track, or in return for the right to mineral exploitation alongside the lines or both. The constructing firms had also taken an active interest in developing market-orientated agriculture where the lines passed and in cultivating a demand for manufactures. Thus, even if the overriding concern in building some of the railways had not been the integration of Turkish agriculture into the world market (as, for example, suggested by Rivkin, who privileges the internal market creation motive)[90], the railway, once it started operating, served precisely that goal. Besides, the Aegean lines connecting Izmir, the outlet for the agricultural surplus of all western Anatolia with its rich hinterland, were obviously motivated by the prospect of moving larger surpluses to the markets of Europe.[91] The lines converging in Izmir accounted for 1314 kms or 40% of the above total. The interior lines connecting Istanbul with Damascus through Konya and Adana (with an extension to Ankara) pass through the agricultural centre of Anatolia, viz. Eskisehir, Afyon, Konya, and Adana. The per capita agricultural production in the vilayets of Ankara, Konya, and Adana in 1913, for example was 27% higher than the per capita agricultural production of the rest of Turkey.[92] In addition to agricultural output, there were copper, chrome, borax, and lead mines, which also contributed to the profitability of railway lines. In fact, the attraction of mineral exploitation rights alongside the Baghdad railway might have influenced the routing of the line.[93]

The existing system of railways inherited by the Republic had been designed to tap the agricultural and raw material surplus of the Ottoman Empire through developing commodity production and purchase.[94] Naturally, no attention had been paid to growing regional inequality or to the growing disarticulation of the internal economy while some parts of it became integrated into an external market. At the level of geography, the distribution of railways exhibited an evident inequality between the market-orientated western regions, the surplus-producing interior, and the subsistence-farming east, northeast, and southwest.

Between 1924 and 1928, the parliament voted funds for the construction of seven new lines, totalling close to 2000 kms. In 1929, about 1000 kms of new lines had been completed and work was in progress on the rest.[95] These new lines continued the same restructuring process that the Ottoman lines had initiated. Their geographical distribution reinforced the earlier trend, which was but an expression of the economic rationale behind the choice of routes. Economic calculation pointed to choices in the direction of the exploitation of potential or actual agricultural raw-material surpluses; thus creating a greater export potential as well as a market for imports which the export earnings would pay for. We shall look at these new lines in order to emphasise the growing role of railways in the commodity-producing sector of agriculture.

The most important lines in question, Ankara–Sivas and Sivas–Samsun, connected the new capital city with the central collection area of the cereals surplus of central Anatolia. Ankara was also on the main Anatolian line (the old Baghdadbahn); thus Sivas became connected to Istanbul as well as to points south. The importance of Sivas province may be gauged through its contribution to the agricultural surplus. In 1927, before the line was completed, Sivas already was the fifth largest cereal-growing vilayet. The vilayet produced 153 kgs of wheat per inhabitant compared to 97 in Turkey as a whole.[96] When we remember that wheat was produced everywhere in Turkey this 57% difference emerges as a certain indicator of the existence of a marketable surplus. The other four wheat-growing vilayets were already connected with the centres of distribution and consumption, and therefore could be considered as having been integrated into the internal market and indirectly into the world market. Konya, the largest producer of wheat, was a main junction on the old Baghdadbahn. The region owed its primacy as much to its natural endowment in terms of fertility and geography as to its location on the railway. The second largest cereal-producing vilayet was Ankara, also on the old Anatolian line, and a traditional market town of the interior. With the moving of the seat of power from Istanbul to Ankara, a large consuming population was also transferred to this city in the form of government and army officials and their families. Thus, Ankara's importance as a market increased as its population grew from 70,000 to 120,000 between 1927 and 1935,[97] and rather than it being a supplier to the Istanbul market through the railway connection, it became necessary to think of Ankara as a potential market for the agricultural surplus. The connection with Sivas would guarantee this.

The third and fourth largest wheat growing vilayets were Manisa and Bursa. Manisa's importance had been recognised early due to its potential in tobacco production, and it had been connected to the Izmir–Kasaba line in 1888. As for Bursa, the railway connecting the city with the Marmara port of Mudanya had been constructed in 1871, although, prior to that too, ample road connections had existed.[98]

Thus the Ankara–Sivas line emerges as a natural step in the policy of agricultural integration. In fact, a long range plan for the development of railways in the Ottoman Empire had been prepared during the period of concession-hunting by foreign builders.[99] This project designed by foreign experts had included a railway linking Sivas with Kayseri and Ankara. The new government realised the plans with a delay of three decades.

Samsun, as was remarked above, was the largest tobacco producer after Izmir and Manisa. The vilayet was also the largest grower of corn and the third largest grower of rice. An important port, it would become the natural outlet of its hinterland with the railway connection. In fact, the richness of the agricultural surplus in the Samsun region was so lucrative that it led to an unprecedented development. In 1927, a group of local producers, relying entirely on their own funds, collected sufficient capital to construct a narrow-gauge line connecting Carsamba, a fertile valley in the Samsun vilayet, to the port. Their operations, however, did not succeed due to the competition of newly introduced motor transportation on a parallel road.[100] This embarrassment of riches resulted in the government's purchasing the loss-making operation in 1929, in the true tradition of nationalising economically inefficient concerns. Two additional lines were to be constructed, mainly to take advantage of mining output. Thus the Irmak–Filyos line passed through coal fields on the Black Sea coast and the Diyarbakir–Fevzipasa line served the Erghani copper mines.[101]

The government's fare policy on railways was also designed to increase the primary production potential of the country. Freight charges had always been a cause of complaint. Foreign-operated railways of the Empire had charged high prices for freight, arguing that because the country was poor, rail traffic was only outward bound, and prices had to be kept high in order to cover costs. During this period and, in fact, until a new fare policy came into effect, imports into Istanbul by sea had been cheaper to transport than domestic transportation by rail. In June 1924, freight rates per ton of wheat were $5.06 from New York to Istanbul by sea route; and $8.84 from Ankara to Istanbul by rail.[102] This situation had encouraged grain imports, but new fares were legislated in 1924 and the share of imports in the provisioning of Istanbul declined. The new fare schedule was a specific one: different rates applied according to the nature of freight. The following basic fares held:[103]

Agricultural products and minerals:	3.30 ks/ton-km
Semi-manufactured materials:	4.05 ks
Manufactured materials:	5.25 ks

More specifically, special tariffs were applied to cereals, flour, livestock, construction material, coal, minerals, sugar beets (i.e. raw materials for industry), and export products. Together with these reductions, cereals became the most favoured cargo, with a tariff declining to 1 ks/ton-km for a haul of 1000 kms. Exported agricultural goods were slightly more expensive to transport to the port of export.[104]

The impact of the railways and lower transport prices can be traced through the increases in the volume of transportation by rail. In 1924, 47.5m kgs of wheat were transported by rail, in 1926 105.7m kgs, and in 1929/30 148.5m kgs. A similar increase was observed in the transportation of flour. From 1924 to 1928/29, the volume of flour transported by rail increased fourfold, that of barley by 40%, fruits by 80%. At the same time transportation of goods entering foreign trade increased. Eggs and tobacco transported by rail increased threefold between 1924 and 1928/29. The growth in the reverse flow of imports could be observed in the shipment of gasoline and oil which exhibited an increase from 7341 tons to 38,043 tons between 1924 and 1929/30. Sugar, which, together with fuel, is among the first commodities demanded by the marketised agricultural sector, also showed large increases: from 7589 tons in 1924 to 18,130 tons in 1929/30.[105]

In addition to railways the government launched a road campaign. In 1924 the length of roads 'open to wheeled traffic' was estimated at 10,000 km. However, only a third of this was considered in good repair.[106] By May 1928, a total of 1089 kms of new roads had been built by the government, and work was in progress on another 2096 kms. It should be taken into consideration that the new roads were higher quality 'chaussée' roads suitable for all year travelling. Of the 1089 kms, 822 kms were described as 'chaussées'.[107] The geographical spread of road-making activity exhibited a bias in favour of the already rich districts of Aydin, Izmir, Istanbul, and Trabzon. The vilayet of Ankara was also the scene of road-building activity, due as much to its being a cereal-growing district as to its newly gained political importance.

Some of this achievement was due to the road tax imposed on the population when the tithe was abolished. The road tax provided the government with revenue, but more importantly with labour. The tax had originally claimed a certain number of work days from all adult males, but it could be commuted to money payments. Poorer peasants preferred actually to offer their labour rather than pay cash. Through this method, the road network expanded.

2.8.3 Taxes on agriculture

In the Ottoman Empire, the most important tax, which, in fact, defined the nature of the imperial system, was the agricultural tithe, traditionally claiming one tenth of the output. It was through the tithe that the agricultural surplus, the ground rent, was appropriated by the state.[108] Therefore, the transformation of the tithe by the Republican government reflects not only the economic policy choices of the government, but also its self-conception *qua* state. The 1925 decision abolishing the tithe should be analysed at three levels: its effect on the development of capitalist agriculture; its effect on the inter-sectoral flow of surplus; and its implication for the identity of the state.[109]

During the first years of the Republic, the tithe was 12.5%, its rate raised in the late nineteenth century. However, from 1923 on there were attempts to lower the percentage and big landlords frequently appealed for its complete abrogation. Finally, in 1925, this tax, 'which represents such a heavy burden on the peasant, and does not provide him with any motivation to cultivate more land',[110] was abolished. During the later centuries of the Empire, the predominant mode of collection of the tithe had been tax-farming. In this method the central bureaucracy received cash payments in advance from local financiers, and gave them the right to collect the tithe in kind. Because the tax-farmer could manipulate the timing and the mode of assessment of the crop, the growers frequently ended up parting with a much higher proportion of their output than the stipulated 12.5%. Frequently, the peasant complained that tax-farmers would wait until prices had changed to claim their share of the produce, which caused rotting and disappearance of the crop under rain and exposure.[111] Thus, the abolition of the tithe increased the absolute amount of the available surplus by eliminating this waste marginally; but more importantly, it shifted a segment of farmers from self-subsistence to surplus production for the market. By making an additional one eighth of the output available to the peasant, the absence of the tithe brought a hitherto marginal, self-providing stratum into direct contact with the market. Its earlier integration into the market economy had been through tax obligation to a commercial capitalist—the tax-farmer. Therefore, the organisation of production had remained traditional. After the abolition of the tithe this stratum possessed a surplus that it could market itself, and was thus introduced into the cash nexus.[112]

This segment of the peasantry may be identified more closely as the grain-producing small-holders of the interior. Their development into commodity producers was through supplying the food surplus which had been lost due to the replacement of grain production on fertile lands by the production of export crops. As such, they grew staple crops, and especially wheat. It was on this stratum of the middle peasantry that the government based its wheat policy in the 1930s. While the depression had destroyed the export outlets of the commercial farmers, the autarkic policy followed by the government included an extensive support programme for wheat production, which, relatively, had its most important positive impact on the middle peasant who had marginally entered the market in the 1920s. The impact of the abolition of the tithe was qualitative on the would-be middle peasant by bringing him to the market, and quantitative on the large farmer through increasing the size of his surplus product.[113]

The second perspective to be brought on the 1925 legislation abolishing the tithe concerns the amount of surplus retained in the agricultural sector. I will not argue that the absolute size of the surplus changed because of the abolition of this tax; although, as was mentioned above, there is some justification in arguing that the farmer would increase his production because of the greater incentives offered, and also that there would be a smaller loss of the harvest due to immediate marketing. In any case this addition to the volume of the surplus would be marginal. The impact on the mode of utilisation of surplus and therefore on the potential and locus of accumulation of capital was, however, considerable.

In 1924, 22% of the government's total revenue and 63% of the revenue from direct taxes consisted of payment from tax-farmers in exchange for the tithe. The actual amount extracted out of the growers was at least 20% higher than the government receipts due to the commercial profit of the tax-farmers.[114]

Between 1924 and 1926, when the tithe was abandoned, the share of direct taxes in the revenue fell from 30% to 21%.[115] We may argue that the share of the surplus extracted by former tax-farmers did not decrease greatly since most of them continued to enjoy a profit on commercial capital engaged in the marketing of the surplus. Did the central authority, as well, continue to appropriate as much of the agricultural surplus as before 1925?

Although the government attempted to replace the tithe with other direct taxes which fell strictly on the agricultural sector, all signs indicate that the actual tax burden of the farmer decreased somewhat. It was recently instituted indirect taxes which made up the major part of the government's budget, not the new direct taxes falling on the farmer. These new direct taxes were the land and livestock taxes, both traditional levies which had lost their effectiveness. With the abolition of the tithe, the tax on agricultural property was raised from 0.6% to 4.8% of the assessed value of the land.[116] This wealth tax, however, was quite ineffectual since the land values upon which the tax was based were assessed in pre-war gold liras. The exchange rate between paper and gold liras was 8 : 1 in 1925, 8.1 : 1 in 1926 and 9.2 : 1 in 1930.[117] Thus, the real incidence of the tax was between 0.6 and 0.8% of the current value of the land. This amounted to between 5 and 6% of total government revenue in the years 1926–29. Public lands, common pastures, and state farms were permanently exempt from this tax. Temporary exemption was also granted to newly reclaimed land and to land given to immigrants and settling nomads. In 1929, the tax ratio was once again raised from 4.8% to 6.5%.[118]

The livestock tax, also an Ottoman tax, consisted of a fixed levy for each sheep and goat alive at the time of assessment. Its original intent had been to tax the wool output. In 1926 this old prestation was revised to yield greater revenue, through a higher tariff for each farm animal.[119] Thus, in 1926, its yield was over twice as much as what it had been in 1924. The livestock tax amounted to between 6 and 7% of total government revenue until 1929. In 1929, the rates prescribed by the tax were doubled. Hence, these two newly raised taxes accounted for 12% of government revenue, on the average, 7% higher than their pre-1925 contribution. We must also mention that both of these taxes were fixed in money terms and therefore fell in real terms between 1923 and 1930 when prices were rising. During the 1930s, the opposite happened, and these taxes became much more burdensome due to falling prices of agricultural output.

The government's loss of revenue in direct taxes was compensated for by increases in indirect taxes, the most important category being the newly instituted consumption and transaction taxes. In 1926, these alone made up 20% of all government revenue. In addition to this, increased prices on salt, sugar, and petrol, all government monopolies, provided for 9% of the revenue in 1926.[120] Most excise taxes and high-priced monopoly items were designed with peasant consumption in mind. In 1931, for example, a rich farmer deputy of the ruling party complained that the new situation for the agricultural population was as burdensome as the tithe, only disguised.[121] Nevertheless, it is certain that the tax burden on the urban commercial and industrial sectors increased after 1925, while the tax burden of the agricultural sector in relative terms did not.

2.8.4 The internal terms-of-trade

Since an effective tax on agricultural output was never reinstated, the main mechanism of surplus transfer out of agriculture became terms-of-trade, or price policy. During the history of the Turkish Republic, the terms-of-trade between agriculture and manufactures have closely reflected the attitude of the government on the question of surplus mobilisation, because prices have been effectively controlled through restrictions on imports and the government's prominent position as a purchaser of agricultural produce.

To calculate the internal terms-of-trade for the agricultural producer, we took the cost of living index in twenty principal Turkish cities prepared by the Statistics Office.[122] This index is based on twenty-six consumption articles all of which are food, processed food, or combustibles – coal and wood. This was taken to be the numerator, indicating the sales price farmers received. For the denominator, an index of Turkish imports was prepared, prices of imports weighted by values, with the assumption that the purchases made by the farmer can be represented by the import package.[123] This exercise gives the result (1929 as 100) shown in column 1 in the table below. Column 2 for the years 1927–29 is the quotient of the wholesale food price index and the 'textile sub-index of the wholesale price index', calculated by Hirsch and Hirsch.[124] Column 3 is the world 'terms-of-trade of food' as calculated according to representative international trade prices.[125] It will be seen that columns 1 and 3 indicate a decline in the price ratios between 1923 and 1925. Then an upturn is sustained over two or three years and 1928 exhibits another slight downturn. The similarity in the movements of the internal terms-of-trade for agriculture and the world terms-of-trade of food indicates that government policy with respect to prices was notable in the 1920s for its absence. In other words, the open economy was allowed to work in such a way as to regulate internal price

	(1)	(2)	(3)
1923	107		107
1924	91		107
1925	90		100
1926	100		100
1927	101	102.5	107
1928	98	110.7	103
1929	100	100	100

movements without any intervention by the state. This was true *strictu sensu* until 1926. In 1926 consumption taxes were levied on sugar and petrol, interfering with the free movement of prices.[126] From then until the end of the decade, no measures were taken affecting the price of imported consumer goods, mostly because the government was restricted in its tariff policy.

The impact of the 'luxury' tax on sugar and petrol on the agricultural sector has to be weighted with the relative value of the consumption of these two items in farmers' budgets. Lacking precise knowledge of this, the price data alone fail to suggest an impact of appreciable degree. In the case of petrol, where the tax had no protectionist aim, the price on the Istanbul retail market increased by 5% while delivery price at the port had declined by 12%.[127] For sugar, the internal (Istanbul) retail price declined by 15% between 1927 and 1930 while the delivery price declined by 33%.[128] In the case of sugar, however, two factories had been established by the government in 1926, and therefore the tax had a protectionist dimension. For exported crops, however, landowners faced world market prices without any tampering by the government. This passivity on the part of the government was, of course, not neutral with respect to the differentiation of the agricultural classes.

2.8.5 Conclusions

The preceding discussion shows that state policy did not attempt to effect a transfer of surplus out of the agricultural sector. Changes in the tax system were roughly neutral, and prices did not move against agricultural producers. Growing market opportunities and high wages due to a favourable land/labour ratio kept agricultural incomes high. The agricultural policy of the state during the 1920s was designed to aid in the reconstruction of pre-war output levels. To this end the government sought to increase the amount of land under cultivation, supported tractor purchases, and legislated firmer rights of ownership on land. A parallel effect was produced by the transportation policy, which was designed to facilitate the marketisation of surplus, and commercialisation of agriculture. Thus, labour scarcity and abandonment of cultivated lands, factors which would cause a decline in agricultural output, were countered in part through government policies. Legislation designed to increase the labour input, facilitate the purchase and use of machinery, together with measures to provide more extended and cheaper transportation facilities to agricultural growers, counteracted the war-time devastation. These measures undoubtedly contributed to the recovery of pre-war levels of production and marketisation.

In addition to these policies, the principal measure taken by the government relating to agriculture was the abolition of the traditional tithe. This abolition allowed the farmers to dispose of a larger share of the surplus, thus increasing their commercialisation potential. With diminished taxes the government could have utilised a terms-of-trade policy aimed at transferring agricultural surplus to the state, or to the urban sector. Our investigation shows, however, that this was not the case, and we conclude that government policies favoured the commercial development of the agricultural sector. They allowed farmers to enjoy higher incomes, and to carry out the marketisation of a larger share of the surplus rather than yielding it through market and non-market mechanisms of control.

2.9 Growth of agricultural output

National income data for the period indicate that agriculture was the most rapidly growing sector in the economy. In constant prices agricultural output increased by 115% from 1923 to 1929, while manufacturing output increased by 56% and income of the commercial sector by 71%.[129] This rapid increase in agricultural output was due in most part to the devastation suffered by land and labour in the more fertile areas of the country. The war had been an accelerating factor for manufacturing production, which was concentrated in the comparative quiet of Istanbul. Western Anatolia and Cilicia, principal agricultural areas, however, had been the theatres of protracted fighting. After the Greek army was driven out of Anatolia, villagers in the Aegean region began to cultivate their fields in safety. Yet, due to wartime deaths, there was an important decline in the number of hands returning to work in agriculture. Thus, the growth in agricultural output is an indication of the extent of recovery of older levels of activity. Since it was not through a massive increase in the labour input that this recovery occurred (immigration into Turkey was only one tenth of the population that emigrated or was lost during the war), we should look at the changes in the capital input.

The data relating to the capital input are mainly impressionistic. Since meteorological conditions played a significant role in influencing output levels, it is difficult to arrive at meaningful estimates of productivity starting from levels of output and the land input. It should be mentioned that meteorological conditions were not always favourable, and yet the period 1923–29 exhibits an increase in output superior to any other six-year period until 1950.[130] We might also note that the overall growth rate in output between 1923 and 1929 occurred despite a considerable downturn in 1927 which was due to a bad harvest. The harvest of 1928 was an improvement, and 1929 brought agricultural output back on the trend line originating in 1923. The years 1930 and 1931 witnessed further increases compared to 1929.

The number of tractors imported has already been mentioned: Turkish agriculture possessed 2000 tractors in 1929 as compared to 220 in 1923. Imports of agricultural machinery also remained at a high level between 1924 and 1929: by weight, agricultural equipment represented one third of the total imports of machinery (5.30m kgs in 1925, 4.73m in 1926, 4.75m in 1927, and 4.43m in

1928).[131] Domestic production of agricultural implements accounted for the largest employment figure among the sub-sectors of 'metal and machine-building industry' in the 1927 census.[132] That agricultural machinery possessed a ready market had been noted as early as 1922 when the concession-hunter Admiral Chester included a factory for agricultural implements among his projects designed to bring about a 'total' development of Turkey.[133] Three years later, a Polish consortium had been formed to sell agricultural machinery in railway depots.[134]

Investment in agriculture was accompanied by an increase in the area cultivated. The cultivation of commercial crops increased as well as the area of grain land. The area sown with wheat, for example, increased by 15% between 1927 and 1929,[135] after pre-war levels of cultivation had already been recovered. The number of sheep and goats increased from 17.2m in 1923 to 24.0m in 1928; and the number of cattle from 4.1m in 1920 to 6.8m in 1927, which was equal to the 1914 level.[136] In one region (Konya), the irrigated area grew by five times over the decade.[137] The productivity of land under wheat cultivation increased due in part to capital intensification. Output of wheat in quintals per hectare evolved in the following manner:[138]

```
1926 :  6.9
1927 :  5.5
1928 :  5.8
1929 :  9.8
1930 :  9.2
1931 : 10.1
```

The results of this development in agriculture before the depression may be summarised in the statement that pre-war levels of activity were recovered with the encouragement of the state.

During the 1920s, market-oriented production in general, and capitalist production in particular, progressed along the lines of integration into the world economy started during the Ottoman period. The integration of Turkish agriculture into the world market was manifest in the proportions of exported output in major crops. We now turn to an evaluation of agricultural exports.

2.10 Agriculture and trade

The world war and the subsequent Turkish war of liberation had severely curtailed the volume of foreign transactions. The first stage in the growth of the exporting agricultural sector was therefore to attain the pre-war levels of production and to recapture its previous markets. This was quickly done in certain crops. Cotton, for example, which had not been developed as an export crop to its full potential, quickly surpassed the pre-war maximum of 1914. Already in 1924, production was 18% higher than in 1914.[139] A similar performance was observed in tobacco cultivation which reached a level superior to the pre-war maximum in 1924 and attained a pre-depression maximum in 1927.[140] Figs and raisins, the most important export crops after cotton and tobacco, lost their relative importance. One of the reasons for this decline was that the production and marketing of these crops had formerly been monopolised by Greeks who were forced to leave Turkey during the postwar exchange of populations.[141] Secondly, figs and raisins required an outlay of capital that did not produce returns in the short run. This condition had led to a domination of merchant capital over the farmers who were largely small producers. Merchant capital had been supplied by Ottoman Greeks and Armenians who functioned as sub-contractors to large foreign exporting firms. Hostilities and the exchange of populations, however, had temporarily upset this mode of functioning. The Izmir region had also witnessed large-scale physical destruction; since it was the main theatre of war, conditions as a whole improved slowly. By the time the Izmir region became ready to export the pre-war volume in 1926, Californian growers had secured protective measures from the American government against Turkish raisins, and had thus robbed the Izmir exporters of their largest market.[142] Nevertheless, in 1927, the fig crop surpassed the pre-war volume, and raisin production was at 80% of the 1913 level.[143] During the 1920s, cotton, tobacco, figs, and raisins regularly amounted to close to 60% of all Turkish exports. Hazelnuts also belonged to the category of exclusively export-orientated fruits. Hazelnuts were exported fresh, destined mostly for the chocolate industry. The principal importers were Italian firms who mixed higher quality Turkish products with local hazelnuts and served as re-exporter to other countries in Europe, notably Switzerland.[144] It is possible to estimate the percentage of output which was exported because the output of the principal growing region is known. In the years 1927 and 1928, out of a total output of 75.9m kgs, 72.5m kgs were exported, representing close to 10% of the value of total exports.[145] Turkey, together with Italy and Spain, was one of the major exporters of hazelnuts. But since Turkish products were of higher quality, and prices did not reflect this quality difference, there were no marketing problems.[146] Turkish exports were limited only by the extent of production. In the reports prepared for the 1931 Agricultural Congress, the emphasis was on the expansion of land under cultivation and more efficient exploitation. The reporters stressed that Turkish exports of hazelnuts faced no competition and could be expanded to increase foreign exchange earnings. In fact, in the 1920s, it was planned to extend the production of hazelnuts to the Izmir region, and the project was realised in the 1930s.[147]

The production of figs in the principal growing region, Izmir, increased from 20.5m kgs in 1923 to 32m kgs in 1928.[148] Its exports in this year amounted to 27m kgs, Britain, the US, Germany, and Italy, accounting for over three quarters of the sales.[149] In 1928, the export of figs represented a value of 4.8m TL, or 2.3% of total exports. Raisin exports in the same year amounted to

15.2m TL, or 8.8%. Turkey's main customers were Britain and Holland and her main competitors Australia and the US.[150] Very early in the integration of Western Anatolia into the world market, raisins had become a principal item of export. In fact, the production of the Izmir region in the last pre-war year had been 69m kgs whereas the post-1923 maximum was 51m kgs in 1929.[151]

In the first half of the 1920s it was hoped that cotton exports would constitute the motor element in the Turkish economy's integration into the world economy. The performance of cotton output and exports provided this outlook with some justification. Indeed, in 1924, cotton production was about 20% higher than in 1914. Between 1924 and 1927 it increased by another 15%. From 1927 to 1929, the area under cultivation and output of raw cotton doubled.[152] In 1922, there were only 3 Fordson tractors in Adana, the main cotton producing region accounting for three quarters of the output. In 1925 there were 100.[153] This rapid development was not entirely generated through responses to the market. Purchasers had taken an active interest in the rapid development of supply. Through the supply of short-term credits and other, non-pecuniary, aid to the growers, they endeavoured to increase the pace of specialisation in cotton culture. Foreign experts arrived in the Adana region to effect improvements in the crop. In 1925 a Manchester firm built a large gin in the region to increase the volume of trade.[154] The Turkish government also joined the efforts to regularise cotton production and shipments. In 1925 a conference was held in Adana with the purpose of studying the production of cotton. A Trieste Bank organised Italian capital to establish a new company to deal specifically with cotton exports. The Liverpool Cotton Association and 'Lancashire milling circles' encouraged the British-owned 'Turkish Trading Company' to establish a cotton seed crushing mill in Adana, the first in Turkey.[155] In 1925, it was estimated that the Adana region alone could potentially produce 1.5 to 2 million bales of cotton.[156] But the actual performance was disappointing. This was due in part to a lack of standardisation and partly to the low quality of Turkish cotton, which was not always guaranteed a stable market. The Adana cotton exchanges, however, had been established, and 'even the most modest farmer [knew] how to follow the market'.[157] By 1927, total production in Turkey was at 180,000 bales, and only about 40% of this was exported. In 1928, the volume of cotton exports decreased by about 6,000 bales or by 8%.[158] One factor in this unsatisfactory export performance was the growing domestic demand for cotton. The domestic manufacture of cotton products had increased during the decade, a trend which was further reinforced after the 1929 crisis. A more important factor was the depression that hit the cotton industry in Europe during 1926 and 1927. In England, for example, 1926 saw a rapid decline of cloth manufacturing which at the time was explained through an uncompetitive cost structure by the employers. At the same time, however, Belgian, German, French, and Italian cotton production activity was also experiencing a slowdown. In 1926 English cotton cloth exports declined by 15% in volume and 23% in value, as a result of which raw cotton exporting countries faced lower demands in 1927 and 1928.[159]

The structural dimension in the overall recessionary tendency was the growing substitution in textiles by importing countries. The industrial West had to switch to a higher technology product from cotton textiles that had traditionally found outlets in the periphery, and which, because of a labour-intensive technology, were the first substituted manufactures. Yet, the problems accompanying such a long-term adjustment process were effective in causing market disequilibria in the short run. Indeed, as Svennilson argues, the industrial history of Europe's early industrialisers between the wars may be regarded as a long crisis of transformation.[160]

Tobacco, which was also developed as an export crop in the nineteenth century, attained a level of output in the 1920s which was consistently higher than pre-war averages.[161] Between 1924 and 1928, output fluctuated between 50 and 60m kgs, with a maximum of 69.9m kgs in 1927, representing the largest harvest in Turkey's history. Generally, one quarter of the crop was used domestically and the rest exported: accounting for between 25 and 35% of all export earnings.[162] Turkish tobacco was mostly of high quality 'Oriental' variety which was used as an essential ingredient in Western mixtures. Competing with Greek and Bulgarian crops, Turkish exporters, nevertheless, could sell all the fine tobacco that was produced.[163] Italy was again the principal customer, purchasing more than half of the sales, yet re-exporting over 90% of its purchase to other European countries.[164] The US purchased another 30% and Germany 15%. Turkey's 3.2% share of the world production could readily find markets and only fluctuations in output due to weather and plant disease meant a decline in earnings.[165]

Both production and exports of tobacco increased up to and including 1926. In 1925, however, the government took over the Régie des Tabacs, formerly a French monopoly over the commerce of tobacco. A new state monopoly began to handle the purchasing and export of tobacco. One of the decisions of the new monopoly administration was to retain a higher proportion of good quality leaf for domestic consumption.[166] Also in 1926, the German government passed a law imposing a fixed duty on all imports of tobacco regardless of quality.[167] This meant that both Italian and German purchases of low quality tobacco declined. As a consequence of these two developments, the international tobacco exchange in Istanbul was glutted with low-quality tobacco.[168] In 1927, for example, although production was the highest it had ever been, exports declined precipitously by 29% in volume and 34% in value, as compared to 1926. Yet in 1929, the share of tobacco in the export revenue was 26%, and it was also the largest item of export.[169]

As a result of growing production and marketisation, there was also a specialisation process. More villages became mono-culture areas submitting to the requirements of the world division of labour. In tobacco cultivation, for example, the average area sown per village increased from 29 donums in 1923 to 142 donums in 1928; while the number of villages planting tobacco decreased from 13,321 to 4674.[170] In Giresun on the Black Sea, 90,000 farmers specialised in the production of hazelnuts; in Adana 46% of the land was used to grow cotton.[171]

2.11 Degree of integration of agriculture in the world market

Together with the growth of commodity production, we can also observe a growing dependence on the world market. Despite the bad harvest in 1928, which caused an 8% decline in agricultural exports in 1929, the average ratio of agricultural exports to agricultural output was 20% from 1923 to 1929. The same ratio in the seven years before the World War was 14%.[172] This 20% average conceals wide variations. In 1927, for example, three quarters of the hazelnut output was exported, 62% of the tobacco crop, 41% of the cotton and 40% of the raisin output were sold abroad. Among the crops destined less directly for foreign markets, 32% of the sesame output, and 17% of the 'beans, lentils, etc.' output were exported. Of the cereals, oats with 17.3% exported, and barley with 7% occupied the front ranks. 2.5% of the potato output and 1.5% of the wheat output were also exported.[173]

When the problems associated with the world crisis hit Turkish agriculture and exports, the policies of the earlier decade figured more starkly in the agenda. In 1931, the government convened an Agriculture Congress, in the preamble of which we read:

The burden of exports is on *agriculture*. The deficit in balance of trade may be covered on the one hand through the encouragement and protection of manufactures capable of being developed in the country and thereby reducing imports, and on the other hand through increasing the *exports*, which face an ever-increasing *competition* in world markets. Therefore increasing our exports requires an increase in our competitive ability in *world* markets.[174] [Emphases in the original]

The text goes on to recommend quality control as one major requirement in the process of gaining competitive ability in world markets. In the reports to the same congress, we have accounts by the actual producers and merchants of agricultural products indicating their views as to the extent of the integration of Turkish agriculture into world markets. As the justificatory note in the beginning of the published accounts makes clear, the underlying purpose of the congress was precisely to assess the possibilities of export promotion in agriculture. To this end, reports were requested from the producers' associations of each of the exportable crops (this included the entire gamut of agricultural produce except those cultivated primarily as animal feed), from government officials stationed in those areas producing primarily for export, and from commercial attachés based in those ports where Turkish produce was exported. Together with information pertaining to general conditions of production – land tenure, agricultural machinery, fertilisers, producers' cooperatives – the reporters were supposed to provide information as to the marketing of the produce. Standardisation, quality control, packing, and commercial credit were the topics which took up the longest sections of the reports, and established the general tone of the endeavour. After the onset of the depression, agricultural producers and exporters seem to have become aware that the government might figure more directly in their attempts at capturing and maintaining a share in world markets.

The pleas to the government, which came at a moment when exporters and commercial producers were anxious to counteract the effects of the world crisis, were also indicative of the degree of integration that agriculture enjoyed before the world crisis. Most significant in this respect were the discussions relating to price formation and commodity exchanges (*bourses*) which performed the role of clearing houses for export markets.

2.11.1 *Commodity exchanges*

The commodity exchange which attracted the greatest attention was the grain and agricultural produce exchange in Istanbul. This exchange was established by the Turkish Chamber of Commerce in 1925. In 1931, the volume of transactions in this exchange was said to be 'the largest in the Balkans except for the Romanian exchange.'[175] At that time it was the major exchange in hazelnuts and poppy, both important Turkish export items. It was hoped that in 11 other items of export Istanbul could establish itself as the major exchange centre of the area, and consequently become one of the 'secondary centres of exchanges, such as Bremen'. The primary centres were those of New York for cotton, Winnipeg for wheat, etc. In this position Istanbul would be the commercial node for the exports of Bulgaria, Greece, and other Balkan countries, whose exports would find outlets through the intermediation of Istanbul-based merchants.[176]

Whether this position could have been attained in the absence of the world depression it is impossible to say; however, the aims indicate that perhaps the actual situation was not too far from that which was sought. In the same report on the exchanges, export merchants complain that closing prices in London, Winnipeg and Chicago reached Istanbul the following morning and not immediately, which points to a high degree of sensitivity to world prices. Such close dependence on the world market had certainly not been customary previous to the institution of this exchange, and it certainly has not been since the 1920s.

The merchants, however, also indicated that the world price fluctuations were amplified in the Istanbul exchange due to an insufficiently developed futures market. The lack of an adequate futures market meant that the products which changed hands were actually brought to Istanbul for exchange, and the inadequate storage facilities in the city forced quick sales in which price fluctuations were magnified.[177] The merchants advocated the institution of a more efficient futures market. This was also to alleviate another problem, which was that the prices in Istanbul not only reflected the world prices, but also the daily arrivals of goods into Istanbul. While arrivals were at a normal and expected level, world price fluctuations remained the only important variable affecting prices; when, however, shipments to Istanbul were disturbed due to an unforeseen cause, prices also reflected this temporary shortage. It was necessary to arrange for the elimination of this undesirable factor. A futures market would achieve the purpose, and prices would only fluctuate at the cue of world markets, as the merchants wanted. In 1931, well into the second year of the crisis, export merchants were still seeking salvation in the world market, betraying a high degree of commitment to Turkey's integration into the world economy.

2.11.2 Prices

As a result of export activity, and following the institutional measures of integration into world markets (such as the commodity exchanges we discussed above), internal prices closely reflected world trends. Not only in markets for Turkey's major export items such as tobacco, raisins, figs, and nuts in which export prices could be expected to determine internal prices, but also in cereal markets, we can observe a narrowing of price differentials. For the following tables we took wholesale prices in Britain, France, and Turkey, and converted British and French prices at the current exchange rate to obtain Turkish equivalents. Since there were no restrictions on currency exchange, the actual rate of exchange sufficiently approximated a free market rate and rendered this exercise possible.[178]

As will be observed in the tables, Turkish prices diverged from British and French prices to no greater degree than these diverged from each other.

Ks/kg at currency exchange rates			
Wheat prices			
	Britain	France	Turkey
1923	7.36	9.60	7.7
1924	9.14	10.75	10.6
1925	10.60	11.50	14.4
1926	11.29	11.84	12.4
1927	10.60	12.55	11.8
1928	9.38	13.04	13.5
1929	9.72	12.15	12.5
Rye prices			
		France	Turkey
1926		8.75	9.07
1927		10.61	9.22
1928		10.24	10.32
1929		9.23	11.05

Oats prices

	Britain	France	Turkey
1926	8.18	7.30	
1927	8.39	8.75	7.89
1928	9.77	9.31	7.64
1929	8.71	9.15	7.13

Barley prices

	Britain	Turkey
1926	9.39	6.83
1927	10.84	8.59
1928	10.34	9.47
1929	9.77	9.48

2.12 Summary and conclusions

The development of agricultural production in accordance with and as a function of world demand has been depicted at some length because foreign trade is considered to be the determining element in the instigation of commodity production. In the context of the present exposition we have dealt specifically with commodity production and the conditions which favour it. I have argued that the period under study witnessed a recovery and a movement along the development of commodity production, due partly to the upward conjuncture of the world economy as a whole, and partly to politico-economic conditions internal to Turkey. The development which began in the Ottoman period had been interrupted by the long stretch of war culminating in the occupation of Anatolia. When the Turkish state was finally established, the years until the world depression witnessed a recovery of the level of production and of exports in agriculture. The conjuncture of the 1920s reestablished the weakened lines of communication with the world economy, and increased the pace of transition to market-oriented agriculture. Yet at the end of our period, there remained a geographically well-defined area outside the domain of the parameters generated in the world market. With the relative contraction of the world economy during the 1930s, not only did the momentum of integration come to an end, but also some units of production withdrew from the market to which their commitment had not solidified.

The mechanisms underlying the particular mode of integration experienced by Turkish agriculture in the 1920s, as well as the factors shaping it, have been analysed in this chapter. A similar inquiry will be conducted on the industrial sector in the next chapter.

3 Structure of the manufacturing sector

3.1 Introduction

Industrial development in the periphery has variously been interpreted as a necessary stage to be reached in an isolated and unilinear history or as an impossible goal attainable only through a challenge to peripheral status. It has become more apparent in the post Second World War era that the location of industrial, like all other economic activity, follows upon the logic of the world economy. Thus, there are no definite rules as to the absence or presence of particular industries, rather the rules of profitability determine the particular development of the means of production. Within such a framework it becomes easier to analyse the structure and the development of peripheral industry.[1]

Before the Second World War most peripheral economies were characterised by the coexistence of traditional crafts whose heritage derived from the peripheral social formation itself, and modern manufactures which were a result of the integration process. Although there are similarities, we must be careful to distinguish traditional crafts from modern small industry, which exists in a much closer articulation with modern manufacturing. Traditional crafts remained literally traditional despite a growing volume of exchanges with the modern manufacturing sector: their types of activity, technology, and markets were not yet transformed under the impact of a changing economy. Modern industry, on the other hand, could be seen as a necessary component of a growing degree of world economic integration. In an open economy, it was the nature and the direction of commercial flows which determined profitability and consequently the nature of investments. Our task in studying the structure of manufacturing activity in Turkey during the 1920s will be to discover the reasons for the non-transformation of traditional crafts into modern manufacturing, the post-integration conditions of their existence, their survival despite competition from modern industry, and their new functions. Similarly the conditions of development of modern manufacturing within the process of economic integration require analysis. These examinations will also show that the apparent duality resulting from the generic diversity and from the manifest differentiations in scale, technology, and market, in fact conceal an integration where traditional and modern manufacturing sectors are linked through commodity flows.

Traditional craft activity in the periphery is distinguished from its counterpart in the core by its lack of transformational dynamic toward modern industry. During an autonomous transition to capitalism in the core, domestic industry, proto-industry, or rural manufactures, as it has been variously termed, provides a channel of primary accumulation through which productive capital develops inside a precapitalist social formation.[2] This particular development of productive capital and wage labour paves the way for the transition to capitalism. Although nationalist versions of the economic history of the periphery argue that in the absence of imperialism traditional crafts would have undergone a similar development to usher in capitalism, an analysis of the position of crafts within a typical peripheral social formation might indicate otherwise. In China, India, or the Ottoman Empire, where the political authority exercised strict control over economic activity, the production of manufactures and their distribution processes were administratively regulated. Unlike the proto-industrialists of the West, the craftsmen of the East could not cater for the needs of independent merchants; their principal market consisted of the central or local political class. Hence peripheral crafts did not constitute an autonomous locus of primary accumulation, either of capital or of free labour. It is, however, true that imperialist penetration did cause a de-industrialisation. As the volume of trade increased, Ottoman manufactures succumbed to the competition from European industry,[3] and the path of primary accumulation through proto-industry was irreversibly closed off.[4] Even if the 'revolutionising path' had been conceivable for the periphery, under commercial penetration it became an impossibility.

The disappearance of traditional crafts, however, was not complete. The degree of integration into the world economy, or the degree of penetration of the peripheral formation by merchant capital varies according to geographical proximity, facility of transportation, and the agronomic capacity to produce surplus. Thus even after a long period of integration we may find in the periphery manufactures characterised by a small scale of production and traditional technology.[5] This is not to say, however, that traditional crafts remain identical with their pre-integration configuration. While there might not be significant changes in scale, technology, and markets, the sourcing of raw materials and capital goods often shift toward provisioning through imports or from 'modern' industry in the cities. Cobblers begin to purchase dressed hides, hand-weaving utilises factory-spun yarn, metal-working craftsmen obtain raw materials from abroad. Nevertheless, crafts can be said to survive because, despite these connections through the purchasing of raw materials from non-traditional markets, the actual activity of production remains traditional, and profitable enough to retain a hold on certain, limited consumption markets, and thus to withstand competition from imports.

There is however, a confusion which must be avoided. It would be wrong to identify all small-scale traditional manufacturing as survivals which have been able to withstand competition from imported manufactures. There is one category which not only survives but in fact owes its existence to the penetration of merchant capital, and that consists of export-orientated putting-out activity. The clearest example of commerce ruling industry in the case of Turkey was carpet-weaving organised by foreign merchant capital, and carried out in traditional forms, mostly domestically. In this case, merchant capital not only conserved but also created a seemingly traditional activity. We shall see that this particular activity occupied an important place both in terms of manufacturing employment and as a proportion of exports.

It is relevant in this context to inquire why certain crafts enjoyed a competitive advantage during the process of integration when others submitted to the competition of higher technology. Transport costs in the case of bulkier goods and the relative inaccessibility of interior areas was certainly one reason. Another reason why traditional crafts would hold some markets captive was a frequently observed differentiation of demand under local conditions. In general, the viability of a traditional craft increased if it utilised a higher proportion of locally provisioned inputs.[6] This allowed for a full exploitation of the cost advantages – while the use of imported inputs led either to the status of small industry conditioned and determined by modern manufacturing (textiles), or to rapid decline (metalware).

When we turn to the establishment of modern industry, an explanation based on the requirements and implications of world economic integration becomes more readily accessible, mainly because this type of manufacturing activity has no history preceding capitalist penetration. As trade with industrial economies increases, its structure undergoes a transformation: while in the beginning only unprocessed raw materials are exported from the periphery, as the volume of trade becomes sufficiently large, a threshold is reached making it profitable to establish activities reducing the cost of transport. This is a particular sort of manufacturing which should be called export-promoting. There is a second sort of manufacturing activity which again does not pose a threat to the degree of integration. In certain branches of manufacturing, transportation difficulties make it imperative that production be carried out near the site of consumption. Breweries, cement factories, and production of essentially non-tradeable goods, such as electricity, fall into this category. Far from reducing the demand for imports, these activities provide an essential component in the construction of a peripheral metropolis, where the demand for consumer goods imports flourishes. As the peripheral metropolis is the privileged site of communication with the core, its consumption pattern closely follows that established in European capitals. Istanbul in the 1920s was an example of such an articulation. Famous Paris shops had branches in Pera, the rich purchased Panhards and not Fords. To adjust the entire gestalt of consumption to that of the core, an infrastructure was required including, for example, apartment buildings with electricity, and surfaced roads. Hence the need for cement factories, electricity plants and the like. This second kind of modern manufacturing we might call import-complementing.

It should not be forgotten that integration into the world economy signifies not only the penetration of goods and merchant capital, but also of productive capital. Although the international flow of productive capital before the Second World War was not of important proportions and remained sub-ordinate to merchant capital, when the differential of profit rates between the core and the periphery was sufficiently large foreign capital moved in considerable quantities. Thus, foreign capital may be considered as one element expediting the manufacturing developments we have mentioned in the preceding paragraph. In fact, the history of Turkey's industrialisation shows that the 'modern' sector during the 1920s developed mostly through the impact of direct foreign investment.

In what follows we shall first comment on the nature of existing data pertaining to manufacture in Turkey during the 1920s. After an analysis of the composition of manufacturing, state programmes differentially favouring the modern sector are detailed. Focussing then on the structure of large firms and foreign capital, the chapter examines the profitability and growth of manufacturing.

3.2 Sources of data

There are three 'industrial' censuses which we will refer to in analysing the development and structure of manufactures in the 1920s. Unfortunately these censuses are not comparable in their coverages, rendering it impossible to present a moving picture.[7] The first census, dating from 1913, covered manufacturing located in a few industrially privileged areas and it included only those establishments which employed more than three workers.[8] The second census was the result of a questionnaire sent by the Ankara government to the provincial administrations under its control. In 1921, when Istanbul, Izmir, Adana, and Bursa, those regions which the 1913–1915 census had specifically designated as high industrial concentration areas, were still under occupation, the Ankara government sought to take an inventory of the 'wealth' of the country. Despite, however, the geographical shortcomings in its cover-age, the census is useful because of its inclusion of small manufactures.[9]

The 1927 census covered all of Republican Turkey.[10] Arguing that most Turkish manufactures consisted of artisanal and traditional small scale activities, its preparers decided to cover all manufacturing activity with the exception of activities carried out domestically. In other words, a separate location designated as a workshop or an atelier was required for the purposes of inclusion in the census.[11] This meant the exclusion of an important portion of domestic textile production. Carpet-weaving, for example, a widely-practiced domestic industry, was, in large part, excluded.[12] For the purposes of abstracting the structure of the Turkish economy in the 1920s, the results of the 1927 census will be used. We shall employ comparisons of the censuses to gauge developments during the decade.

As was indicated, our second concern is to identify the contribution of the state and foreign capital to the development of modern manufacturing. For this purpose we employ statistics relating to firms which received privileged treatment under the Law for the Encouragement of Industry;[13] and data compiled on the participation of foreign capital in Turkish corporations. Our main source on foreign capital is a study conducted on the basis of firms incorporated in the 1920s, although we also make use of scattered – chiefly anecdotal – accounts.[14]

3.3 Overall character of manufacturing

Manufacturing establishments were, on the whole, small in size as measured by the numbers of workers employed. Out of a total of 65,245 manufacturing establishments in 1927, 23,316 employed one person, that is to say the owner-proprietor was also the sole worker; and 4914 'firms' consisted of one owner and his immediate family. These two categories made up 43% of all manufacturing establishments. Another 36% of establishments belonged to the category of 'employing 2 or 3 workers', that is one or two wage earners in addition to the owner. When we look at manufacturing sub-sectors, we see that with the exception of electricity, paper, and extractive industries where firms employing 4 or more persons were a majority, small firms dominated.[15] In the industrial census the labour force in manufacturing is given as 257,000, while the population census indicates that 300,000 declared themselves as working in manufacturing. The difference is presumably due to domestic workers. Of the non-domestic workers, 64% worked in firms employing 4 or more persons. Of course the number of establishments is not an appropriate index to measure the relative importance of small manufactures in industrial output. For that purpose we have to rely on estimates of output and calculations derived from the number of workers employed in artisanal vs. 'industrial' concerns. None of the censuses mentioned above include estimates of industrial output by firms; therefore our account concerning the share of output due to artisanal production relies on scattered data.[16] On the basis of censuses and the ILO data on artisanal production, we are able to argue that there were geographical and sectoral distinctions between modern and traditional manufacturing, as well as differences deriving from the time of establishment. We shall now investigate the differences along these three dimensions.

3.3.1 Geographical and temporal concentration

In terms of geographical location, artisanal production dominated in smaller towns and in the countryside, while larger manufactures were found in larger cities. Contact with the world economy increased the chances for the establishment of production units of 'more modern' size. This, of course, is in accordance with the model which sees the genetic origin of modern manufactures in the integration with the world economy. In the 1927 census, we can see that out of 2052 manufacturing establishments employing more than 10 wage earners, Istanbul and Izmir accounted for 816, or 40%.[17]

According to the population census of 1927, 25.7% of total 'industrial' employment was in Istanbul and Izmir.[18] In all manufacturing sectors Istanbul accounted for a disproportionate share of large-scale establishments. Out of the total 212 textile firms employing more than 20 workers, 62 were in Istanbul; in paper and its products the figure was 21 out of 33, in metallurgy and machine construction 20 out of 53, in the chemical sector 8 out of 15. Even in wood products, which is a resource-based sector, the figure was 16 out of 99.[19]

In contrast, small cities were characterised by the predominance of small-scale manufacturing. Although in absolute numbers more craft production took place in larger cities, small towns were characterised by the relative dominance of crafts. In the absence of a transportation network facilitating the movement of goods to the interior, large areas remained outside the reach of imports. As was mentioned above, the road and railway networks were designed primarily to move exportables to ports. This meant that areas without export potential relied on their own resources for the provisioning of manufactures, and obtained only the most essential of the new consumables from outside markets. Villages in the interior purchased kerosene and sugar but not woollen cloth or hosiery, which were locally manufactured.

The 1921 manufacturing census is valuable in determining specificities depending on the date of establishment of manufactures, although it concentrates on the geographical area remaining outside the large cities and dominated by small manufactures. According to its findings 76,216 workers were employed by 33,058 manufacturing establishments, or an average of 2.3 workers per establishment.[20] In 1927, however, the average number of industrial workers per establishment was 3.9.[21] We can, in fact, calculate how much of this difference was due to the time dimension. While the average number of workers in 1921 was 2.3, production units established between 1921 and 1927 within the same geographical area were of an average size of 4.6 workers.[22] In Izmir (which is included in the 1921 census 'for comparison', although the figures were not based on direct questionnaires) the 1921 average of manufacturing employment was 6.6 workers.[23] In 1927 this average was 7.9. This indicates that establishments in Izmir which began operating between

1921 and 1927 must have been of an average size of 27 workers.[24] Even if this figure is an exaggeration, we may conclude that manufacturing establishments starting production in the 1920s were, in general, larger in scale than already existing ones. Newly established manufacturing tended to be more 'modern' in the sense of conforming to the scale norms of more developed technology.

In fact, there is one piece of evidence which corroborates the view that the relative importance of crafts declined in the 1920s. According to this finding on cloth weavers, the number of looms in operation in a small town in Western Anatolia, Buldan, declined from 1000 during the Greek war to 600 in 1929, to increase to 2000 in 1938.[25] The evidence suggests that the open economy of the 1920s and the competition of imports undermined the viability of crafts, although these were resurrected once the economy became more autarkic in the 1930s.

3.3.2 Sectoral concentration

The predominance of small-scale manufacturing was not only locationally and temporally determined. There were certain sectors characterised by large numbers of small-scale workshops where other sectors could be considered as modern. In other words, the division of manufacturing into traditional, small-scale manufacturing and 'modern' manufacturing can be observed not only along geographical and date-of-establishment lines, but also through activities. Thus, one reason why the average scale of manufacturing inside the boundaries of the 1921 census was inferior to the average scale in the whole of Turkey is that the 1921 area was characterised by a higher concentration of textiles. 46% of the workers in the 1921 census appear to be working in textiles, with an average worker concentration of 1.8 per establishment.[26] This division of activities according to greater or lesser dominance of crafts can be seen in Table 3.1. In this division of manufacturing activity, craft production is dominant in all of the sectors except in 'paper and products'. The four most clearly artisanal sectors

Table 3.1 *Distribution of the labour force and scale differences among manufacturing sectors for 1927.*[27]

Industry sectors	% of establishments employing less than 4 workers	% of the manufacturing labour force in the sector	Average number of workers per establishment
Food, tobacco, leather	78	43.0	3.9
Textiles	74	18.7	5.1
Wood	83	9.5	3.1
Paper and products	49	1.1	8.0
Metal-working	89	13.2	2.3
Construction materials	57	4.8	4.3
Chemical industry	72	1.2	4.5

are: food, tobacco, leather; textiles; wood; and metal-working. The figure for the food, tobacco, leather sector overstates the average number of workers because of the inclusion of the tobacco industry with 95 workers per establishment. Excluding tobacco industry we would get a concentration of 1.6 for food processing and leather manufacturing.[28] The metal-working industry was of a divided structure also. It consisted of workshops manufacturing traditional metal implements, and larger sized units producing more modern equipment. In the latter class we find, for example, an automobile assembly and an airplane assembly plant which were in operation at the time of the census. Similarly the category including 'typewriters, electrical machines, other electrical implements, manufacturing and repair' employed an average of 6 workers per plant. Yet small workshops were predominant: two thirds of the metal-workers were found in the sub-category of 'furniture and agricultural machines manufactured from iron or lead' where the average plant size was 2.2 workers.[29]

According to the ILO data we have already mentioned, artisanal production was predominant in textiles. These estimate that three quarters of the cotton cloth produced in the country originated in artisanal production. The clothing (apparel) industry was entirely artisanal while hosiery was losing ground to the newly developing factory sector. Carpets and knitted wool were also products of the artisanal sector. The only branch of textiles where modern industry occupied a preponderant position was in silk. Here artisans contributed only 10% of the spinning and 30% of the weaving output.[30] These estimates concerning textiles are borne out in the 1921 census. The figures are 'of doubtful value', but they indicate that there were 20,057 shops or factories in textiles employing 35,316 workers. In terms of scale, preparation and the weaving of silk cloth the largest workshops were for silk. Here, the average number of workers per shop was 28.[31] These 1921 figures, however, reflect the situation prior to the exchange of populations, and, therefore, give inflated estimates for the 1920s.[32]

In the leather industry 28% of the total output was estimated to have been produced by the artisanal sector; footwear, however, was entirely produced by small workshops employing less than four workers. The same situation obtained in the case of carpentry and furniture production. Two thirds of the oil-presses, which were used especially in olive-oil production, were found in small workshops. The soap industry had also developed as a by-product of olive-oil production and there too artisanal production accounted for more than half of the total output.[33]

3.3.3 The composition of manufacturing output in 1927

Taking the sectoral output minus the figures for raw material inputs as a rough measure of value added, we observe that food, textiles, metals, chemical, and wood manufacturings, which jointly accounted for more than 93% of the total

Table 3.2 *Value added and labour force by industry sector*[34]

Industry	Value added (Output – raw materials) (Current TL)	%	Labour force	%
Food, tobacco, leather	127,878,074	64.4	110,480	43.0
Textiles	36,571,042	18.3	48,025	18.7
Metals	7,982,901	4.0	33,866	13.2
Chemical	7,294,268	3.6	3,107	1.2
Wood	6,968,270	3.5	24,264	9.5
Mining	6,933,481	3.5	18,932	7.4
Paper	2,604,847	1.3	2,792	1.1
Construction materials	2,020,341	1.0	12,345	4.8
Other	1,764,353	0.9	2,589	1.0

value added, were also the sectors with the highest proportion of small-manufacturing, with respectively 78%, 74%, 89%, 72% and 83% of the establishments employing less than 4 workers.[35] It can thus be argued that those industries contributing most to total value added in manufacturing were also the most dispersed ones. The manufacturing sector as a whole was characterised by the predominance of traditional craft production, catering to local markets. Most of its output was consumer goods; capital goods accounted for a maximum of 10.5% of the net output (metals + construction materials + part of the chemical industry).[36] This meant that investment in relatively capital-intensive concerns required imported producers' goods. Small-scale manufacturing, on the other hand, was characterised by a very low capital–labour ratio.

As may be seen in Table 3.3, the sector processing agricultural products – food, tobacco, leather – was by far the largest in terms of its contribution to value added. If we look more closely at the composition of this sector, we see that it consisted of two distinct components, one engaging in activity orientated to the export market, and the other to the internal market. For example, footwear manufactures, grain mills, bakeries, confectioneries, breweries, and the two sugar refineries belong to the second category, while fruit preparation and drying, vegetable oils (in large part), tobacco preparation, and canneries belong with export-oriented activity. In fact, this was the most important manufacturing sector which realised value added through export markets. There was also a locational distribution: while export oriented sub-sectors were found in the immediate hinterland of ports, grain mills, bakeries, and leather industry were most uniformly dispersed. 'Almost every village boast[ed]a water-mill to process wheat and other cereals.'[37] There were 13,152 workshops manufacturing footwear, with 32,154 workers. Among these establishments only 46 employed mechanical power, and only 649 more than 6 wage-earners. Similarly, 5196 workers staffed 1963 tanneries.[38]

The second most important manufacturing sector was textiles, which was also a widely dispersed sector with a total of 9353 establishments. About one quarter of its workers were employed in spinning and weaving of cotton; one third worked in the clothing sector; one fifth were employed in carpet-weaving. The rest of the textiles sector consisted of spinning and weaving of wool and silk.[39] Most of the output of textiles was meant for the domestic market, and yet it was far from satisfying domestic needs. Between 1923 and 1929, textiles accounted for between 35 and 45% of imports, while raw cotton was regularly exported.[40] Apart from the insufficiency of manufacturing capacity, it was also the case that cotton grown in Turkey was of low quality and short-fibred. Therefore, cotton cloth manufacturers in the modern sector preferred imported yarn. Weavers using hand-looms, however, purchased yarn from Adana manufacturers.[41] Wool yarn was also regularly imported, because wool produced in Turkey was coarse and dirty, best fit for carpets.[42]

It was estimated in 1932 that half of the cotton cloth output in Turkey was produced domestically on hand-looms.[43] The output of such domestic activity was also consumed locally. There were larger firms – only 12 of which used mechanical sources of energy – located mostly in Istanbul, Adana, and Izmir, which produced for a larger domestic market.[44] They supplied the villages and small towns with coarse white cloth (kaput bezi) utilised for diverse purposes. Domestically spun wool provided mostly for the carpet-weaving industry (46% according to estimates for 1928).[45] About one quarter of the raw wool was exported, and the rest divided equally between factories and domestic manufacturing. The army was the chief customer of the coarse woollen cloth manufactured from domestic wool.[46] Urban customers consumed imported woollen clothes and cloths produced from imported wool-yarn.

The silk industry had suffered a gradual decline since the mid-nineteenth century, and the Greek war had further disrupted the industry centred around Bursa. In 1927 only 2400 workers were employed in spinning and weaving of silk.[47] This was due to a secular decline which had accelerated through the departure of the Greek population. In 1914, there were 41 spinning establishments in Bursa, but by 1926 only 12 were left, and three of them were French-owned, supplying silk yarn to cloth-weaving firms in France.[48] Meanwhile the silk industry in Greece developed rapidly, due to the influx of immigrants from Turkey, whose previous occupations had been in the silk trade. In one case a village of 550 refugee families had been established in the Peloponnesus, specialising entirely in silk.[49] The Greek production of raw silk increased by three times between 1922 and 1926, and the production of silk cloth increased by 3.1 times between 1925 and 1930.[50] Greek exports of silk also increased while during the same period Turkish silk exports declined in relative value; and the export of silk cloth was gradually replaced by the export of silk cocoons.[51] As the Bursa secretary of the Chamber of Commerce commented: 'The exporting of cocoons . . . is one factor creating the present problem in our silk industry.'[52] A manufacturing export had been transformed into a raw material export, with the consequent decline of the industry of transformation. Parallel to this development, Turkish consumers began to prefer imported silk cloth, which, although less durable, was better suited to new fashions.[53] The Turkish silk industry never recovered from the impact of losing Greek artisans and merchants in the movement of populations.

Of the output of the textile sector, only carpets constituted a channel of integration with the world market: 60% of the carpet production was exported. This industry was organised by merchant houses on the basis of putting-out methods. According to one estimate in 1927, 67, 854 workers were employed in carpet-weaving.[54] Presumably most of these worked at home, since, according to the 1927 census, which only covered separately located workshops, this industry employed 9167 workers.[55] By far the largest establishment was the Oriental Carpet Company in Izmir, although it had shifted some of its activity to Greece. This company, apart from operating its own workshops, acted as the chief source of merchant capital to domestic manufacturers.[56]

Although the departure of Greeks helped establish a carpet industry in Greece, the impact on the Turkish carpet-weaving sector was not as destructive as in the case of silk. In 1929 there were 135 carpet-weaving workshops in Greece, all established after 1922.[57] This industry, which had not existed before the immigration of Anatolian Greeks, boasted 11,000 specialist refugee women workers in 1928.[58] Production in Turkey, however, did not decline, although difficulties were encountered because of the new Greek competition in export markets.

3.3.4

There is a definitional problem involved in treating manufacturing establishments in the two groups of crafts and modern industry. The customary dividing line for a factory – a minimum of ten workers – would leave us with 98.7% of establishments and 67% of non-domestic workers in the crafts sector; proportions which would increase if domestic industry were also included.[59] Despite the ambiguities involved in such a definition, for the purposes of identifying the locus of modern manufactures, size serves as the most appropriate proxy. We have found that sectoral concentration in manufacturing, geographical location, and date-of-establishment of plants provided data that correlated with the size distribution of manufacturing plants. We shall see through an investigation of larger firms that the division also applied to differences in sources of capital and the use of modern technology.

3.4 The modern sector

The overall picture of the industrial sector indicates that crafts continued to be the major part of the manufacturing sector during this stage of peripheral integration. It is also possible, however, to derive conclusions from the data presented above relating to the existence of a post-integration manufacturing sector. While crafts are part of the pre-existent social formation, new industries corresponding to the requirements of peripheral integration derive from a super-imposition. During this super-imposition process native capital develops only as an adjunct to penetrating capital, and to a degree that does not threaten the dominance of the latter. During this stage of its infancy, native capital may not be expected to undertake an important role in modern industry investments.

In the case of Turkey the inability of native capital to undertake investments required by modern technology was remedied to some degree through the aid of the state in guaranteeing certain pecuniary privileges to firms conforming to requirements set out in legislation. Through the Law for the Encouragement of Industry, the state promoted approved firms. It was among these establishments that most domestically financed modern manufactures were to be found.

A second source of modern industry was foreign capital. Even the most radical demands in the Izmir economic congress of 1923 had specifically warned against the interpretation that foreign capital would be kept out of Turkey.[60] In fact most participants argued that foreign capital should be allowed to invest freely in those projects requiring large initial outlays. Although in absolute terms direct foreign investment amounted to a small sum, its relative significance in the development of modern industry was considerable. Two thirds of the capital in manufacturing firms incorporated in the 1920s was of foreign origin. An analysis of foreign investment confirms the peripheral industrial structure hypothesised above. Its activity remained trade-complementing and did not hinder greater commercial integration. We shall analyse modern manufacturing through an investigation of state-promoted manufacturing and foreign investment in the productive sphere.

3.4.1 Encouragement of industry

The 1913 Law for the Encouragement of Industry was still in effect when the Republic was established. In 1923, however, during the Izmir economic congress, the participants proposed the institution of a more comprehensive programme to encourage industry. The report drafted by the industrialists urged the state to create the conditions for the establishment of large scale industry in order that 'Turkey would also march toward progress', and further proposed that the state itself should undertake certain projects which were beyond the scope of private investors.[61] In the final text, which was voted on by the entire assembly, the government was asked to modify the 1913 law according to the needs of the industrialists, which were that privileges accorded by the law should not be extended to foreign firms, that the industrialists themselves should decide which raw materials would be imported freely, and that the government should prefer to purchase domestically manufactured goods up to a price differential of 20% to the favour of imported material.[62] It was not, however, until May 1927 that the new law was voted in by Parliament. Among its stipulations were tax-exemptions, land grants, permission to import investment goods without payment of duties, reductions of freight fares, and a promise that government offices would purchase the output of favoured firms up to a price differential of 10%. The kinds of establishments which would enjoy the privileges granted were carefully specified. In general, a certain level of mechanisation (existence of mechanical power amounting to a minimum of 10 hp) and scale (based on employment) were required.[63] Although smaller establishments could also benefit from some of the privileges, it seems that the bureaucratic operations were sufficiently off-putting to encourage only the larger firms to apply for licences. The joint complaint of the industrialists in the 1930 congress was that it was forbiddingly difficult to apply and be granted a licence and that only the larger firms obtained any benefit through the workings of the law. The reports all urged the extension of the law's stipulations to what they called 'intermediating' small industry.[64] Nevertheless, while 341 establishments dating from before 1923 benefited from the law, and 299 more were added to the list up to 1926, 435 firms obtained licences in 1927, 1928, and 1929.[65]

3.4.2 Characteristics of approved firms

There are no statistics relating to the situation of approved firms in 1927 or 1929. However, by looking at their situation in 1932 we can draw certain conclusions. In 1932, the average number of workers employed per establishment in 1473 such firms was 38.[66] Compared to the overall figure for manufacturing in 1927, 3.9, the difference is striking. 'Approved' firms were close to modern factories. The average 'approved' firm used machines requiring an energy of 79 hp.[67] In the 1927 census the same figure was only 0.6.[68] 'Value-added' (output minus raw materials) per approved firm was 43,300 TL, and for the establishments in the 1927 census only 3080. 'Value-added' per worker was 1220 TL compared to 780 TL.[69] These encouraged firms probably utilised a higher level of imported machines as capital goods.

Table 3.3 *Percentage of imported raw materials in output*[70]

	Licensed firms (1932)	All firms (1927)
Food, tobacco, leather	5.6	3.1
Textiles	19.4	11.2
Metals	57.1	19.5
Chemical industry	19.9	15.2

The ratio of imported raw materials (current inputs) to total output was considerably higher in these firms than in the overall sector, as can be seen in Table 3.3. In terms of geographical dispersion these firms conformed to the pattern of larger establishments in the 1927 census: 47% were in Istanbul and Izmir.[71] Their distribution into broad industry group was not significantly different from the 1927 establishments except in the case of textiles. In 1927 14.3% of the establishments were in textiles while among the licensed firms the proportion was 24%. There were, however, none engaged in clothing among the approved textile firms whereas 49.8% of the 1927 textile establishments were found in the clothing sector.[72]

The ten-sector division is too crude a device to gauge the differences in the composition of output between the two groups. Yet it can be concluded from scattered evidence that manufacturing closer to the retail end of production was not proportionately represented among the firms benefiting from the encouragement. Approved firms were found in higher-technology sub-sectors. Most of the cement factories, both sugar refineries (which were actually owned by the government)[73], all important mines (although only 1% of the approved establishments were mines, 16% of the 'value-added' in the approved sector originated in mining),[74] all the larger oil-presses, and the machine-tools sector were 'encouraged' by the government. Encouragement was not the cause of modern industry: its impact on the formation of modern manufactures was only marginal. Yet its existence indicates that government measures also recognised a distinction between modern and traditional manufacturing. Statistics were collected on the basis of such a distinction, and this fact has allowed us better to gauge the importance and characteristics of the modern sector.

3.4.3 Characteristics of foreign capital

Foreign capital in its undertakings was more selective than the government in its encouragement. Although there had been direct foreign investment in the Ottoman Empire, government borrowing had consitituted by far the larger part of the foreign capital inflow to the economy. Direct investment by foreigners had increased during the Young Turk period, and had taken the form of railway construction and commercial firms. When the Republic was founded in 1923, there was an estimated £ 63.4m or 500m TL of foreign capital. This sum was distributed in 94 firms only 12 of which were in manufacturing, and 6 in mining.[75]

In the 1923–29 period foreign direct investment in industry gained a new momentum. Foreign capital took on the role of mobilising most of the larger scale investment in manufactures. In January 1924, a new law was passed liberalising the conditions of property ownership by foreigners.[76] As mentioned above, the participants in the Izmir congress were especially careful to declare their non-hostility to foreign capital. Even the 1927 law for encouragement of industry did not exclude manufacturing firms owned by foreign capital. Thus, in 1929, in addition to pre-war concessionary firms such as in mining and in public works a number of recently established corporations could also be observed.

According to balance of payments figures, new foreign investment in Turkey amounted to 6.5m TL in 1926, 5.3m in 1927, 8m in 1928 and 12m in 1929.[77] Since these figures include purchases of property by foreigners it is difficult to establish the proportion that represents investment for profit. There is, however, a remarkable study attempting to estimate the share of foreign capital in Turkish corporations established between 1920 and 1930. From the figures in this study it can be calculated that the total paid-up capital in firms with foreign participation incorporated between 1920 and 1930, was 31.5m TL.[78] This figure conforms to the total foreign capital inflow obtained from balance of payments accounts. In fact, we know from the distribution of shares in firms with foreign participation that the Turkish contribution was largely confined to providing access to the bureaucracy. In a typical distribution, foreign nationals would own more than 90% of the shares and the usually sole Turkish founding member only a nominal amount. Thus, 'foreign participation' almost always meant foreign ownership.[79]

Of this 31.5m TL as paid-up capital, 66.6% was in productive concerns, divided into 66.4% for manufacturing and mining and 0.2% for agriculture. Foreign capital's share in the total amount of paid-up capital in Turkish corporations established in the 1920s was 43%. Its share in the paid-up capital of mining and manufacturing firms was 67%. In absolute amounts foreign capital represented 21m TL of investment in production as against 10.5m TL of Turkish capital.[80] Of course, it should be remembered that these figures include only those investments in incorporated firms. There was no foreign investment in smaller concerns, in crafts etc. However, these figures are useful for an analysis of the structure of our second group of 'modern' manufacturing.

Before beginning to analyse the productive investments of foreign capital it should be repeated that mining and manufacturing accounted for about two thirds of the direct foreign investment between 1920 and 1930. The rest of the foreign capital was to be found in the tertiary sector: banks, trading companies, insurance and concessionary concerns in foreign trade. Thus one third of the foreign investment in the 1920s was directly related to merchant capital, and two thirds were to be found in the productive sphere.[81] Of the 21m TL of productive investment 5.5m were invested in electricity, gas works, and other non-tradeable municipal services. Investment in such municipal services for the large peripheral cities which were in close contact with the centre was typical of late nineteenth century movements of capital.[82] The second largest category was investments in mining. Here, we observe the enclave pattern where productive capital was invested only to produce exportable output. The product of mines did not become an input for domestic industry; instead it was sold abroad as raw material for industry in the centre. The third largest branch of foreign investment in the 1920s was cement, with 4m TL. As was discussed above, cement manufacturing is an essential component of a certain quality of construction which becomes prevalent with integration into the world economy. Cement, however, is forbiddingly expensive to transport. For this reason it constitutes the first 'modern' industry which develops in peripheral economies. In addition to one cement factory which had been established prior to the war, foreign capital invested in 4 more cement factories in the 1920s, three in Istanbul, and 1 in Ankara.

The fourth largest investment category was the food processing sector. While in public works and cement, foreign companies were dominant within the sectors as a whole (with 90 and 91% of the capital respectively), in food processing foreign companies provided only 52% of the total paid-up capital. However, this 3.4m TL was divided into 3 firms as opposed to 19 firms of entirely Turkish capital accounting for 3.2m TL. The largest of the 3 firms was a brewery in Istanbul, originally established prior to the war. The other two firms were engaged in the processing of cereals.[83] Here again we observe the familiar pattern of investment in those goods whose high transportation costs make imports forbiddingly expensive. Hence, as we might expect in a relatively open economy where the domestic market is not protected by tariff barriers, most of the productive foreign capital investment was placed in sectors which did not compete with imports. Foreign capital in manufacturing, therefore, rather than preventing the further extension of the world division of labour, complemented it.

In addition to their sectoral specificity, foreign capital investments reflected larger scales, and higher geographical concentration. In the manufacturing sector the average capital was 825,000 TL for foreign firms, while only 180,000 TL for Turkish concerns.[84] In textiles, for example, 9 Turkish companies were established during the decade as opposed to 3 companies dominated by foreign capital. Turkish firms, however, were of much smaller scale: their total paid-up capital amounted to only one third of the capital of foreign companies.[85] Furthermore, only four of these companies were located in Istanbul, the rest being in small Anatolian towns.[86]

All of the manufacturing foreign investment was orientated to the domestic market. Towards the end of the decade, however, we observe attempts – notably in textiles – to invest for the export market. In 1929, for example, a mill-owner from Alsace, representing Maison Baudry de Cernay, had arrived in Bursa to investigate possibilities of investing in cotton-spinning. The object was to export the yarn to Alsace, where it would be woven into cloth.[87] Similarly, first the French, then the Italians, had invested in spinning in the Adana region, with the intention of exporting the cotton yarn rather than the raw cotton.[88] These planned and actualised foreign investments belonged in the category of export-promotion attempting to benefit from low wages.

The figures we have given so far pertain to foreign capital participations in 'Turkish' firms. As such they do not include direct investments in subsidiary branches by 'multinationals'. Such subsidiaries were established for catering to the growing internal market. Besides Swiss pharmaceutical firms, and Nestlé's chocolates, American companies were also represented in the form of a Columbia record factory, and more importantly by an abortive investment by Ford in a car and tractor assembly plant.[89] Ford had obtained free-zone rights in Istanbul for this plant, which started operations in 1929. It had a capacity of assembly of 80 cars per day, and was planned to be a plant serving 'as distributing centre for ports in the Black Sea and the North East generally'.[90] With the advent of the depression, the plant ceased its operations. A similar but smaller enterprise had been in operation in Izmir. 'Baladour, the only automobile supply and repair station in Smyrna, does a very profitable business and cannot assemble cars fast enough', reported *The Economist*.[91]

That banks and commercial firms would be established in the commercial centres of Istanbul and Izmir was to be expected. Investment in mining was determined by the geographical location of mines. In the manufacturing sector, too, there was a geographical concentration: all foreign firms were located in the three largest cities. In contrast, this was true for only half of the similar firms established with Turkish capital.[92] Small-scale local accumulation found its outlet in small productive firms established in provincial towns, while larger volumes of capital in the metropolitan cities was either engaged in the non-productive spheres of commerce and finance or went into partnership with foreign capital to establish larger-scale manufacturing firms.

Although foreign ownership of capital was disproportionately represented in non-productive spheres – banking and trade – it is significant that two thirds of the new investment in the 1920s was directed to mining and manufacturing. This indicates that, both in its absolute contribution and in its role in providing the motor of industrial growth, foreign capital took on a new role during the young Republic. Such a development was due to many factors: the stage of growth of Turkey's economy, overaccumulation in the core countries especially after 1926, and pressure by Turkish banks and merchants to replace foreign capital in banking and commerce. We shall discuss the latter development in subsequent chapters.

3.5 Profitability and growth

Between 1923 and 1929 value added in manufacturing increased by 50% in constant prices. During the same period the contribution of the manufacturing sector to national product declined from 13% to 10%.[93] This, however, was in large measure due to the fact that industry had not suffered as much destruction as agriculture during the war years. Consequently, the growth rate of industry was less a result of reconstruction and recovery, factors which inflated the figures for agriculture. Nevertheless, manufacturing activity in general was not lucrative in the 1920s. The 50% overall rate of change in value added conceals a wide variation in profitability: while some new and profitable firms were established, many old ones, facing competition from imports, went into bankruptcy.[94] The 1920s could not be considered a period of secular boom for the whole of the manufacturing sector.

Among manufacturing firms cement factories and flour mills obtained the highest returns.[95] Both of these products were protected by tariffs, as well as through high transportation costs. There was also a sellers' market in cement because the government in Ankara was building a new network of public buildings, and reconstructing the war-destroyed interior of the country. Domestic production of cement could provide for only half of private consumption; when demand by the public sector, which was even greater than private demand, was added, and under conditions of protection, cement factories obtained 39% profits on paid-up capital in 1928, and 36% in 1927.[96] These profit rates attracted foreign capital, which established two new plants near Istanbul in 1928 and 1929.[97] It was claimed in 1929 that since the new factories were of larger scale and used modern technology, they could compete with Marseilles cement and that 'the customs duties may be decreased to more reasonable and world rates such that the country's construction needs would be more widely provided for'.[98] In fact, the specific duty on cement was lowered in the 1929 tariff by 20%.[99]

The only other item for which the 1929 schedule lowered the rates of protection was flour.[100] In the generally protectionist trade regime of 1929 (it increased most specific rates by more than three-fold – see below) cement and flour were the two items whose imports were exceptionally liberated. Since the manufacture of these two items had also been unusually lucrative in the 1920s, we may surmise that the political authority, through the liberation of imports, sought to redress the balance in favour of the merchants. It appears that in addition to production and transportation barriers, another reason for high profits in flour production was that the manufacturers could speculate on inventories. In 1928 they obtained 32% profits because they had accumulated stocks and the prices in 1928 were favourable.[101] In 1929, however, they doubled their stocks hoping for a more protective clause against flour in the new tariff law.[102] When their hopes failed to materialise – because certain countries could export grains and flour to Turkey under special arrangements and because the rate on flour was lowered – twice as many bankruptcies as in the previous year ensued.

On the other hand, the largest category of manufacturing firms – in terms of declared capital – was in textiles (weaving and spinning), and their profitability was low. Of the 3.6m TL of capital in textile firms, 2.2m TL was accounted for by 5 firms which, in 1928, together obtained 5% returns on their investments.[103] The remaining 9 firms closed their accounts with deficits. It was the larger firms which survived in the face of competition from imports. Smaller firms which 'lacked the minimum necessary conditions required by industrial firms did not possess economic value and strength'.[104]

Although its growth in terms of output is undeniable, the manufacturing sector was in a precarious position during the 1920s. As could be expected of a relatively open economy, imports could normally prevent the development of competitive lines of activity. There were, however, industries for whose development peripheral integration created a conducive environment. These industries prospered and were favoured by foreign and native investment. State subsidies, on the other hand, were an attempt to encourage the development of a modern sector of manufacturing. In terms of numbers of firms established, the encouragement programme could be considered a success. Yet this encouragement does not seem to have greatly modified profitability conditions. Political inducement merely complemented the market rather than supplanting it as in later practice. Government intervention only had a marginal impact.

3.6 Relationships between the traditional and modern manufacturing sectors

We have so far discussed the two generically separate components of the manufacturing sector. It was argued that the composition of manufacturing reflected a division between the traditional and modern sectors. Their distinctness was manifest along different dimensions: scale, type of technology, date of establishment, nature and volume of output, and location. However, the co-existence of two separate sectors did not imply their independence. Indeed, we discussed above one crucial relation of dependence: the traditional sector purchased current and capital inputs from the modern sector. This provisioning of the traditional sector had at first been undertaken by merchant capital through imports which had replaced locally obtained inputs. The modern sector in time began to produce some of these formerly imported inputs. The major example is cotton yarn; but dressed skins as input for the footwear industry, metal tools for various crafts, metal nails, tin cans, boxes and metal pails, chemical dyes for textiles and carpets may also be mentioned in the same category.[105] Whether they obtained inputs from the modern sector or through imports, crafts could not be considered as an isolated sector surviving solely because of 'distance' from the world economy and out of its reach.

The figures for imported inputs, which we have already mentioned, demonstrate only one aspect of this flow. According to these 1927 figures, in textiles 22%, in paper and its products 69%, in metal-working 43%, and in the chemical industry 26% of the raw material and intermediate inputs were imported.[106] Although the utilisation of imported inputs was not divided proportionally among crafts and the modern sector, it is obvious that with a preponderance in terms of employment and output, the traditional sector commanded a significant volume of imported inputs.

Although traditional crafts were in general directed to domestic consumption and local markets, there were significant exceptions where artisanal production was organised under the domination of merchant capital, with its output realised in the national market. In this category were local crafts which were raw material-based, such as stone-working in Eskisehir, and knife manufacturing in Bursa. These crafts retained their artisanal character where the producer owning the workshop was also the seller of the wares.[107] There was, however, a second category which could be described as putting-out activity. In Denizli, for example, a province neighbouring Izmir, there were 8000 looms, with 30% of the population dependent on the domestic activity of weaving cotton cloth. Merchants supplied the yarn, which was factory-produced, and purchased the cloth at rates perpetuating the indebtedness of the producers. Although weavers owned their own looms, they were unable independently to finance their raw material requirements, and were 'in reality workers confronting merchants and intermediaries. Their relationship with the yarn merchants was that of employer and worker.'[108] In Antep, in south-eastern Anatolia, the relationship had evolved a degree further such that the looms were also owned by the merchants organising production, paying very low wages to the artisans. The division of labour imposed on the artisans was such that in the production of cotton cloth there were seven different stages.[109] With such a structure, the craft had been transformed entirely, such that no single artisan owned the means of production to undertake all stages of manufacturing. This organisation of crafts, with whole cities specialising in the production of one type of output, was a typical case of pre-industrial capitalism. Here too, the value created by the artisans was effectively tapped by merchant capital, and utilised by the capitalist sector.

In addition to these mechanisms acting through the circulation of commodities, another flow between the crafts sector and the modern sector characterised the 1920s. In contrast to subsequent experience – especially after 1950 – when urban population increased due to the rural exodus, the balance between urban and rural population moved against cities in the 1920s.[110] One contributory factor was the Greek emigration. We have mentioned above that more than half of the emigrating Greeks from Turkey had been urban-dwellers, employed in commerce or manufacturing. Especially in Izmir, the role of the Greeks in the manufacturing sector had been considerable. These changes in the balance of populations translated into a labour shortage in urban areas. This shortage, however, did not 'pull' a population from the countryside: when employment was created in the modern manufacturing sector, the demand was met by labour released from artisanal shops gone bankrupt.[111] The hypothesis can be advanced that the high degree of workers' militancy, and the degree of labour organisation which occurred in spite of interdictive and proscriptive measures was due in large part to the origins of manufacturing labourers. These were either of working class origin or former urban artisans, seasoned in industrial conflict or recently déclassé. In spite of labour militancy, workers did not obtain significant rights during the decade. Among the demands put forward in the 1923 Izmir congress only the official recognition of the 6-day week was put into effect.[112] The semi-martial law legislated following the 1925 Kurdish rebellion brought censorship and suppression of all legal labour activity. Nevertheless illegal strikes and associations continued to exist, as can be seen in the rich labour history of the period.[113]

3.7 Integration into the world economy through imported capital goods and raw materials

The integration of the economy through its manufacturing sector into the world market proceeded through the demand for imported capital goods and raw materials as well as through the institution of a division of labour where peripheral industry specialised in certain lines of activity. For such a specialisation to occur, it was necessary that these industries were established following technological and commodity norms devised in the centre. Thus the increasing specialisation itself is the principal factor in the growth of a 'derived' demand for imports. In 1927, the manufacturing sector used up 29.4m TL of imported raw materials, and another 13.5m TL of imports could be designated as investment goods for the manufacturing sector.[114] (This figure only includes those items which can unequivocally be said to serve as capital goods in manufacturing. It does not, for example, include sheet metal or trucks.) As was mentioned above, the import requirements of 'modern' industry both in capital goods and raw materials was higher than those of the traditional manufacturing sector, which mostly dealt in the transformation of locally accessible raw materials through the use of traditional technologies. The share of such imports in the total purchases of Turkey from abroad was 20% in 1927.[115] In other words, 20% of Turkey's imports depended on the development of the manufacturing sector. This figure should be another reminder that the peripheral economy, although integrated to the world economy through merchant capital, does not generate only consumption and mercantile demand for imported goods. In addition to merchant capital's investments such as in railways and ports, the investments of productive capital, remaining within the purview of peripheral development, constitute a market for the centre's exports, and thus further the ties of integration.

3.8 Summary

In this chapter the structure of the manufacturing sector was described, and it was stressed that the modern sector of manufacturing did not develop in spite of and as a force countering peripheral integration into the world economy. Rather, it was precisely the degree of this integration which warranted and required a certain development of modern industry, a development encouraged by the state, and partly implemented by foreign capital. It was also shown that the duality between traditional and modern manufacturing should not imply the isolation of these sectors from each other. Together with peripheralisation there results a change in the input structure of traditional manufacturing: while its output may compete with imports, it begins to utilise intermediate inputs obtained from non-local markets. One reason for this change is that peripheral raw materials now begin to be exported abroad, and intermediate goods manufacturing stagnates in the periphery. As a result traditional crafts are now related to the modern sector through a demand for factory-produced inputs, and thus contribute indirectly to the demand for imports.

In the last section we attempted to evaluate the total performance of the manufacturing sector. Unprotected against competition from imports, manufacturing activity remained limited in scope, and did not attain sufficient momentum to guarantee a sustained growth performance. Nevertheless, Turkey in the 1920s may be characterised as in that stage of peripheral development when the forces described in the beginning of this chapter were in operation to induce investment in certain sectors of manufacturing activity. In addition to crafts – whether transformed by merchant capital or remaining within the traditional nexus – there was a modern manufacturing section, albeit in its infancy. Of the 300,000 persons declaring their occupations to be in manufacturing,[116] exactly one half were wage-earners in establishments employing four or more workers, and one quarter were labourers in establishments employing ten or more workers.[117] This industrial activity responded to the expansion of the domestic market, where demand was conditioned by a strong cultural interaction with the urban centres of Europe. Peripheral manufacturing took on the role of complementing the trade pattern of Turkey's world-economic integration.

4 Trade relations with the world economy

This study attempts to describe the structure of a peripheral formation and to trace the relationships with the world economy which shape it. It is, of course, principally through trade relations that a formerly external area becomes a periphery of the world economy. While this incorporation is brought about, merchant capital constitutes the main mechanism of peripheral structuration – the process whereby the economy in question is shaped to accommodate the hierarchical division of labour in the world economy. Such an accommodation does not consist merely of a market integration: it is also necessary that merchant capital transform certain existing products into commodities, and actively induce the production of new commodities. Thus, in the economic transformation of the periphery, trade relationship constitutes the impact that provides the important momentum. In the following we shall describe the overall importance of trade, its organisation, and the composition of merchant capital. The actual relations with (peasant) producers will be more extensively dealt with in the following chapter.

4.1 Importance of trade in the national economy

Between 1924 and 1928, average annual exports accounted for 11% of the national product. Imports, on the other hand, reached 23% of the GDP in the latter half of the decade.[1] Although these figures do not provide overwhelming evidence that trade relations were the principal factor shaping the economy, we shall argue that they constituted the main dynamic in the development of commodity production. In the case of exports, the 11% represented a commodity composition which was nine tenths agriculture based, and accounted for more than one half of non-grain production. It seems, therefore, that the extra-subsistence output of the agricultural sector was in large part conditioned by the existence of markets in foreign trade. Transformation of agriculture through commodity production – both historically and in its 1920s dimensions – was directly linked with the existence of foreign markets. Hence a discussion of the magnitude and mechanisms of foreign trade is crucial for an understanding of the implantation of commodity production – and integration into the world market – in agriculture.

The second point is about the relative historical significance of the figure for the proportion of foreign trade in national income. The ratio of imports to national income has never been higher in the history of the Ottoman Empire or Turkey.[2] It would not be misleading to say that the Turkish economy of the 1920s had been integrated into the world market to an extent which it has not experienced since. This extent, however, fell short of the degree of integration of most of the Latin American countries, while it was comparable to the degree of integration of other peripheral countries such as Bulgaria or Yugoslavia.[3]

Another perspective to bring to the trade performance of Turkey is the development of trade in the world as a whole. The years after the war represented a conjuncture of recovery and reconstruction. This period of recovery was followed by a precarious boom which lasted only until the crash of 1929.[4] In the last four years of this boom the volume of world trade increased by 19%, and that of European trade increased by 22%.[5] Turkey's foreign trade volume peaked in 1925, showed a decline up to 1927, recovered in 1928 and levelled off in 1929. Thus, it was in 1925 that Turkish trade volume as a proportion of world trade was highest. Between 1927 and 1929, Turkey's share in total world trade was 0.3%.[6] Once again, this share has not been equalled since then.

4.2 The trade regime

The mercantile activity of the 1920s took place in what was nearly a free-trade environment. Before 1914, the Ottoman Empire was bound by international treaties to observe a certain customs tariff. The Porte could not change the rate of import duties, nor could it introduce rates to apply to specific items. Thus a protectionist trade policy was an impossibility. In 1907, after long negotiations with Turkey's creditors, import duties were increased from a level *ad valorem* of 8% to 11%, still without allowing the institution of specific protection.[7] During the War the Young Turk government was at relative liberty to take measures concerning external economic relations and it introduced a specific tariff in 1916 which was designed to be protectionist.[8] During the occupation following the War, the Ankara government, in order to adjust these specific rates to rising prices, increased them five-fold. In Istanbul, which was under occupation, the occupying powers reverted to the 11% ad valorem rate in 1921.[9]

After the Ankara government unified the country, it set out to revise the specific tariff of 1916 (modified in 1920) through increasing the schedules on certain commodities by twelve-fold (on the basis of the 1916 rates). These commodities were chosen with the intention of protecting domestic agricultural products, and prohibiting luxury imports.[10] However, the protective nature of the 1920 modification had somewhat eroded as the lira fell against gold by 36% during 1920–23.[11]

The government's unilateral decision was to come under scrutiny during the

Lausanne peace talks. Here, Turkey accepted that the specific rates should remain unchanged for five years, that is until 1929. For certain items, however, the twelve-fold increase of 1923 was decreased to a nine-fold increase. Otherwise, the signatory countries would be subject to the rates introduced in 1916.[12] These countries regularly supplied over half of Turkey's imports.[13] The non-signatory countries, together with the nine- and twelve fold increases in certain commodities, had to face a rise from five- to eight-fold in unprotected items. It should be remembered, however, that the Turkish gold lira, which constituted the basis for 1916 rates, was worth 7.3 paper liras in 1924 and 8.7 paper liras in 1929.[14] Therefore the changes in Lausanne, and the subsequent alteration of the rate for non-signatories was equivalent to a preservation of the 1916 schedule.

If we consider all taxes on imports (including excise taxes), these amounted each year to about one quarter of the value of total imports during our period.[15] This, however, is a gross figure and does not reflect the rates of actual protection in commodity groups. Calculations for 1928 indicate that the duties varied widely in proportion to the value of imported items between different commodities. Table 4.1 shows those commodity groups which were significant in the composition of imports, and the calculated rates of protection. The weighted average of the rate of protection on these items in 1928 was 12.4%. That is to say that to import a package worth 100 TL, composed of the six groups in proportions equivalent to their share in total imports, required 12.4 TL of duties to be paid. (The rate would have been higher in earlier years since the Turkish lira depreciated and foreign prices increased over the decade, both acting to lower the importance of a specific tariff.)

In September 1929, the new trade regime came into effect. As the Lausanne treaty had authorised Turkey to institute new tariff rates beginning 5 years after the signing of the treaty, merchants and industrialists had for some time been lobbying and preparing studies on tariffs to influence the government's

Table 4.1 *Share in total imports and rate of protection by commodity group*[16]

Commodity group	Share in total imports (%)	Rate of protection (%)*
Cereals and products	3.9	23.4
Colonial supplies and confectionery	9.2	14.9
Cotton products	23.5	12.4
Wool products	7.1	11.9
Metal products	11.8	6.8
Petrol and oils	5.0	11.8
	60.5	

* Import duty as a percentage of value (*ad valorem* equivalents)

decision.[17] The final tariff which came into effect reflected the balance of power between the merchants and the manufacturers, but it also bore the imprint of the coming crisis, which had already been felt in certain sectors of the economy – especially in the cotton-growing and exporting sector – since 1926. The schedule which was finally legislated was not as protective as later historiography suggests. Closer investigation shows that the move towards autarky during the 1930s was due to a monopoly regime rather than solely to tariffs.[18] In fact, it seems that the 1929 schedule by itself would not have greatly disrupted the domination of merchant capital had the world crisis not followed. Sufficient concessions had been given to the merchants, and industrial protection was not accorded where it might have mattered.

4.3 Composition of imports

The composition of Turkey's foreign trade can be summarized as the import of manufactured consumer goods and colonial staples while raw materials and luxury primary produce were exported. This composition of imports is within the expected peripheral pattern. During our period the largest single item of import was textiles, accounting on average for 40% of the import bill. Other manufactured material consisted of consumer goods made of metals, invest-ment goods in the form of tools and mechanical power sources; and means of transportation (most of which consisted of private cars) made up appro-ximately 20%. Colonial staples: sugar, coffee, and tea amounted to an average of 10% of import expenditure; kerosene and petrol to another 5%. The remaining quarter of imports was made up of various consumer goods, foodstuffs, and raw materials. The exact figures for 1926 are shown in Table 4.2. These proportions changed during the decade, due both to secular developments and short-term shifts. In order to discuss the representative structure, we continue with the example of 1926.

Table 4.2 *Value composition of imports 1926*[19]

	% of total value of imports
Cotton, wool, silk, linen goods	44.2
Sugar, coffee, cocoa, tea	8.6
Machines and tools	4.3
Petrol and derivatives	4.4
Metals, iron, and steel	9.4
Transportation vehicles	1.2
Cereals	2.6
Glassware	2.6
Leather and furs	2.8
	80.1

In 1926, imports of manufactured goods constituted 85% of all imports. This amount represented approximately 38% of the manufactured commodity flow in the economy. In other words, while domestic manufacturing output was 363m TL, imports of manufactures amounted to 220m TL.[20] Out of this 220m TL, between 30m and 35m TL represented investment goods, which approximately equals the amount of domestically produced investment goods.[21] In finer classifications, items which were not produced inside the country at all and whose total supply was entirely due to imports can easily be identified. Iron and steel, paper, glassware, and engines could be cited in this category. Among consumption items, domestic production supplied only about one eighth of cotton fabric and one fifth of woollen materials consumption. The rest was imported. Over 90% of the refined sugar, as well as 60% of the cement consumed was imported.[22] As was mentioned above, for cotton and woollen yarn and cloth imported and domestically produced items were not substitutes; for commodities like cement, and sugar, however, domestic production could substitute for imports and in fact we do observe such a substitution throughout the 1920s.[23]

4.3.1 Conjunctural disturbances

If we look at the conjunctural fluctuations in the structure of imports, the most important shift is observed between 1925 and 1926, when the share of grains and flour imports declined from 9.4% to 2.6%.[24] The reason for the decline should be sought in the delayed reconstruction in agriculture after the devastation of 1914–22, but also in the exceptionally good harvest of 1926. In fact, although bad weather conditions prevailed in 1927 and 1928, flour stocks could supply some of the consumption demand.[25] Imports of grains and flour in 1928 increased only to 70.2m tons from a low of 23.5m tons in 1927 (compared to 207.8m tons in 1924).[26]

It should also be mentioned that, in looking at the structure of imports during the 1920s, the year 1929 presents a problem. As was discussed above, importing merchants and consumers were aware that the liberal trade regime which had made Turkey into a relatively open economy was coming to an end in September 1929. For this reason, merchants wished to import a maximum of highly demanded foreign goods in order to earn speculative profits when the new protective regime was established. As a result, the trade deficit doubled in 1929. Although it was an unfortunate year for Turkey's agricultural exports whose earnings declined by 20m TL, imports increased by 25m TL.[27] More importantly, however, the structure of imports shifted to favour consumer goods which could be easily speculated on.

4.3.2 Secular trends

Aside from short-term fluctuations in grain purchases, and the specificity of the year 1929 when importers increased their purchases due to the expected

Table 4.3 *Import trends 1923–29 (million kgs)*[28]

	Metals	Machinery and tools	Petrol and grease
1923	34.0	2.6	49.7
1924	97.3	8.6	58.3
1925	128.2	12.5	82.5
1926	124.0	14.5	76.1
1927	109.3	12.5	87.9
1928	175.2	13.7	101.4
1929	183.9	14.1	112.3

changes in tariffs, the composition of imports exhibited stability or secular trends in certain items. Table 4.3 shows the volume of imports of selected items where a steady increase is observed. In terms of value, the share of these three items against which there was no domestic competition increased from 10.8% in 1923 to 22% in 1929.[29]

On the other hand, imports of cotton goods declined in relative importance. While their share in total imports was 32.8% in 1924, this figure declined to 30.6% in 1926 and 23.5% in 1928.[30] Although domestic production of cotton goods increased during the decade, this increase did not imply a decline in the absolute quantity of cotton imports: 26.3m kgs were imported in 1924; 30.4m in 1926, 23.3m in 1928, and 27.4m in 1929.[31] Thus the changes in the relative share of cotton imports in total imports were due on the one hand to a relatively stable volume of cotton goods imports while total imports were increasing, and on the other hand to the fluctuating – and after 1926 declining – unit price of cotton goods in the international market.[32]

In woollens a similar situation was not observed. Although domestic wool yarn production doubled between 1924 and 1929, both the relative share and the quantity of woollen imports increased steadily until 1928.[33] We have already mentioned that the domestic production of cement and sugar increased during the decade. In 1924, 24m kgs of cement was produced while in 1929 the figure was 71m. Despite this increase, the volume of imported cement did not decline and remained constant at around 55m kgs. The production of sugar was begun in 1926 and increased to 8.1m kgs in 1929. During the decade sugar imports did not decline, yet the share of domestic production had increased to 10% of the total supply by 1929.[34]

The share of final goods – textiles and food – in total imports declined steadily from 74% in 1923 to 67% in 1925, and to 52% in both 1927 and 1928. These shifts indicate growth in the domestic manufacturing sector. As the output of manufactures increases, the complementary requirements from foreign markets change. The implicit assumption here is that the pattern and level of consumption demand of manufactures is a more stable datum, relatively independent of the domestic volume of manufacturing output. In this situation, domestic manufactures develop by competing successfully against

Table 4.4 *Export trends 1924–29 (%)*[35]

	1924	1925	1926	1927	1928	1929
Tobacco	29.3	31.4	36.6	27.7	31.2	26.3
Raisins	11.4	5.7	6.7	4.7	8.7	6.3
Cotton	7.3	7.0	8.0	6.0	6.0	5.5
Figs	6.9	4.2	3.3	2.7	3.0	3.4
Hazelnuts	4.7	7.3	6.0	6.5	5.8	2.9
Wool	5.1	2.7	4.7	5.8	6.5	6.1
Opium	3.8	3.8	4.5	3.0	3.0	5.5
Eggs	2.3	2.4	2.4	3.4	3.4	4.1
Total	70.8	64.5	72.2	59.8	67.6	60.1

imports because they have cost advantages due to transportation and/or low wages. This development requires the importing of capital goods and raw materials which are not produced domestically. Thus, the process of 'import substitution' also creates a new demand for imports of a different kind. Of course, the period we are dealing with is too short to reveal the entire dimension of the described process. Nevertheless, the secular trends which can be observed – relative decline in consumer goods imports and increase in the proportion of capital goods and raw materials imports – might only be understood through such a perspective of structural transformation.

4.4 Composition of exports

We have already mentioned the predominance of certain agricultural products in the composition of Turkish exports. With minor fluctuations due to weather conditions, the structure of exports remained stable during our period. Table 4.4 sets out the share of principal export items in total export earnings. In addition to these foodstuffs and raw materials there were two manufactured items which were of importance: olive-oil and carpets. Carpet exports came to between 3 and 4% of export earnings; and olive-oil fluctuated between 0.2 and 5.5% due to the two-year cycle of the olive crop.[36] As is obvious in this table, the change in the structure of production was far from affecting the composition of Turkey's exports. These retained a traditional pattern and only fluctuated with weather conditions and world demand.

4.5 Trade partners

Turkey's trade partners were the old trade partners of the Ottoman Empire with one major exception: Italy, due to the importance of Trieste, had now become the principal partner – at least ostensibly. In imports, England, France, and Germany each held about 15% of the Turkish market. Turkey's exports were purchased by the same countries with the addition of the US. Around half of total exports went to the four major countries, each having an approximately equal share.[37] Italy, however, appears in statistics as the major partner with an average of 15% of the import share and one quarter of the export share. The port of Trieste during the 1920s served all of Eastern Europe as well as Austria and Germany. As sea-transport was the cheapest transportation available, Turkish imports would be loaded in Trieste and arrive in the ports of Istanbul and Izmir. Exports from these ports were carried to Trieste first and then re-exported by Italian merchants.[38]

During this period German industry remained a major supplier of the Turkish market, but seems to have improved its position in certain markets connected with machinery and electrical equipment. In the trade in steam engines, for example, Germany held 90% of the market in 1928.[39] Later in the same year, the American attaché reported that Germans controlled the market for electrical supplies and 'had a grip on the market in hardware'.[40] In 1928, the British attaché reported that machinery and metal exports to Turkey had gradually come under German domination.[41]

During most of the nineteenth century, the British economy had maintained a privileged relation with the Ottoman Empire. It was only when imperialist rivalry accelerated during the last quarter of the century that Germany gained in importance in Ottoman trade. Especially after the end of the depression German capital began to enter the Empire in greater quantities. In fact, we may argue that it was the differential impact of new German investments that partly balanced the repatriated earnings from old – especially British – capital which, in themselves, would have caused greater problem in the balance of payments. The inflow of German capital was certainly an important element in the Young Turk decision to enter the War on the German side. During the War years, British and French representatives and economic agents were ousted from the Empire and Germany and her allies enjoyed a virtual monopoly over Ottoman trade. After the armistice and during the occupation period, trade with Germany had naturally declined. But a few years of recovery and reconstruction had sufficed for German industrialists once again to compete for markets in the new Turkey. Towards this end, German merchants, mostly agents of industrial concerns, had established a chamber of commerce in April 1924.[42] Nevertheless, after losing the first war for world supremacy Germany had to wait for the second war in order to substantially increase its share in Turkish trade (when it reached 50%). During our period the German share in Turkey's imports remained at around 15%.

4.6 Trade figures

In macro terms, Turkey's trade with the rest-of-the-world did not exhibit a trend common to other peripheral economies. During the 1920s, peripheral economies with the exception of dominions and recent areas of settlement earned more from their exports than they spent on imports. In other words, this category of countries as a whole exported more value than they imported and had a surplus on their balance-of-trade accounts. Frank rightly analyses this phenomenon as a form of peripheral exploitation.[43] It would be wrong, however, to claim that all peripheral countries suffered the same exploitation. The Ottoman Empire had always been an exception in this regard. Due in part to imperialist rivalry, in most years during the nineteenth century the Empire received a net capital inflow – in the form of state loans or direct investment. The absence of direct colonial domination and the fact that the governing class in the Empire constituted a large market relative to the exporting potential of its producers resulted in a secular excess of imports over exports. The same situation continued during the first years of the Republic, although to a smaller extent. For one thing, world-wide capital movements had declined in importance; and, more saliently, the Ottoman Empire, when it was reduced to Republican Turkey, had lost some of its richer provinces and more attractive resources. Nevertheless, between 1923 and 1929 Turkey continually experienced a deficit in its balance-of-trade, or rather enjoyed an import surplus, and some of this surplus was financed through an inflow of foreign capital. Its export earnings fell short of its import expenditures as can be seen in Tables 4.5 and

Table 4.5 *Balance-of-trade 1923–29 (million TL)*[44]

	Imports	Exports	Deficit
1923	144.8	84.7	60.1
1924	193.6	158.9	34.7
1925	241.6	192.4	49.2
1926	234.7	186.4	48.3
1927	211.4	158.4	53.0
1928	223.5	173.5	50.0
1929	256.3	155.2	101.1

4.6. The official figures in Table 4.5 understate imports because they omit government purchases from abroad. They also understate exports because the customs figures were calculated on the basis of wholesale or exchange prices, and did not include the costs incurred by the merchant during the process of bringing the freight on board.[45] A revision of the figures was carried out by the 'Supreme Council of Economics', an advisory body instituted in 1927 to advise the government on economic policy matters.[46] According to the new estimates the trade balance of Turkey was as shown in Table 4.6.

There are grounds, however, for suspecting the validity of these new figures. Firstly on the grounds of consistency: with such deficits in the commodity balance it becomes impossible to account for the means of payment for this excess of purchases from abroad. Secondly, and this is a much more conclusive

Table 4.6 *Revised balance-of-trade 1926–29 (million TL)*[47]

	Imports	Exports	Deficit
1926	259.7	209.0	50.7
1927	239.2	180.6	58.6
1928	248.5	197.7	49.8
1929	283.8	175.0	108.8

criterion, the figures thus obtained do not concur with the trade figures obtainable from the statistics of Turkey's trade partners. For example in 1926, British statistics show a value of £3,000,932 for imports from Turkey. At the average 1926 rate of 929 Ks = £1, this figure comes to approximately 27.9m TL, whereas the figure given in the Turkish statistics is 21.3m TL. In 1927, the British figure comes to 27.6m TL, while the Turkish statistics show 16.8m TL.[48] It is more difficult to carry out the exercise for Italy (Turkey's most important trade partner) since the Italian figures do not include re-exports. However, the differences should remain important even after transportation costs are allowed for.

The principal reason for the understatement of export figures in these revised estimates was the transactions tax of 2.5% which was imposed on export earnings starting in May 1926.[49] Therefore, merchants had an incentive to underdeclare their revenues and illegal exports received a boost. In fact the Supreme Council warned against official statistics in their Report on the balance of payments for the year 1927: 'Although customs statistics may be considered as the surest of the items in the balance (of trade), the differences between market prices and those declared to the customs officials may not be neglected. Valonium, for example, which is entered in the registers at 21 TL per kg could not be obtained at the factories for less than 30 TL. This under-valuation of up to 25–30% can be observed in the declared price of exported tobacco etc.'[50] Thus a contemporary student of the subject concludes that official figures should be augmented by at least 10% to reach true export values (this increase being in addition to the inclusion of delivery costs and taxes to obtain f.o.b. values).[51]

The new figures, taking into account underdeclaration and illegal exports, increase the value of commodity sales abroad by around 10%. Hence the trade deficit, although it does not disappear, decreases to some extent. (Estimates are only given for 1927–29, because underdeclaration is assumed to be less important before the transaction tax of 1926.)

This revision decreases the amount of the balance-of-trade deficit to be explained. Yet we still have to analyse the means of covering the gap in foreign exchange earnings. After all, we do know for certain that, in the uncontrolled currency market and free-floating exchange rate situation of the 1920s, the

Table 4.7 *Revised figures for exports and for the trade deficit 1927–29 (million TL)*[52]

	Exports (f.o.b.)	Underdeclaration and illegal exports
1927	180.6	18.0
1928	197.7	22.5
1929	175.0	15.5

	Revised value of exports	Revised deficit in balance of trade
1927	198.6	40.6
1928	221.2	27.3
1929	190.5	93.3

Turkish lira depreciated constantly during the decade. Contemporaries regarded this depreciation as the incontrovertible and sufficient proof of the gravity of the balance-of-payments situation.[53]

4.7 Patterns in the balance-of-trade

Turkey had trade account deficits with all of its major trading partners except for the US and Italy. Germany and England could offer what the US offered at more competitive rates due to the ease of transport and communications, yet the US continued to demand tobacco, figs, raisins, and carpets from Turkey. Italy, on the other hand, re-exported most of its exports from Turkey and thus obtained middleman's profits through a three-way trade.[54] Some of the deficit was made up in Turkey's trade with other peripheral countries: Greece, Syria, and Egypt. To Greece and Egypt the major export item was tobacco; Greece also purchased raw cotton and eggs while Syria's main import was live sheep.[55] Thus a picture emerges in which Turkey had a trade deficit with industrial core

Table 4.8 *Turkey's trade balance with its partners (m TL)*[56]

	(– sign indicates an import surplus)	
	1926	1928
Europe including USSR excluding Italy and Greece	– 76.1	– 73.8
US	15.6	17.4
Italy	14.7	5.2
Greece, Syria, Egypt	14.2	19.6
Others	– 16.7	– 18.4
Total	– 48.3	– 50.0

countries from which it purchased manufactures, but a trade surplus with Italy, acting as intermediary in the marketing of Turkey's exports, and with three peripheral countries to which it sold raw materials and animal products. Table 4.8 sets out these relations for the years 1926 and 1928.

It can be seen from the table that the trade surplus with Italy (representing goods which were actually sold to Europe) fell well short of covering the deficit arising principally from trade with Britain, France, and Germany. The dollars earned from the export surplus to the US served to lower this deficit, while peripheral trade was in balance.

4.8 Balance-of-payments

The margin of protection in the 1920s, an average weighted rate of 12.4%, was very low compared to other peripheral countries. To give one example, Argentina applied an average rate of 23% for cotton manufactures imports, 31% for woollen products, 18.5% for iron and steel products.[57] Relative to international examples, Turkey's trade situation could certainly be termed free. This free-trade situation in a country devastated by war, and therefore in need of urgent reconstruction, naturally implied a high level of demand for imports. The economy taken as a whole consumed more than it could produce, and this was reflected in the secular trade deficit. The revised figures for imports and exports were given above. According to these the excess of imports over exports in the 7 years between 1923 and 1929 was about 350m TL; a sum equivalent to approximately 5% of the total GNP of the period, and a much higher proportion of the output of the monetised sector.[58] This continuous trade deficit was financed in some part from abroad; that is to say through an inflow of foreign capital and foreign loans.

Table 4.9 *Balance-of-payments (1926–28) (m TL)*[59]

Item	(−sign indicates an excess of debits over credits) Debits	Credits	Net
Merchandise trade	249.1	209.6	− 39.5
Services	5.1	15.1	10.0
Interest and dividends	7.9	0.8	− 7.1
Tourism and Remittances	8.6	8.2	− 0.4
Government account	8.9	5.9	− 3.0
Total current account			− 40.0
Capital movements	1.3	8.4	7.1
Increase in short-term credit (residual)			32.9

We will now analyse the balance-of-payments accounts to show the composition of foreign transactions and to determine the magnitude of the foreign contribution to the financing of the trade deficit. Table 4.9 shows the balance-of-payments account for the average of the three years 1926, 1927, and 1928. 1929 is not included because of the exceptionally high trade deficit of that year, and the years from 1926 on were considered since revised trade estimates are available for them.

An analysis of the balance-of-payments indicates that the current account balance was in deficit due to the import surplus and to the repatriation of returns to foreign capital. (It must be mentioned that the payment on the debt that Turkey inherited from the Ottoman Empire did not begin until 1929,[60] therefore the 7.9m TL interest and dividends are the returns on private foreign capital: both to actual foreign investment and to credits advanced to Turkish merchants.) The excess of services derived from the charges that the Istanbul port authority levied on transit trade.[61] As will be discussed below, most of Turkey's 'services' imports are concealed in the trade account, because Turkish trade was conducted through the purchasing of the services of foreign shippers. The excess in services exports, however, was only sufficient to balance the current account deficit arising from items other than merchandise trade. Therefore the financing of the trade deficit required a surplus on the capital account.

In the three years under consideration, there was an inflow of 23.7m TL foreign capital invested in Turkey. This inflow, however, only decreased the annual deficit to 32.9m TL. In fact the inflow of capital should be gauged against the outflow of profits and dividends, which are the returns to foreign capital invested. These two sums were in an approximate balance: new incoming capital equalled the repatriation of profits generated by already invested capital. Thus long-term capital movements may not be appealed to in order to explain the financing of the current trade deficit. This sum has to be explained through another inflow of foreign exchange. The preparers of the balance-of-payments table have chosen to label this residual as 'the increase in short term indebtedness'.[62] This reasoning would indicate that a growing volume of short-term credits were advanced to Turkish merchants every year such that the level of indebtedness would be higher by 32.9m TL between 1927 and 1926, and between 1928 and 1927. This would be a plausible account if the volume of trade had also increased by the same proportion. Assuming that short-term credits were advanced for purposes of imports and exports, a growing volume of trade would require a growing level of short-term indebtedness to mobilize a higher quality of merchandise. In reality, however, the volume of trade remained stable between 1925 and 1928.

Another hypothesis might be that although a stable volume of trade was maintained, business conditions had worsened during these years such that the turnover of merchandise was much slower and therefore merchants required relatively greater working capital. Thus with the same volume of marketed merchandise, merchants would require higher levels of credit to supplement their own investments and this working capital would be supplied by foreign creditors. There is no doubt that this latter hypothesis will explain some part of the increase in the supply of short-term credits. For, beginning with the fall in world cotton prices in 1926, a slackening of demand had affected all agricultural commodity markets. Growers of export crops (cotton, tobacco, and hazelnuts in particular) had speculated on ever-increasing demand, and loans from banks as well as encouragement by the government had made possible the expansion of cultivation and output alike. With the change in world market conditions, however, these growers were soon in a position where they could not fulfil their obligations. Confronting widespread indebtedness and potential bankruptcy, banks began to restrict credit, thereby worsening the situation. We might surmise that in the last half of our period the advancing of short-term foreign credit was undertaken more by the direct trade partners of Turkish merchants and less by foreign banks in Turkey. However, the total short-term credit might have increased due to – what then seemed – temporary difficulties in trade.[63]

It is impossible conclusively to identify the sources of financing of the trade deficit. Although there is reason to believe that short-term indebtedness might have increased, there is equal justification for doubting that this increase would have attained the volume suggested in the balance-of-payments tables. Two other possibilities remain: bullion movements and outflow of foreign currencies which had been circulating inside Turkey. The Central Bank estimated in 1934 that, between 1925 and 1929, 53m TL worth of gold was exported by private individuals.[64] In other words, the gold hoarded during the Ottoman period and the wars[65] was used to finance purchases from abroad during the Republic. It should also be mentioned that some portion of this gold was obtained through contraband export trade in the East. In a practice which continues to this day, smugglers sold live animals to Syria and Iraq, and obtained gold in exchange, which subsequently found its way to import markets in the West.

Another means of payment – though without the same documentary evidence – was the foreign currencies which had been circulating in the Empire. During the occupation of Turkey by foreign armies, foreign currencies had circulated freely. It was in 1925 that a judgement of a court in Eskisehir prohibited the circulation of foreign currency inside Turkey.[66] According to this decision, contracts could not be concluded in foreign currencies, which effectively meant that the Turkish lira was the only legal tender. Hence, after 1925, there was an incentive to part with foreign currency held for saving or transaction purposes. We are unable to estimate the amount of foreign purchases financed through this means; if not as great as the export of gold, it was certainly not negligible.

We may conclude that the considerable trade deficit that Turkey enjoyed between 1923 and 1929 was financed in part through the growing volume of short-term trade credits advanced by foreign purchasers and banks to Turkish growers and merchants, and in part by the export of gold and foreign currency. We will discuss the reasons for this expansion of credit in the following chapter.

4.9 Terms-of-trade

It is usually argued that there is a secular tendency in the terms-of-trade to move against the exporters of agricultural goods and raw materials. This worsening in the terms-of-trade would mean that more goods have to be exported by the peripheral economy to finance the same amount of imports; or, failing an increase in the volume of exports and with a stable volume of imports, the peripheral economy would experience a growing deficit on its trade account. In order to determine whether an adverse movement in terms-of-trade contributed to the trade deficit, we calculated price indices of Turkey's imports and exports. The calculation was carried out by finding unit prices for thirty categories in the trade statistics. Then weighted averages of prices were computed, based on the value composition of trade in 1926 and in 1928. The resulting price indices for imports and exports are given in Table 4.10.

Table 4.10 *Price indices for imports and exports* [67]

Years	Price index for imports		Price index for exports	
	1926 weights	1928 weights	1926 weights	1928 weights
1923	93	101	71	79
1924	99	104	102	118
1925	101	105	110	128
1926	100	106	100	118
1927	101	107	90	106
1928	96	100	87	100
1929	97	100	82	97

As will be seen in the table, the prices of Turkey's imports were fairly stable during the period except for a decline in the last two years. This resulted from the manufacturing boom in 1928 which produced a worldwide decline in prices.[68] On the other hand prices of exports exhibit a rapid downturn after 1925, declining by around 25% up to 1929. This movement was conditioned by a world-wide trend of overproduction and falling agricultural prices beginning in 1926, which is often considered to be the factor triggering the subsequent depression. The immediate cause of world-wide declining prices was excess supply and growing stocks of agricultural products. The general index of world primary product prices declined by 30% between 1925 and 1929 which closely reflects the behaviour of Turkey's export prices.[69]

Not all of Turkey's export items, however, were influenced by world

Table 4.11 *Turkey's terms-of-trade*[70]

Years	1926 weights	1928 weights
1923	77	79
1924	103	114
1925	109	122
1926	100	111
1927	89	99
1928	90	100
1929	85	96

conditions. Cotton was the least exceptional, yet tobacco, nuts, and raisins all proved relatively resistent to the general decline in prices during the 1930s. However, between 1925 and 1929, tobacco and raisins confronted their own problems in addition to adverse world trends. As was shown in Chapter 3, exported tobacco declined in quality and had to face new competition, while the US market was closed to Turkish raisins. Hence the parallel movement in Turkey's export prices and world prices for primary products was partly due to specific conditions. Nevertheless, Turkey's terms-of-trade moved in the same direction as the world price ratio between primary and manufactured commodities. Table 4.11 sets out the net barter terms-of-trade (P_x/P_m) for Turkey, using both 1926 and 1928 weights.

The worsening of the terms-of-trade followed the decline in the export price index. After the most favourable year of 1925, the terms-of-trade declined by over 20% up to 1929. This means that Turkey in 1929 had to export 20% more commodities in order to purchase the same amount of imports as in 1925. Or, from another point of view, Turkey's trade deficit in the years 1927–29 would have disappeared had 1925 prices prevailed. With the described behaviour of prices, however, although the volume of exports was maintained, the value of exports declined.

The worsening of the terms-of-trade constituted a mechanism through which a growing inequality in exchange resulted. Assuming that the movement of prices did not reflect relative changes in total productivity, Turkey had to exchange 20% more labour time at the end of the decade, in order to be able to purchase the same amount of labour time as it had in 1925. This does not imply that the exchange in 1925 was an equal one as regards labour time, only that the degree of inequality of the exchange increased against Turkey, and in favour of Turkey's trade partners.[71]

There is one other mechanism relevant to exchange prices between exports and imports, which occupied an important place in discussions by contemporary students of Turkish trade. As Turkey mostly exported agricultural crops, with a definite production cycle, its exports increased after the harvest: that is to say in the months of September, October, November, and

December.[72] Its imports, however, were more evenly distributed throughout the year. Thus foreign purchasers' demand for the Turkish lira increased in Autumn, causing an appreciation of the currency. Assuming that prices were quoted in pound sterling, Italian lira, or French francs, Turkish growers and merchants were disadvantaged due to this appreciation, since they obtained fewer Turkish liras for a given amount of foreign currency. It also meant that the foreign currencies purchased by banks in Turkey could be sold at a higher price in terms of the Turkish lira once the exporting season was over, yielding a handsome profit to these banks.[73]

In fact, seasonal movements of the exchange rate were not as regular as this argument seems to suggest. Since the Turkish lira was on a trend of depreciation what we do observe is a temporary set-back of the trend during the last quarter of the year. In 1924, for example, the price of the pound sterling moved from 9.28 TL in April to 8.67 TL in October, and to 9.17 TL in January 1925. In July 1927, the pound was worth 9.50 TL; it fell to 9.31 TL in November, and rose back to 9.74 TL in January 1928; fell to 9.37 TL in September, increased to 9.91 TL in the January of 1929.[74] In as much as the profits from this fluctuation accrued to foreign banks, there was a loss to Turkey's balance-of-payments account. But, even if the profits were captured by local banks which did not transfer dividends abroad, there was a loss suffered by Turkish producers and merchants. It was partly the recognition of this loss which prompted Istanbul merchants to institute a commodity exchange designed to even out the fluctuations in the prices of Turkey's exports. On the other hand, the attention that foreign banks received because of this temporal arbitrage prompted the government to promulgate a law in March 1927 stipulating that all foreign exchange operations involving more than 500 TL had to be conducted at a newly established Exchange for foreign currency through Turkish Exchange brokers.[75] Although foreign banks complained, this lucrative source of profits was thus transferred to native capital. Both seasonal and secular movements of prices increased the payments difficulties of Turkey. They contributed to the formation of the trade deficit, and increased the inequality of exchange where larger quantities of exports had to be traded in order to obtain the same quantity of imports.

4.10 Exchange rate

The excess demand for imports compared to the foreign demand for Turkey's exports was manifest in the declining price of the Turkish lira. There were no restrictions on the exchange of foreign currencies until the end of 1929. Since there was no state bank either, exchange rates obtained in the Istanbul market fully reflected the free play of supply and demand. The Turkish lira during the 1920s was a floating currency, and the contemporaries gauged its value according to the rate of exchange against the pound sterling.

Aside from the seasonal fluctuations which were mentioned above, a trend of

Table 4.12 *Exchange rate annual average and depreciation*[76]

Year	TL per £	% depreciation from preceding year
1923	7.62	—
1924	8.12	6.6
1925	8.90	9.6
1926	9.29	4.4
1927	9.43	1.5
1928	9.58	1.6
1929	10.07	5.1

depreciation is clearly discernible in the TL/£ exchange rate (see Table 4.12).

The constant loss of value of the lira was especially disturbing for Turkish merchants who signed futures contracts with their foreign counterparts. Operating with advanced credit they had to pay, in addition to interest, the margin of depreciation during the period of maturity. Since the lira was expected to depreciate, creditors always quoted the sums involved in foreign currency, and businessmen new to Turkey were forewarned to do so.[77]

Despite these expectations, the lira stabilised after 1926. In 1929, however, to the disastrous harvest of 1928, and to the inflated import demand before the new tariff law, was added the required payment of the first instalment of Turkey's share in the Ottoman foreign debt. Fearing a moratorium on exchange, merchants and bankers began to speculate against the Turkish lira which reached its lowest point in December 1929 (11.15 TL to the £).[78] It was after this 'crisis' that the government began to take measures in order to control the foreign exchange market, which after three years culminated in the establishment of the Central Bank.[79]

The cost-of-living index, calculated on the basis of 26 consumption items, increased by 20% between 1923 and 1929,[80] while the lira depreciated against the pound by 32%. If the prices paid to Turkish producers were based in some part on the costs incurred by them – that is to say if the prices of Turkey's exports did not entirely form in the world market – then we can argue that depreciation made Turkish products cheaper for the world. In as much as the prices of Turkish exports formed in Turkish liras rather than in pounds or dollars, the cheapening of the lira meant a gain for foreign purchasers. Since, however, Turkey had negligible importance in the price formation of its imports, these, in turn, became more expensive for Turkish consumers. This mechanism resulting from the differential between the depreciation of the currency and the internal rate of inflation is one aspect of the worsening terms-of-trade.

4.11 The organisation of trade

In each epoch of the world market, and for each specific economy, trade has been carried out through a different organisation. The organisation of foreign trade in Turkey in the 1920s reflected both the degree of development of the Turkish economy, and the particular conjuncture of the world economy which was already experiencing the beginnings of an overproduction crisis. We shall describe the mechanisms through which foreign trade was conducted.

Imports which had been contracted for, mostly arrived by sea at one of the larger ports: Istanbul, Izmir, Mersin, or Trabzon. The purchasing was conducted either by trading companies specialising in foreign commerce, or through the agencies (or agents) of foreign firms exporting to Turkey.[81] There were also retail companies operating in Turkey which had their own purchasing agents carrying out external transactions for them. It seems, however, that, during the 1920s, trading companies had lost ground and direct purchases through foreign companies' agents posted in Turkey had become prevalent.[82] Trading companies incorporated in Turkey were low-profit making concerns in the 1920s,[83] and among the newly established companies during the decade trading firms accounted for only 3.75% of the paid-up capital.[84] It was a field where foreign capital found it preferable to be working from an outside base: only one third of the paid-up capital in this activity was invested in firms with foreign capital participation.[85] Another indication that companies specialising in imports were not very profitable may be seen in the history of the Turkish Export-Import company, established by high bureaucrats and deputies in 1924.[86] The company, which also boasted British participation, attempted to engage in foreign trade but soon realised that only through obtaining monopoly rights for government imports could it become a profitable concern. When the monopoly rights were not obtained due to adverse political sidings, the company had to close down despite its powerful backers and impressive collection of capital.

In fact, the recommendations and the demands of consular reports, of commercial attachés, *The Economist*, and the *Revue du Commerce de Levant* also make it obvious that the organisation of the import trade depended largely on foreign manufacturing companies sending their agents to find consumers for their products. Both official and unofficial reports indicate those areas where manufactures produced in one country might compete favourably with those which had already captured the Turkish market.[87] Consular officials and reporters alike exhort manufacturing firms to seek markets in Turkey. This situation is not surprising within the context of the world economy in the 1920s. Towards the second half of the decade the signs of a crisis were already visible: agricultural as well as manufacturing stocks were growing. Productivity increases in industry with wages rising less rapidly had created a situation of insufficient demand. Hence there was an intense competition over markets among oligopolistic suppliers. Within this competitive struggle both capital concentration and centralisation through vertical integration were observed. Manufacturing firms growing bigger also set up their own sales departments, and of course these developments were reflected in Turkey's imports: they were predominantly purchased from sales agents of foreign manufacturers, while trading companies had to accept lower rates of profit.

Once the imported goods arrived in the ports, they were purchased by Turkish merchants who either were themselves retailers in large cities or transported the goods inland to be sold to shopkeeper–merchants in the towns of the interior. These shopkeeper–merchants acted as wholesalers for the smaller town or village retailers who made the trip to the larger town in order to purchase enough commodities to be sold until the next trip. At the consumption level this trade network was most visible in the case of imported yarn and hosiery and of kerosene and sugar. These were imported commodities available at the village store. In order to purchase a metal tool or a pail, much less frequent transactions, the peasant would himself make the trip to the town.

The propagation of imported goods in the interior followed the pattern of integration into the world market through the transportation network. Internal trade followed the development of the railway. As the Supreme Council of Economics reported: 'Our railways reflect the limits of commercial development with an almost perfect correlation'.[88] However, since railways connected ports – the openings to the world market – with the interior, and other roads served to feed into the railways, 'the new phase of internal trade which started with the railroad era has manifested itself in the inter-regionalisation of commercial movements'.[89] In other words, while most coastal regions specialised in export-oriented production, railways made it possible for the interior regions to indirectly participate in the new division of labour by more readily transporting and selling their surplus to the coastal regions.

Export trade articulated with internal trade in the same fashion. The majority of exports consisted of commodities produced expressly for the foreign market. Exports of surplus products, collected by merchants after the output was in the hands of the producer, were rare. As in the case of the egg-merchants, recounted above (section 2.5), this procedure involved the penetration of commercial capital to the interior in order to collect sufficient surplus produce to be sold at a point of export. For most exportables the producers were under contract with the merchants at the time of production, and received the money for their expected output in advance.[90] This mode of 'à *livrer*' contract, in fact, meant that the merchant also acted in a money-lending capacity. We shall deal with this case in the next chapter. There were, however, several stages through which exports had to pass. The contracting merchants or trading firms who were in direct contact with the producers were themselves contracted to foreign purchasers. These foreign merchants, who were agents of manufacturing or large retail firms, arrived in Samsun or Izmir at harvest time in order to select and price the goods they were willing to buy for their companies. American tobacco purchasers, British and French agents buying figs, raisins, hazelnuts, and cotton thus conducted at least 50% of the export trade.[91]

Another channel of exports was the agents of Turkish companies abroad.

They were called 'brokers' and were employed in the marketing of Turkish goods in the countries where they were based. Some larger Turkish firms had proper branch offices but most employed free-lancing agents.[92] This mechanism could not have accounted for a significant proportion of the export trade except in the case of traditional connections.

One last category was the exporting done by foreign firms undertaking production in Turkey. The Oriental Carpet Company, which both employed workers in plants and putters-out weaving carpets for it, acted as an exporting firm as well. A similar arrangement could be observed in the case of mining firms. Balia-Karaaydin mines, extracting lead and silver, owned not only a narrow track leading to a small port on the Aegean, but also the port facilities. The same was true for Fethiye-Koycegiz chrome mines.[93] Foreign capital in 1924 controlled 6 mining companies[94] and 11 out of the 20 mining concerns established during our period were foreign controlled.[95] Except for one company which had been established to mine coal, all the foreign firms extracted minerals for the export market.[96] The firms founded by Turkish capital, however, were predominantly orientated to the domestic market: five mined coal, and one exploited a quarry.[97] The specificity of foreign mining companies was that they acted as their own marketing concerns and carried the output to the port of export without having to deal with intermediaries. The mining sector was responsible for between 2 and 3% of total exports.

4.12 Foreign capital in trade

It was impossible to carry out exporting procedure except in ports. This was partly due to the absence of administrative offices: there were no customs gates in the interior, and commodities for export could not be insured at railway stations.[98] Therefore, the actual procedure of exporting had to be done at the ports, with the result that intermediaries were required to bring the goods to customs gates and that there was a concentration of export-related activities at port cities. This concentration was parallel to a division of labour between native and foreign merchant capital. It also signalled the mode of articulation between internal – domestic – trade and external or foreign trade. Internal trade, together with its required linkages, was mostly conducted by native merchant capital, while foreign capital engaged in external trade. The division of labour was most readily visible in the dominance of foreign capital in activities at the ports of trade. We have already mentioned that importing was, to a large extent, conducted through the agency of foreign manufactures. In exporting, too, the insuring, transportation, and marketing of Turkey's exportables were undertaken by foreign capital. There were, for example, 44 foreign insurance companies operating in Turkey in 1928, whereas only nine Turkish insurance firms were in existence.[99] Of those insurance companies established in the 1920s, 6 were owned by foreign capital and only 2 were registered as of entirely Turkish ownership.[100]

The dominance of foreign capital in the final stages of exporting operations was even more evident in transportation. Exported commodities were carried almost exclusively by foreign ships. For short hauls such as from the Black Sea ports to the Soviet Union, to Greece, and to Italy, Greek freighters dominated;[101] Italian and other foreign ship-owners monopolised longer hauls. Turkish ships called only at Piraeus and at Alexandria and carried a small proportion of the exports to Greece and Egypt.[102] It was estimated that Turkish shipping was responsible for only 5% of all exports.[103] Otherwise the Turkish merchant marine was confined to internal coastal trade. Especially after 1926, when a law was passed forbidding foreign ships to carry people and freight between Turkish ports,[104] Turkish ship-owners attempted to benefit from the lack of competition by purchasing second-hand ships in poor condition in order to expand their fleets.[105] In fact the total tonnage of the Turkish merchant marine increased from 28,125 tons in 1923 to 86,967 tons in 1929. However, 78 of the 119 ships involved had been built in the previous century.[106] In 1927, 15,074 ships called at the port of Istanbul. In terms of tonnage, those carrying the Italian flag dominated with 22.2%. British ships came second with 18.3% and Greek ships fourth with 13.9% of the freight capacity. Turkish ships accounted for 14.4% of the tonnage, but the average Turkish vessel had a capacity of 170 tons while Italian ships were of 2200, British 2130, and Greek 1250 tons.[107] It is evident that Turkish vessels were confined to coastal traffic, and that the export trade to foreign ports was conducted by foreign vessels.

Aside from the loss to Turkish merchants of a potential source of income in insurance and transportation, this two-tier trade, through which the final exporting was carried out by foreign merchants, made possible the intervention of Italian merchants in the marketing of Turkish goods. As was mentioned above, the Italian share in Turkey's exports reached as high as 27% in 1926. Foreign merchants based in Trieste purchased high quality Turkish products such as hazelnuts, olive-oil, and tobacco, mixed these with local produce or imports from other Mediterranean countries and re-exported these products at prices which yielded profits of intermediation.[108] The Turkish commercial attaché in Trieste describing this procedure lamented the potential loss through this trade which 'makes it seem that trade with Italy and even Greece is in our favour but in fact is not at all'.[109]

There had also been a recent transfer of offices as some exporting firms, formerly based in Izmir and Istanbul, had moved their operations to Greece or Italy. These moves had come as a response to the mass emigration of the Greek population out of Anatolia. Individual Greek merchants, and Greek merchant houses of Izmir had been, before the war, the almost exclusive intermediaries through which both the export and import trade were conducted. Although in the later part of the nineteenth century these firms had lost ground to foreign firms, which had themselves established offices in Izmir, Greeks continued to predominate in the internal commerce that fed the export trade.[110] Therefore, immediately after 1923, foreign exporters found themselves in a situation with no intermediary suppliers, which prompted a considerable number to abandon their Izmir offices for new locations in Athens or Trieste.[111] The Anatolian Greeks who relocated in Athens, on the other hand, put their earlier connections with European firms to use in competing successfully against previously established local Greek firms.[112]

The fear that the new Turkish government – with legislative and tax privileges abrogated – would impose restrictions and taxation on foreigners, was another factor pushing foreign firms out of Turkey.[113] Again, however, this was a short-term development; when the fears proved groundless, and as Turkish merchants began to fill the lucrative intermediary position, the flight of foreign merchant capital stopped and the flow reversed in Turkey's favour. Nevertheless, the departure of Greeks resulted in Izmir losing her position as the principal port of export in Turkey. In the 1920s it ranked second behind Istanbul.

4.13 Competition against foreign capital

Turkish merchants after 1923 were, no doubt, well placed to capture the positions left vacant by the Greeks. This replacement, however, did not alter the earlier-established division of labour whereby Turkish merchants acted as the internal agents and intermediaries of foreign capital, which, itself, controlled the direct links with world markets. The recognition of this subordinate position led Turkish merchants to voice their grievances and to organise in order to capture a higher share of mercantile profits. 'A national export trade is the external reflection of our economic independence' was a maxim offered by a reporter to the 1931 Agricultural Congress.[114] In fact, his estimate was that only 15% of the value added accruing to the exported commodity between the producer and the final consumer was captured by Turkish merchants or carriers. The rest was 'lost' to foreign agents. Prices of Turkish products increased as a result of these mediations, causing the same reporter to complain that had Turkish merchants themselves been able to market the produce, prices could be maintained at lower levels and a larger share of the world market would be captured.[115] This observation indicates that the cost of production was probably lower in Turkey (in its traditional export crops) than in competing countries such as Greece, Italy, or Spain; a difference resulting most probably from a lower remuneration of labour. Merchant capital appropriated the cost differential in the form of high profits from Turkey's exports.

One reason why Turkish exports had to be sold at lower prices than they would ideally command was that, Turkish ports having insufficient facilities, lines of transportation were established with only a few foreign ports, the major one being Trieste.[116] This situation created a monopsony position for Italian merchants where they could bid the prices down to a certain extent, but it also meant that merchants had to calculate the future expenses to be incurred during re-exporting, and pay correspondingly lower prices to the Turkish wholesalers.[117] Another effect of the concentration of Turkish export produce in a few ports was to create a buyers' market and therefore lower the prices that foreign importers had to pay, which reflected back on the prices offered to Turkish wholesalers and producers.

These various mechanisms acting to lower the share of Turkish merchants in foreign trade came under attack during our period. Policy measures were proposed and government aid solicited in the hope of capturing a higher proportion of the profits accruing to merchant capital. Of course, the appeal was directed to a mercantilist sense of national gain, but only competitive tactics, remaining within the confines of a free market, were put into practice. The most immediate measures consisted of increasing the size of the merchant marine – so that more of the trade would be conducted by Turkish shipowners – and organising Turkish merchants in order to exercise a degree of control over the formation of export prices – so that a better bargaining position could be attained against foreign exporters. It was also believed that an improvement of port facilities would create greater opportunities for merchants, although not much was to be accomplished on this score. There was a promising suggestion of establishing a free zone inside the port of Istanbul which potentially could have been instrumental in attracting a greater volume of transit trade, thus opening up new opportunities to Turkish merchant capital. The plans for the free zone, however, did not materialise until after the downturn in the world economy.

The improvement of the Turkish merchant marine could not be carried out within a short period or through administrative measures. Turkish capitalists did not have a sufficient level of capital accumulation to envisage replacing large-scale foreign shipping.[118] In fact the Supreme Council reported in 1928 that Turkish shipping capital might attempt to capture the Black Sea trade, which involved short hauls and required small ships,[119] consisting mostly of wheat imports from Romania and coal imports from the USSR. Greek ships had dominated this trade, but since it could be carried out without large vessels, Turkish shipowners did have a chance in the competition. Although there was a slight improvement between 1923 and 1929 in the proportion of Turkish ships calling at the ports of Istanbul and Izmir,[120] by the end of our period the picture was substantially unchanged with Turkish shipping firms undertaking coastal trade and foreign ships competing among themselves for the longer hauls.

The improvement of port facilities, however, was of continuing concern. Exporters, and shippers alike complained of the insufficiency of the facilities, of the bureaucratic problems and of the time spent in loading and unloading ships. These complaints especially concerned the Istanbul Port Authority which was a private company established by political favourites who did not have much knowledge about the workings and the needs of the port, and were themselves surprised to see how much revenue their government-granted monopoly yielded.[121] The port remained incapable of handling the traffic because there was not enough docking space. Most of the loading and unloading had to be done in two stages: the goods were brought to or from larger ships in small boats, because only smaller boats could dock.[122] Warehouses were inadequate, and dock-workers were lazy and careless. On top of all this, there were bureaucratic requirements of papers to be filled, permits to be granted, etc. The paperwork required even for provisioning usually took a whole day. The dues and taxes collected by the Port Authority and other official bodies were extravagant.[123] It was calculated by the Supreme Council on Economics that a ship unloading a freight of 3000 tons had to pay various official dues equivalent to 448.8 TL in the port of Istanbul, whereas in Salonica or Piraeus it would pay only 107.9 TL and in Varna (Bulgaria) 122.4 TL.[124] Provisioning, refuelling, watering and the fees paid to loaders were also more costly in Istanbul than in the ports of neighbouring countries.

None of these conditions improved during the 1920s, which was felt to be the principal reason preventing the development of a transit trade through Istanbul. Istanbul had formerly been a transit port before the war, serving especially the European trade with Russia and Iran.[125] The decreased volume of trade of the Soviet Union was one factor in the decline of Istanbul as a centre of transit trade. Another factor, however, was the quality of services obtainable at the port of Istanbul.[126] 'For Istanbul to become an important port of transit, it has to possess a harbour, warehouses and docks equipped with modern vehicles which would be incomparable with the facilities existing today', commented the Council.[127] The president of the Port Authority, himself, lamented the inadequacy. The tonnage of ships calling at Istanbul had declined by 45% between 1910 and 1927;[128] according to the Council, the establishment of a free zone in the port might bring the traffic back,[129] and Istanbul could once again attain the status that its geographical location warranted, and which it had lost to 'Piraeus, Salonica, and even to Port Said, Genoa, and Trieste'.[130]

In 1926 the government appointed a special commission to inquire into the feasibility of creating a free zone in Istanbul.[131] The free zone would be a special area in the port where Turkish customs and regulations would not apply and which would contain modern facilities and adequate warehousing in order to attract trading firms dealing with proximate markets.[132] It was speculated that the Black Sea trade with the Soviet Union and Romania, and the Asian trade with Iran and other Middle Eastern countries, might employ the free zone for stocking goods and as a central point of collection.[133] This role that Istanbul was to play was thought of in conjunction with its role as the centre of exchange for commodities such as tobacco and carpets.[134] It was imagined that similar exports of neighbouring countries would find a market in Istanbul. Although the Parliament voted a law on the establishment of a free zone (June 1927), the intention did not materialise. As the correspondent to *The Economist* pointed out, the scheme would have involved considerable capital outlay, and 'in default of Turkish capital, the money must obviously come from abroad'.[135] Steps were not taken to attract such an investment of foreign capital, and the government itself did not show any zeal in carrying out the original intention. When the Depression arrived two years later, the only application of the law had been in the granting of free zone rights to the Ford Motor Company where it was to assemble cars to be sold in Turkey. With the Depression the scheme was forgotten, without having contributed to the reattainment of Istanbul's transit position.

The government's initiative in attempting to favour Turkish merchants and shippers had in large part been a response to demands by the merchants' professional organisation, the Chamber of Commerce. Chambers of commerce had been in existence in Istanbul since the 1870s. In addition to the Turkish chamber, which was the last to be established, there had been British, German, and French associations. The Turkish association, which had had its most active period during the war, fell into an eclipse with the occupation.[136] Foreign merchants monopolised all trade with Istanbul between 1918 and 1923. After the Republic was established, the Turkish chamber re-commenced its activities in earnest. In September 1925 a law was passed granting Turkish chambers of commerce 'semi-official' status.[137] With this law, chambers were considered as professional organisations and therefore legal bodies.[138] In August 1926 the Turkish Chamber in Istanbul voted to apply to the Ministry of Commerce demanding the denial of legal status to foreign chambers of commerce.[139] In September the correspondent to *The Economist* reported that the British association could no longer use the word 'chamber' in its title.[140] In 1927 all foreign merchants dealing in Istanbul had become members of the Turkish Chamber of Commerce. There were 1595 foreign merchants as members of the association and 8451 Turkish ones.[141]

The Chamber of Commerce, grouping together the merchants of Istanbul, acted as intermediary between them and the government. Its main endeavour was to secure protection and support for Turkish merchants against foreign traders. The first demand of the Istanbul merchants from the new government had been for measures to 'strengthen Turkish shipping against the competition of foreign companies'.[142] When foreign companies were forbidden coastwise trade in Turkish waters, the Chamber reacted jubilantly, celebrating the occasion with numerous telegrams to Ankara.[143] In 1927 and 1928 reports were drafted asking for the protection of the Turkish merchant marine, and complaining of Greek monopoly in Black Sea transportation.[144]

A constant complaint and the unchanging subject of special reports was the inadequacy of the port of Istanbul. The Chamber sought measures to improve the facilities; sent delegations abroad to study the possible means of improvement; and tried to influence the government in finding ways of creating a more suitable lifeline connecting with the world market. In this connection, the free zone scheme attracted the attention of the merchants. In August 1926, they sought to secure representation at the committee appointed by the Ministry of Commerce to study issues relating to the establishment of free zones.[145] By the end of the year a report had been drafted evaluating the potential offered to Turkish merchants through the institution of a free zone.[146] It stated that a free zone would open new opportunities for Turkish shippers; that if Turkish merchants were better informed about the conditions of trade in Russia, Iran, and Bulgaria, these countries could become the 'hinterland' of Istanbul, and Istanbul could develop as the centre of world trade in certain commodities such as carpets.[147]

Another activity of the Chamber which was significant in the attempts of the Turkish merchants to capture a greater share of the profit from foreign merchants was the establishment of a commodity exchange. In July 1924, the Chamber appointed a committee to investigate the means of 'carrying out a wish that the Chamber had for many years entertained', namely the establishment of a commodity and grains exchange.[148] In November of the same year, the exchange had commenced to operate. Its functions would be 'the organisation of commercial transactions, balancing of the market, prevention of speculation, and enabling the transaction of commodities at their value'.[149] In fact, within a short period, the Istanbul commodity exchange became the centre of price formation and quality determination. It was there that merchants could follow price fluctuations in the world market, apply for the settlement of disputes, determine quality, and carry out transactions. The exchange also organised a rudimentary futures market, thereby attempting to control the wide price fluctuations in agricultural commodities. However, since the terms allowed for a maximum of 31 days delay in delivery, the measure was not effective, and prices continued to fluctuate seasonally.[150] Thus, the commodity exchanges of Istanbul and other cities only marginally contributed to the protection of Turkish merchants from price fluctuations which meant that prices still declined when crops were brought to the market during the harvest season. Nevertheless, the existence of an exchange meant that the market power enjoyed by a few buyers against a large number of sellers, was, to a certain extent, broken. This organisation of the market provided Turkish merchants with better information and allowed them to bargain for prices closer to those obtained in the world market. Such a development, of course, would directly affect the relative profit shares of native as opposed to foreign merchant capital.

It should be emphasised, however, that these gains by native merchants cannot be taken to imply a nationalist economic policy by the state. The Ankara government responded – mostly favourably – to demands by the merchants of Istanbul, but did not itself take initiatives to further nationalise trade. In fact, the history of trade monopolies shows that the government did not have a consistent policy against foreign merchant capital.

The according of monopoly rights to importers of certain items had been a privilege of the Porte until the trade treaty of 1838. After this treaty, the system was dismantled since Britain had insisted on 'free trade'. The Turkish government reinstated the practice after 1923, and sold the monopoly privileges of importing certain articles to foreign firms. The match monopoly, for example, was conceded to a Belgian group in December 1924; the French firm Minelite, manufacturer of explosives, obtained in 1927 the monopoly of importing gunpowder and other explosives.[151] The spirits and alcohol monopoly (which also included a manufacturing concession as well as a marketing monopoly) was given to a Polish consortium, Natchalna, in June 1926. This latter group, however, entered financial difficulties, and the government took the monopoly rights back within a year.[152] Of the trade monopolies only the Regie des Tabacs was challenged by Turkish merchants. This company, which was a by-product of the Public Debt Administration set up in 1881, had exclusive rights in the purchasing and exporting of Turkish tobacco. As it was the sole purchaser, the growers frequently complained that they were not given just prices for their produce. Merchants equally complained that they could not partake of the profitable tobacco trade.[153] The move to oust the Regie in 1925 was ostensibly intended to withdraw monopoly trading rights from a foreign company. In fact, the government began to operate a tobacco monopoly to manufacture cigarettes for the internal market. Yet in 1927 the entire export trade of tobacco was in the hands of foreign firms. The largest among these was the French firm Tabacs d'Orient et d'Outre Mer; the Belgian firm Fumaro, and the Dutch firms Commerce des Tabacs Turcs and Tabacus, followed in importance.[154] Undoubtedly, tobacco growers had profited from the dissolution of the monopsonist Regie des Tabacs, but Turkish merchants could not benefit from this situation to replace foreign capital: they acted as the local extensions of foreign firms. Like the Serdarzades in Trabzon (whose firm went bankrupt in October 1929) they purchased from the growers in the hinterland in order to sell to American, French, or German merchants at the port.[155]

It would therefore be wrong to interpret the competitive endeavours of Turkish merchants as part of a nationalist – anti-foreign capital – policy pursued by the government. The native merchants wanted a larger share of the commercial revenue, and for this reason they sought government aid; without, however, constituting a nationalist platform. The government, for its part, had no qualms about dealing with foreign capital and never pursued a nationalist policy, although it accommodated some of the competitive demands of Turkish merchants.

We can conclude from this account that Turkish merchants could not be considered entirely unsuccessful in their attempt to capture a larger share of the value accruing to merchant capital.[156] In a situation where merchant capital claims as profits the difference between purchasing price from the producer and selling price to the final consumer, the endeavour of Turkish merchants was to capture a higher proportion of this profit. Foreign merchants had historically held the dominant position in Turkey's trade, and had therefore been able to capture the commercial profit out of unequal exchange. Indigenous merchant capital had been content to articulate into foreign merchant capital in a subordinate capacity. After 1923, Turkish merchants began to make use of the newly-achieved political sovereignty in order to ameliorate their position vis-à-vis foreign merchants: by gaining the coastal shipping monopoly, they achieved protection of national shippers; and by instituting the Turkish Chamber of Commerce, and commodity exchanges, they attempted to ameliorate their bargaining position against foreign merchant capital.

4.14 Summary

In this chapter we brought two perspectives to the importance of trade in the peripheral formation of Turkey. The first perspective treated the country as a unit inside the world economy and accordingly the discussion was conducted along essentially mercantilist categories. Thus the institutional framework within which trade took place and its economic importance were discussed. In the same line of analysis we compiled the available data on the commodity composition of imports and exports, and on Turkey's trade partners. More relevant to a study of the peripheral structure, we then examined the direction of economic flows in Turkey's foreign relations. It was discovered that there was a continuous trade deficit which gained permanence in large part because of the worsening terms-of-trade for Turkey. In fact, if the prices and the exchange rate of 1925 had prevailed, Turkey's trade deficit would have disappeared in the latter part of the decade. Given the volume of the trade deficit, an investigation of the other accounts in the payments balance was required to discover the means of payment for the deficit. We found that the trade deficit was compensated for by a surplus in short-term capital movements, and the outflows from Turkey of gold and foreign currencies.

The second perspective consisted of a description of the organisation of trade and of the competition between native and foreign merchant capital. Here we were concerned with the implantation of market relations and commodity production in the economy; and with the means whereby foreign merchant capital articulated with the internal economy. Merchant capital, however, is not a homogeneous entity. The functional division of labour between different kinds of merchants also defined the areas of activity of native as against foreign capital in trade. Turkish merchants during the 1920s attempted to capture a higher share of the profits accruing to merchant capital. While their endeavour was not without success, foreign capital still dominated and organised external trade at the end of our period. Turkish merchants, on the other hand, could be said to have captured the positions left vacant by the departing Greeks, who, before the war, had been the main intermediaries of foreign capital in the Ottoman Empire.

In Chapter 5, we turn to another mechanism – banking and credit – whereby a fraction of capital – interest bearing capital – serves to articulate the periphery into the world economy.

5 The importance of credit

5.1 Introduction

In this chapter we shall investigate the organization of credit in various sectors of the economy. Since the structuration of the economy proceeded mostly through the activities of merchant and interest-bearing capital, it becomes important to analyse the network of credit as it reflected the processes of articulation and structuration. Credit, or money created by financial institutions, is one form of the universal equivalent which gains additional importance under capitalism. Thus, its relative status in the economy will depend both on the use of other forms of money and on the functioning of financial institutions. For this reason we shall first discuss money supply in the economy, and then the organisation of banks.

The discussion on banks gains further importance because this sector enjoyed lucrative rates of profit, and was the most rapidly growing sector within the economy. For this reason it became an attractive field of activity for native capital; and it was in banking that Turkish capital gained the largest ground from foreign capital. This transfer was actively supported by the government, partly in response to complaints from merchants and industrialists about credit shortage. But the analyses of the institutional background of credit in banks will also provide us with a total perspective on the articulation and relative status of the three sectors of activity we have so far discussed. Banking capital acts as the accountant and manager of social capital, allocating funds to where they earn the highest rates of return. Thus, the discussion on banking and credit should provide us with an understanding of the total rationality of the peripheral economy.

Finally, it is through a discussion of the lowest form of credit, incarnated as usurer's capital, that we will approach the articulation of subsistence production with the capitalist economy. We shall attempt to demonstrate that interest-bearing capital is the principal force serving to dissolve subsistence economies, to extract value from peasant production, and to structure this production within a peripheral mould.

5.2 Money Supply

The importance of money in any commodity producing economy is that it serves the function of a universal equivalent against which all commodities are measured and are exchangeable. The manufacturers, as well as merchants, require the commodities in their hands to be convertible into their money equivalents. It is not, however, only real purchasing power which determines the volume of transactions thus conducted. The availability of the general equivalent, in other words the existence of a publicly recognised medium of exchange, is also necessary. In general, economic agents have access to as much purchasing power as their share in total income. There is, however, a mechanism which gains importance especially under capitalism, that enables the command of purchasing power in excess of that obtained through the exchange of a commodity: this is the mechanism of credit, equivalent to money created by banks. In addition to the money printed and sanctioned by the government, there is an additional stock of money, created by the banks, and accessible to the receivers of credit. These borrowers thus have access to extra purchasing power, in excess of what they obtain through selling commodities they are in possession of.[1]

The credit mechanism gains additional importance in a situation where monetisation, and consequently the demand for money, increases while the supply of fiduciary money remains constant. For in this situation the growing use of money for transactions requires either an increase in its velocity of circulation, or an increase in its supply to answer the new needs. If the money supplied by the state does not increase, bank money gains importance due to its being the incremental supply. Because banks can decide to whom they will make the additional money available, credit policy comes to determine the differential monetisation of the economy. This new monetisation follows the logic of commercial articulation and proceeds through the opening-up of the subsistence sector to commodity exchange. In other words, it is merchant capital which introduces commodity production and exchange. Therefore, the logic of capitalist penetration requires that differential monetisation should be conducted by merchant capital, and that bank money should foremost be made available for purposes of trade, to merchant capital.

In fact, the monetary situation in Turkey during the 1920s favoured the banks' control of the differential accessibility of money, because there were no means available to the state for carrying out monetary policy. There was no state bank, therefore a policy of discount rates could not be imagined; and the Republican government undertook to keep constant the volume of paper money it had inherited from the Empire. Hence the level of state money remained fixed – and insufficient – until the end of our period. The banks, therefore, enjoyed unusual freedom in designing an ersatz monetary policy through creating bank money, and making this money available to those activities that they found credit-worthy.

Aside from the locally circulating notes of the Ottoman Bank and the ill-fated bank notes of the Porte, the use of paper money during the Empire had remained limited.[2] The main medium of exchange remained gold, of which around 60m TL worth of coins were struck during the nineteenth century.[3] In fact, a concession given to the Ottoman Bank, which made of this foreign bank the official state bank and therefore the sole issuer of paper money, effectively prevented the government from increasing the money supply through other means.[4] Thus, when the War began in 1914, the money stock of the Empire consisted of the gold and silver coins (these of smaller de-nominations, notably the 20 ks piece–mecidiye) struck by the Porte, the Ottoman Bank notes, and foreign exchange, which circulated freely among the merchant community.

With the beginning of the War, the capitulations were abrogated, and with them the restrictive concession enjoyed by the Ottoman Bank. The Young Turk government found able financiers among their German allies who instructed them to issue paper money which would be theoretically convertible to gold stored in Berlin banks. Thus 159m TL worth of paper money was printed (in Germany) and issued up to the end of the War.[5] Since, however, gold coins also remained in circulation, there soon developed a new exchange ratio; and by the end of the War one gold lira exchanged for five paper liras.[6]

During the hostilities most of the gold had been driven out of circulation; some found its way to Germany through trade, and more was privately hoarded.[7] On the other hand, some of the paper money had been destroyed, notably in the Izmir fire of 1922. Some estimates put the amount of paper money destroyed in Izmir at up to 30m TL.[8] This should not be surprising as the circulation of currency in general and paper money in particular was confined to the highly monetised areas of the country, and Izmir was certainly the export centre and the most cosmopolitan city of the Empire. Thus the Republic in 1923 inherited a money stock consisting in most part of what remained of the War-issued paper money – between 130m and 140m worth in banknotes and 8m to 10m in coins[9]– and, less importantly, still circulating gold coins and foreign exchange.

Having lived through the war-time inflation, and fervently believing that national prestige required a strong currency, the Republican leaders were committed to sound finance. In any case, in 1925, the Ottoman Bank was given an extension of its privileges as state bank – and therefore as the sole issuer of paper money – until 1935.[10] The only change in the supply of paper money between 1923 and 1929 was cosmetic: it occurred because the worn banknotes were recalled and exchanged with newly printed ones (printed in London by the firm of Delarue) in 1927.[11] At the time, the Ottoman Bank congratulated itself on having accomplished this task smoothly and within a short period of six months.[12].

By the end of the decade Turkish paper money was the sole medium of exchange. The foreign monies circulating, especially in the Western part of the country, and inside the merchant community, had found their way abroad, and the remaining gold had become exclusively an object of hoarding. Only in a small region in the South-East where illegal transactions with the Arab world much influenced the local economy and where the common currency was perforce gold coins, did paper money remain a subordinate medium, whose price relative to gold was quoted every day.[13]

While the volume of paper money remained constant, the institutional base of credit money – bank deposits – increased rapidly during the 1920s. In the absence of cheque accounts, the difference between demand and savings deposits consisted of a differential of 1% or 2% in the interest rate offered to depositors. The interest on demand deposits ranged from 1.5% to 4% depending on the nature of the bank and its geographical location, while the interest on savings deposits could be between 3% and 6%.[14] We have precise figures on the volume of total deposits in Turkish banks – which means banks incorporated in Turkey and owned predominantly by Turkish capital. For foreign banks these figures are more difficult to obtain. In the cases of branch offices there were no published accounts; for foreign banks dealing exclusively in Turkey, however, there are utilisable figures. Table 5.1 sets out the total

Table 5.1 *Total deposits in Turkish banks and the Ottoman Bank (m TL)*[15]

Years	Turkish banks	Ottoman Bank
1924	16.7	n.a.
1925	52.5	n.a.
1926	44.3	n.a.
1927	63.3	127.6
1928	91.9	151.9
1929	133.5	n.a.

deposits in Turkish banks and the Ottoman Bank. For 1928, figures for eight foreign branch offices out of fourteen in Turkey indicate another 28.1m TL in deposits.[16] The French-owned Bank of Salonica accounted for half of this sum. We can estimate that total deposits in foreign banks, excepting the Ottoman Bank, did not exceed 40m TL. Together with this estimate, the total of deposits

Table 5.2 *Bank deposits (m TL)*[17]

Years	Savings deposits	Total deposits	Demand deposits (residual)
1926	10.3	129	119
1927	16.9	212	195
1928	22.5	284	251
1929	27.2	343	316

Table 5.3 *Money supply and share of fiduciary money*[18]

Years	Money supply (paper money and coins + demand deposits) (mTL)	Share of fiduciary money %
1926	269	56
1927	345	43
1928	401	37
1929	466	32

in 1928 comes to 284m TL. On the assumption that the change in total deposits was parallel to the growth in savings deposits (for which data are available) Table 5.2 is constructed around the figures for 1928. We can now calculate the total money supply, and the share of bank money in the money supply. (Paper money + coins will be taken as 150m TL.)

When we define money supply as fiduciary money plus demand deposits, the gradual rise to dominance of bank money is evident. By 1929 only one third of the money supply consisted of paper money and coins; two thirds was under the control of the banking sector.

Money supply more than doubled during our period, which indicates that the growing needs for a circulating medium were met to some extent. While, in 1924, the stock of state and bank money per capita was less than 20 TL, in 1929 it was close to 40 TL. During the same period total product increased from 1204m TL to 2073m TL in current prices, or by 72%.[19] This increase was mobilised through the rise in the velocity of circulation of the base money (paper money + coins) accomplished through the growing volume of bank money.

Before we investigate the manner in which the banking sector managed and allocated the rising stock of bank money, we will look at the institutional composition of that sector.

5.3 Banks

In the Ottoman Empire there had been individual money-changers, lenders, and financiers; in fact, those among them who lent to the state had collectively been known as 'Galata bankers'. It was not until 1849 that a bank supported by the government was established by two of these bankers in order to prevent the depreciation of the recently issued paper money. Three years later this Bank of Constantinople had closed, and in 1856 the Ottoman Bank was founded.[20] Although the corporation was registered in London, its main activity was centred in Istanbul, and several branch offices were maintained in the Empire. At its formation, the Ottoman Bank was designed as a purely commercial bank; since, however, the services of a lending bank which would also undertake the issuing of paper money were required by the Porte, the Ottoman Bank was conceded the status of a state bank in 1863 and changed its name to Imperial Ottoman Bank. Despite the assumption of the duties of a state bank, the Imperial Ottoman Bank continued to function as a commercial bank, and as the intermediary of most of the British and French direct investment in the Empire.[21] Other, smaller, banks were also set up by foreign capital; notably to facilitate German economic penetration through both trade and direct investment.

The first Turkish bank, the Agricultural Bank, was established in 1888. It was granted, as its capital, an additional 1% added to the land tithe, and was supposed to lend to farmers to help improve agricultural production in the Empire.[22] This aim, however, was not satisfactorily carried out: the state remained the main beneficiary of the bank's funds. Until the Republic, the Agricultural Bank did not receive deposits from the public and remained insignificant in its contributions to the financing of agriculture.

During the pre-war period the main operations of banks were in mediating and managing the public debt, and in administering foreign investment in the Empire. They were mostly established in order to facilitate the valorisation of money capital (loans) and productive capital (investments) originating in Europe. Thus, during this period, banking capital fits the classic definition of 'finance capital'.[23] In contrast, banks during the 1920s were engaged predominantly in the financing of trade, and acted independently, rather than as extensions of particular capitalist concerns.

A significant stage in the development of Turkish banking was the Young Turk period and the War years, 1909–18. During these years 15 banks were established in Istanbul (6 by foreign capital) and 11 banks in Anatolia.[24] While the Istanbul banks were to undertake the entire range of banking activities, Anatolian banks represented associations of local merchants, established in order to provide the means for competing against the domination of foreign capital in the export trade. Commercial growers and traders hoped to secure a control over local credit markets in order to free the small growers from monopsonist foreign companies and as a means of gaining a foothold in the export trade.[25] These small-scale financial enterprises, which found fertile ground during the War – both because French and British capitalists were forced to leave, and because agricultural prices increased – did not prove to be durable operations.

Turkish banks established in Istanbul were fruits of a declared policy of the Young Turks: to sponsor the development of a native bourgeoisie. The most important among these – the National Credit Bank – was established in 1917, and enjoyed the open support of the government. The ministry of finance purchased one eighth of its shares and the rest were to be sold exclusively to Ottoman subjects.[26] This semi-official bank of the Young Turk period merged in 1927 with the Business Bank, the semi-official bank of Republican Turkey.

Another development during the War was the proliferation of branch offices of German, Austrian, and Hungarian banks. As the Central powers gained a dominant role in Turkey's external economic relations, so did their banks locate in Istanbul in order to manage the financial aspect of their businesses. When the War was lost by the Central powers, the occupation period witnessed the return of the branch offices of Allied banks. It was then that the American Express Company, and branches of French banks such as Credit Lyonnais and Banque de la Seine, were established in Istanbul.

The Republic took over this motley inheritance. In 1924 there were 17 foreign banks; the two large Turkish banks, the Agricultural Bank which had become an independent corporation in that year and the National Credit Bank; and 16 other Turkish banks mostly of insignificant scale.[27] The largest bank in terms of deposits and operations was still the Ottoman Bank. In 1924 it maintained 39 branch offices, most of them in Turkey and others in Palestine and Egypt.[28] The two other important foreign banks were the Bank of Salonica, and the National Bank of Turkey. The Ottoman Bank was a joint British – French venture while the Bank of Salonica was controlled by French capital. The National Bank of Turkey had been established in 1908 by a British group headed by Sir Ernest Cassel. It was set up as a rival institution to the Ottoman Bank which had gradually come under the domination of French capital.[29] German banks which had been active during the War and had later closed their offices recommenced their activities when the Republic was established. The Deutsche Palästina Bank had not stopped its operations, while the more important Deutsche Bank re-opened its branch office in Istanbul on 1 January 1924.[30]

German interests had been successful in retaining a foothold in Turkish banks. In 1924 the director of the Turkish owned Agricultural Bank was a former director of the Deutsche Bank. This German financier, who had left the country after the Allied victory had applied to the Ankara government in September 1923 to re-assume his duties. The French foreign office went to work in order to prevent the Germans from obtaining 'this position which is so important'. French diplomats in Ankara lobbied in favour of a French banker, a former director of Credit Foncier, but the position remained with the former director.[31]

This success of German financiers was followed by another coup when German interests took over the second largest Turkish bank, the National Credit Bank, 40% of whose shares were by now owned by the government, apparently in the hope of replacing the Ottoman Bank as an official bank. By extending a 5m TL credit, Deutsche Bank placed another one of its former directors as the director of this important Turkish bank.[32] Deutsche Bank thus obtained exploitation rights in the Ergani copper mines together with the rights to construct and operate a railway to the mines, a concession which had recently been granted to the National Credit Bank. By January 1925, Deutsche

Bank had opened branch offices in Izmir, and another German financial
concern, the Deutsche Orient Bank, had installed in Turkey, also contemplat-
ing branch offices in Izmir 'for the purpose of increasing trade between Turkey
and Germany'.[33] Thus, the German attack in banking could be seen as
accommodating the attempts of German manufacturers and merchants to gain
greater influence in the Turkish economy. In January 1925 the French
Embassy reported that it had become impossible to compete with German
banks: they offered very good terms and took over much of the risk from their
creditors.[34] In this way, they especially attracted Turkish importers.

While German banks gained importance, the French-controlled Imperial
Ottoman Bank dropped the adjective 'imperial' from its title, and signed a new
charter with the Republican government to continue as the official state bank
with the exclusive privilege of issuing bank-notes. In exchange the Ottoman
Bank had to extend a 5m TL loan to the government, and deposit 2m TL with
the Agricultural Bank.[35] The government, however, obviously did not consider
the Ottoman Bank as the official bank suited to its needs. It was continuously in
search of formulae to establish commercial banks, and – after 1927 – a state
bank.[36]

British and French banking interests had expected a resurgence in the
commercial status of Istanbul after the war. They had believed that the city
would continue as the central point of Russian and Romanian foreign trade –
a position it had occupied during the War.[37] These expectations, however,
proved to be unfounded. In fact Romanian banks left Istanbul after the War;
and other foreign banks did not enthusiastically invest in their Turkish
branches. We may argue that the reason why foreign banks were in relative
regression was to be found in the changing pattern of foreign economic
relations. During the nineteenth century, trade-expanding infrastructural
investments had to be undertaken with large capital outlays. Most often, these
investments were financed by banks which could mobilise the sums involved.
During our period, however, productive direct foreign investments were of
smaller scale and primarily in the manufacturing sector. They were usually
undertaken by single firms, and did not necessitate the organisational facilities
offered by a bank. On the other hand, all the obvious regions producing export
crops had already been connected with the ports, implying that foreign
merchant capital now concentrated on exploiting the trade potential which
had already been mobilised. Foreign banks, in fact, did both promote and
respond to trade opportunities. In the Adana region, for example, the Banco di
Roma planned to open two branch offices following upon the success of the
Italian cotton trading company, SITMAC.[38] We have already mentioned that
German banks took an active interest in the expansion of trade with Germany.

The years 1923–29 also witnessed the continuation of a movement which had
been initiated during the Young Turk period: formation of local merchants'
banks with small capital. Twenty-four such banks were established during these

years outside Istanbul and Ankara.[39] They brought together as founders large landlords and local merchants, and aimed at supplying the credit requirements of commercial activity – export agriculture as well as local extensions of foreign trade. Before the Republic local banks had sought to compete with the monopoly of foreign merchants and Greek minorities in the credit market. After the wars and the exchange of populations, the gaps which were left in the organisation of money markets provided attractive outlets for local Turkish capital. It was such prospects that mobilised landlords, merchants, and often the deputies from the region who provided the crucial link to Ankara, to come together in forming banks. In 1928, these local banks collected less than 3m TL in deposits, although their share in the total paid-up capital of the banking sector was higher than their share in the total volume of deposits.[40] Their importance in constituting organised credit markets where informal usurious practice reigned was limited but undeniable. Not all of these banks prospered, however. Among those which lasted the few years until 1929, many could not weather the depression of the 1930s and the competition from the expanding national banks.[41]

The most important development in the Republican period was the formation of national banks under the sponsorship of the Ankara government. The new government attempted to establish banks capable of competing against foreign banks on a national scale. Initial capital for such endeavours was mobilised either through the persuasive powers of high officials, in which case merchants of standing brought their funds together; or directly, through the state budget. The Business Bank was a good example of this process. A law had come into effect in November 1923, less than a month after the declaration of the Republic, authorising the Minister of Commerce 'to establish a reconstruction bank for the purpose of assisting in the reconstruction of destroyed areas'.[42] The indirect outcome of this legislation was the establishment of the Business Bank (Is Bankasi) in August 1924. Sponsored by the President of the Republic, its shares purchased by reputable merchants and deputies, and managed by the outgoing minister of economy, the bank from its very foundation enjoyed official privileges. Starting with two branch offices in 1924, by 1929 it had 28. Between 1925 and 1929, it reported annual profits averaging 36% of own-funds. In 1929 its deposits had increased to one third of the total deposits in Turkish banks; the number of its depositors had increased to 33,466 by 1930.[43] In 1927, it absorbed the National Credit Bank through a merger. The ostensible reason for the absorption was that the Business Bank was in a precarious financial situation, having extended an unorthodox volume of credits. It could 'sort out its immediate problems by acquiring considerable assets' from the Credit Bank.[44] On the other hand, there was no apparent reason why the National Credit Bank should be absorbed by its new confrère and not vice versa. The Credit Bank had better assets and was in a more established position vis-à-vis the commercial world. But the outcome did not surprise contemporaries, who saw in the decision a move by the Ankara government designed to eliminate the last traces of Young Turk influence in the economy. The Is Bankasi was a 'favourite son' of the Ankara official circles emancipating themselves and the country from a rival heritage. But we could also see in the establishment of Is Bankasi an attempt to provide Turkish capital with a truly 'national' bank untainted by Ottoman heritage. The National Credit Bank still had a foreigner as its director whereas the new bank would be managed by a top bureaucrat whose reputation among native capitalists was impeccable. Thus the establishment of the Business Bank and its later growth signified both the installation of Turkish capital in a lucrative field, and a response by the government to constant demands by native merchants and industrialists for a sympathetic credit institution. In fact, the overall success of the Business Bank was due to overt support by the government. Pressure was exerted on Turkish businessmen to choose this bank over others,[45] and there were campaigns in local journals, 'probably inspired by Ankara' thought the French consul in Samsun,[46] to secure deposits for Turkish banks.

The Business Bank was not the only state-sponsored financial institution. The Bank of Industry and Mines was established directly by the government in 1925, specifically for the purpose of extending credit to state-owned manufacturing companies.[47] There were 11 companies which the bank was obligated to supply with long-term credit. Although it was the sole institution extending long-term loans to industry, its activity was confined to its designated clients; and it received a small amount of official deposits. During the etatist period this bank was transformed into the main investment bank of the state sector. Another government project was a realty credit bank (Emlak ve Eytam Bankasi) designed to specialise in extending mortgage credit. This bank was moderately successful, and in 1929 had managed to attract about 5% of the deposits in Turkish banks. Its main activity consisted of providing funds for the public construction works in Ankara.[48] The projects which did not materialise were fanciful. In 1926, for example, after a tour investigating the credit shortage in the economy and the problems that this shortage caused, the minister of commerce announced a new project to form a national bank of credit. He proposed that there should be a levy of 10% on all private wealth and the proceedings should be used to establish a large bank which would solve the credit problem and 'get rid of foreign domination in banking'.[49] The project was received sarcastically in Istanbul circles but seems to have been entertained in Ankara for at least a month. Again in 1926, the press reported that the government planned to establish a large bank with a capital of 90m TL.[50] (When the Central Bank was finally established in 1933, its entire capital was 10m TL; in 1927 the paid-up capital of the Business Bank was 2m TL.) This bank was to finance the public works undertaken by the government, and its shares were to be subscribed by municipalities, the government, and other banks.

The government's endeavours were particularly persistent in the project for setting-up a central bank. It is a telling fact that for the establishment of this bank which would be the Bank of Turkey all the projects involved some foreign financing. During 1928 negotiations were held with various American bankers (Marcus Reich, Kuhn Loeb, the American Oriental Bankers Corporation, an international bankers consortium representing various banks) for a loan to the Business Bank of $30m to $60m in order to establish a central bank.[51] In 1929, negotiations were held with German banks, and German experts were invited to study the means of establishing a state bank.[52] When the Central Bank was finally established in 1933, it was of more modest proportions but was still partly financed by foreign capital.[53]

On the whole, Turkish banks had been successful during the 1920s although they did not radically supplant foreign banks. The newly-established Business Bank and the transformed Agricultural Bank began to attract a growing volume of deposits. From 1924 to 1929, deposits in Turkish banks increased eight-fold, and reached 40% of total deposits.[54]

The overall impression of the period is that foreign banks did not try very hard to attract deposits. A French consul, for example, reported that if he 'were not of other interest, [he] would today become a client of Turkish banks', because they offered better service to their clients.[55] This success of native capital in capturing part of the lucrative banking business did not, however, imply that Turkish merchants and industrialists had easier access to credit. Although the accusation was then made, it does not seem that foreign banks were discriminating against Turkish business. There was, according to would-be borrowers, a general shortage of credit, and banks could choose their debtors following orthodox banking principles. Foreign merchants, representing large firms and with sound collateral behind them, were naturally favoured. Manufacturers had even less luck than Turkish merchants. In a situation where a general dearth of capital reigned, industrialists required investment banks extending long-term credit. Bankers, however, preferred loans on a short-term basis to uncertain long-term propositions. A bank which would finance the long-term requirements of industry was a constant demand of the industrialists; from the Izmir congress in 1923 until the 1930 Industrial Congress, the same complaints and demands were voiced.

Government efforts fell much short of satisfying the demands of the manufacturers. The Bank of Industry and Mines confined its operations to state-owned industry, and thus responded to the needs of the government but not of the private manufacturers. Another state bank supposed to extend credit on mortgage confined its operations to public construction in the new capital city. Foreign banks had been hesitant in entering this area of operations because uncertainties in ownership and inheritance laws made mortgages of doubtful value.[56] On the other hand the Business Bank, from its establishment, was managed on a principle of high profits, which under the circumstances was equivalent to extending commercial short-term credit.

In fact, during the 1920s, the foremost banking activity was located in foreign trade, for both foreign and native banks. For this reason, it is difficult to observe any substantive changes ushered in with the relative development of Turkish banking. As the American commercial attaché had written in 1924:

The import and export business, which constitutes the whole life of a country without manufacturers, fully occupies the capital of the banks not devoted to public works enterprises, and bankers have no inducement to extend operations to reach the whole body politic as is the case in more highly developed states . . . Nothing is likely to alter this situation except the development of sound native banking on a scale to compete successfully with foreign banks.[57]

Although native banking did develop, and gained some ground against foreign banks, its lines of activity remained those preferred by foreign bankers, namely 'the import and export business'. Profit-making banks within an uncontrolled market had no other choice. Therefore, it is possible to conclude that the movement for national banking was an extension of the competition in the mercantile sector. Native merchants, in their struggle to capture a larger share of the surplus realised in trade, required access to hospitable credit institutions. The development of national banking satisfied this requirement to some extent, but its impact on the trend of development which until then had been accommodated by foreign banks was negligible.

5.4 Credit in general

Credit in the economy originated in three organisational forms: banks, merchants, and usurers. These organisationally distinct forms are related through the valorisation process of their capital. Banks mobilise money such that it starts the circuit of capital. Extended as credit to merchants, money serves to purchase commodities which will then be sold for profit. Either the bank or the merchant may also extend credit to producers, who have to purchase fixed and current inputs – from merchants – in order to carry out production. We can show that the banker earns interest by providing money advances and waiting; the merchant earns a profit through unequal exchange (buying low and selling high); and the producer obtains a profit because the value of his inputs is less than the value of his output. The boundaries between these roles, however, become difficult to distinguish when the producer faces the merchant who borrows from bankers and extends credit on promise of delivery of the producer's output. For the producer, the merchant acts the roles of both merchant and loan capital. Consequently his profit is an amalgam of interest and mercantile gain. Interest-bearing capital, on the other hand, if it could expand its organisational network, could also tap the potential gains offered by the producer's demand for funds. Yet in Turkey, as in all peripheral economies, there was a dual money market conditioned by the institutional requirements to which banks had to submit, and by the inaccessibility of the organised market to producers. It was this duality which allowed for the fusion of loan and merchant capital.

The conditions of credit were very different in the two markets, served respectively by banks and usurers or merchants. Different kinds of guarantees and sanctions were imposed; terms of payment, and of course, the rates of interest were qualitatively different. Yet the two markets continued a parallel existence: there were banks as well as usurers, but the markets were also articulated to a certain degree. The funds mobilised by usurers sometimes derived from loans obtained in the organised money market; their repayment always required the marketisation of the producer's output, its conversion to money, and therefore the intervention of the merchant.

We have already mentioned that the capital for local banks was provided in large part by merchants.[58] Foreign banks found their initial capital in direct foreign investment, but their current funds – in deposits and in earnings converted to capital – derived from their dealings with merchants. In a society where hoarding of precious metals was by far the most common form of saving, bank deposits originated in the business sector rather than in households. The small share of savings deposits within total deposits is another indication that banks drew their current funds from business.[59] Foreign banks, more exclusively given to commercial activity, received a much smaller volume of savings deposits than Turkish banks.[60] Thus, merchants' current accounts were the main source of loanable funds in banks. In spite of the flows which might be traced among the two money markets and merchant capital, their organisational forms remained distinct. We will now describe the conditions of credit extension by each of these sectors.

5.5 Bank credit

Foreign banks had originally been established in Turkey with the intention of financing specific investment projects. Although they had gradually changed into commercial banks carrying out all banking operations, they had not become native banks. As the American attaché remarked, they were 'only slightly interested in the country in general, rarely even owning [their] own place of business and moreover very nervous about becoming unduly involved locally'.[61] This nervousness in part derived from an uncertain legal environment. Although the Turkish government did not take any direct measures against foreign capital, the capitulations had been abrogated, and foreign business was now under the jurisdiction of Turkish law. During this period of reconstruction, it was often difficult to ascertain which laws would be applied, especially in matters of property ownership. Moreover, when they had functioned as investment agents, foreign banks had not required the institutional supports that lending banks normally enjoy: a banking law, rediscounting, and short-term government securities. During the 1920s, when they did require them, the Turkish political economy offered no such guarantees. Thirdly, foreign banks, as all foreign investment, had to protect themselves from possible losses due to the depreciation of the Turkish lira.

For these reasons foreign banks shared a common ambition: 'a quick turn-over on every transaction'.[62] Instead of using the credits which were accessible to them from abroad, they relied on their initial capital and on funds obtained locally. If they lent foreign currencies, the repayment had to be in foreign currency; but potential borrowers were reluctant to assume the risk of exchange rate depreciation. In fact, they often did not even lend the Turkish lira funds available to them because they converted their earnings into foreign currency, hedging against the depreciation of the lira.[63] In 1925, the Ministry of Finance notified these banks that if they continued converting their liquid funds into foreign exchange instead of extending credit to their clients, the public would be asked to withdraw their deposits, and foreign exchange transactions might be restricted.[64] For their part the banks complained that Turkish businesses did not practice proper accounting and consequently credit-worthiness was difficult to assess.[65] They, therefore, extended credit against strong collaterals such as merchandise consigned to them, or to the most reputable merchants.[66] Since it was a creditor's market, they could afford to choose their clients, and obtain handsome interest rates. Businessmen had to be on correct terms with banks.

This situation changed somewhat after 1925. Is Bankasi (the Business Bank) was established in 1924, and had begun earnestly to engage in commercial operations. The Agricultural Bank had been transformed into a commercial bank, starting to lend to merchants. The Turkish Bank for Industry and Commerce was established in Istanbul, and its founder declared that he intended to support Turkish business.[67] At the same time German banks had started to establish branch offices in Turkey. These developments created a new atmosphere of 'aggressive' banking. German banks were reported to offer very good terms to borrowers;[68] the Business Bank, a French consul claimed, actually forced Turkish merchants to extend their operations on borrowed funds;[69] the Agricultural Bank allocated its capital to its new branches in trading localities.[70] This development was a break from the more conservative practices which had been the rule among the old foreign banks. Turkish banks were judged to be audacious, as they took unjustifiable risks from the point of view of orthodox banking principles. 'Leur système n'est pas très bancaire au point de vue européen', summarised the French consul in Samsun.[71]

In fact, the year 1925 witnessed an expansion of commercial activity and credit. Especially in the cotton growing region of Cilicia, both merchants and growers borrowed funds in order to expand operations. Tobacco and hazelnut growers in the Black Sea region were also drawn by optimistic prospects, inflated through an unprecedented availability of loanable funds.[72] The expanding volume of trade and rising prices of Turkey's exports justified these expectations. Yet in 1926, the optimistic outlook suffered an abrupt reversal. Cotton prices declined, together with the prices of tobacco. Merchants and growers found themselves with stocks which could not be marketed without accepting a loss. Importing merchants in Istanbul were immediately influenced as they could not market their wares in the interior of the country where incomes had declined drastically.[73] One outcome of this situation was that loans could not be repaid on schedule. Cotton-growers, for example, who had mortgaged their plots to expand operations, did not have sufficient money even to buy seed (November 1926).[74] As a result of widespread defaults on loans, banks became more prudent. In March 1927, they were reported to lend 'only against secure collateral'.[75] In 1928 and 1929 this situation continued, forcing farmers in particular to resort to usurers.[76] Those businessmen who could borrow from banks thus obtained high returns through an arbitrage between the bank credit market and the informal money market.[77]

We can estimate the average annual level of bank credits in 1927 to have reached between 320m and 350m TL.[78] Somewhat over one third of this sum was advanced by Turkish banks, among which the Agricultural Bank had the highest share with 41m TL and the Business Bank came second with 32m TL.[79] Most of the credit was advanced by foreign banks: the Ottoman Bank alone was responsible for 177m TL, or more than half of total bank credits.[80] If a parallel movement of credits and deposits is supposed, we can estimate that the annual level of bankers' credits increased from around 100m TL in 1924 to around 400m TL in 1929. The relative share of Turkish banks in these figures, which denote no more than orders of magnitude, must have grown as well: from less than one quarter to over one third.

5.5.1 Bank credits to manufacturers

Among bank credits, short-term merchant credits were predominant. It has already been mentioned that investment loans to industry were non-existent except in the case of the official Industry and Mining Bank. Short-term credits were advanced to manufacturers on the same terms as to merchants, but this type of credit could only be employed in supplementing circulating capital.[81] Manufacturers complained of the situation and hoped for the establishment of a manufacturing credit institution. In the 1930 industry congress, regional reporters repeated the same formulae: 'In our region manufacturing credit is non-existent. It is of utmost importance that an industry bank be established... Private manufacturing has to rely on its own re-sources... National banks advance [only] a small aid through discounting bills'.[82] Some banks advanced credits in the form of current debt accounts from which manufacturing firms could draw money. However, 'it [was] impossible to utilise these credits because banks [could]ask for a repayment of the money withdrawn with only a week or two week notice. Therefore, the manufacturer [had] to be always ready to repay the sum involved. Such a credit only serve[d] an immediate need, and [had] to be quickly repaid.'[83] In the absence of credit availability, manufacturers were reluctant to invest their funds in fixed capital, fearing that at the time of need they would be left without any working capital.

Manufacturers saw a solution in the establishment of a bank for industry, but also in earmarking a certain proportion of the loanable funds in Turkish banks for manufacturers.[84] 'It would not be reasonable to expect any benefit for our national industry from foreign banks', declared a reporter.[85] But national banks also preferred borrowers other than manufacturers, to the extent that even when applying for short-term credits against inventory, manufacturers were told that banks had filled their credit quotas.[86] It can be surmised that the reason for such a discrimination was the greater convertibility of merchants' – imported or exportable – wares to money when compared with the manufacturer's output. As collateral which might have to be quickly sold, commodities entering foreign trade involved less risk for banks.

5.5.2 Bank credits to agriculture

Bank credits for agriculture were more abundant than for industry. There was the Agricultural Bank, which had been set up as an agricultural credit institution although it had started to extend credit to merchants as well. Secondly, commercial banks also made some credit available to agriculture because the export trade required the cultivation, harvesting, and marketing of export crops. Such credit, as we shall see, served exclusively the needs of export-oriented agriculture.

The Agricultural Bank extended three kinds of loans to farmers: property mortgage, personal guarantee loans, and loans on consignment of valuables.[87] Loans on the mortgage of farmland had originally been intended as long-term credit designed for purposes of technical improvement. In fact, before 1924 these loans had been extended for three-year periods. After the re-organisation of the Agricultural Bank, a ceiling of one-year was imposed, and therefore these loans came to be used predominantly for purposes of circulating capital. Even before 1924, only the larger farmers could benefit from this source of credit, because loans were extended up to 50% of the value of the land owned, and this value was assessed by the Agricultural Bank itself.[88] However, the assessments were greatly undervalued, with the result that the amount of credit obtainable by small peasants was insignificant. Total credit based on property mortgage was around 18m TL between 1926 and 1929.[89]

Personal guarantee loans had been designed as a means to extend credit to poor peasants who did not have enough land or property to mortgage.[90] The bank, however, required partial coverage of the loan by material guarantee. For this type of credit too, the terms of repayment, which had been up to three years before 1924, had been shortened such that the ceiling on maturity was 9 months.[91] The average turnover of this credit was estimated to be twice annually.[92] Most of the credit was, in fact, extended on a seasonal basis, and served to cover the costs of harvesting. Growers of 'tobacco, opium, cotton, grapes, figs, our most important export crops, and those special crops such as sugar beet and rice were the recipients. . . The short terms, and the fact that the Bank gave the credit in small amounts, assured the liquidity of loanable funds, and made it possible for the actual farmers to benefit.'[93] If seasonal credits had to be renewed, then the Bank required a mortgage: in this way personal guarantee loans became short-term mortgage credits.[94] This type of credit increased from 8m TL in 1924 to 18m TL in 1929.[95]

The third kind of credit that was extended to agriculture was credit on consignment of crops, gold, or stocks and bonds. This category accounted for two thirds of the total agricultural credit,[96] and had clearly been transformed into commercial loans after 1924.[97] Merchants would collect the crops from the growers, and then borrow funds by depositing these crops at the Bank's warehouses. At first a sum equivalent to 50% of the value of the marketable output could be borrowed; in 1928 this percentage was raised to a maximum of 85%.[98] Loans extended on the basis of valuable papers were of an entirely commercial character, as farmers did not ordinarily own stocks and bonds. Within this category only the loans against gold could be considered as benefiting farmers, since hoarding of gold was commonly practised. These loans amounted to a maximum of 75% of the gold and silver deposited at the Bank and were of less than 1000 TL per farmer.[99] Between 1927 and 1929 credits extended on gold reached 2.5m TL. Together with the estimated 2m TL, that the peasant received against consigned crops, they made up the total short-term credit reaching actual farmers. Total credit based on consignation was 10m TL in 1927, 13.5m TL in 1928, and 17m TL in 1929.[100]

Thus of the credit seemingly destined for agriculture, only a relatively small portion directly reached farmers; the rest being employed by merchants dealing in agricultural commodities, and especially in export crops. This development was manifest in the changes in the network of the Agricultural Bank's branches. Between 1924 and 1929, the Bank closed down 83 of its offices in small towns. On the other hand, it increased the number of its offices in city centres by 19.[101] Those offices remaining in the countryside were concentrated in the export orientated regions: the Aegean and the Black Sea Coasts, and Cilicia.[102]

Of the part which reached farmers, the credit distribution among different strata of the peasantry benefited large and middle farmers producing predominantly for the market. Poor peasants could not benefit from the mortgage-credit alternative which made up most of the credit allocated to agriculture.[103] Especially after 1926, when the value of property began to be reckoned according to the market value of its output,[104] farmers growing export crops obtained a more privileged position. Among the farmers who could obtain bank credit against consigned crops, those who benefited most were the 'merchant–producers', that is to say merchants with share-cropping type arrangements with growers.[105]

It should also be mentioned that the ceilings imposed on various kinds of credits acted to bring about a particular distribution of loans among the different strata of the peasantry. There were two types of constraints: first, the amount of funds that each branch office had to work with was fixed by the central administration of the bank. Those branch offices in regions without large agricultural surpluses were allocated smaller sums. Secondly, maximum credit obtainable by a person was limited. The personal guarantee loan designed to aid small peasants was fixed at 30 TL and could be raised to 100 TL only with the permission of the central office.[106] Although there were no limits on credit obtained through consignment of commodities or valuable papers, loans which could be obtained by depositing gold at the bank were fixed at a maximum of 1000 TL per person.[107] It is significant that pawning of gold – which should be the most convertible of commodities – was thus penalised compared to the depositing of other commodities. These two constraints served to limit the funds obtainable by small farmers as compared to larger commercial farmers who had access to other kinds of collateral than gold or personal promises.

In addition to the Agricultural Bank, small local banks established through individual initiative also extended credit to agriculture. However, in their case the preference given to merchants dealing with export crops was more evident. Most of these banks had been founded by merchants and large farmers, who were also the main beneficiaries of the loans. In their declarations of intent, they gave preference to mercantile operations over agricultural production and frequently planned to engage in trade themselves. One bank which constituted an exception also proves this rule. The National Bank of Aydin, established in 1914 in the richest province of the Aegean region, declared as its intention 'to extend credit to fig growers in the province of Aydin for purposes of production and marketing'.[108] However, when the availability of more profitable opportunities became apparent, the bank began to extend credit to mercantile activity. After 1927 it did not loan to farmers, and limited the period of maturity of its credits to three months.[109]

There are two conclusions to be drawn from this account of agricultural credit. First, as in the case of manufacturing, agriculture did not receive a significant share of the total bank credit; close to nine tenths of the credit disposed of by institutional loan suppliers was received by merchants. Secondly, in the absence of an official credit market accessible to smaller farmers, their principal source for borrowed funds was the informal money market, usury. This means that by far the greatest number of producers in the economy, who produced the largest portion of both the output and the marketable surplus, were subject to the exploitative mechanisms of the informal money market. These two complementary outcomes were equally conditioned by the institutional and economic parameters of the banking sector.

5.5.3. Bank credits to trade

'Almost every shipment of goods to and out of the country calls for a bank advance or bank credit equal to 70% or 80% of its value', declared the

American attaché in 1924.[110] In fact, merchants borrowed in order to purchase goods from growers, they required advances from buyers in order to pay their earlier debts, and in order to be able to buy from abroad. In a situation characterised by a general dearth of capital, the merchant worked with borrowed funds. This was an attractive solution because despite the high rate of interest, the profit rates in trade allowed for satisfactory returns on mercantile enterprise. Thus, the trade sector in the economy could work within the institutional structure of credit accessibility, and predominantly with bank money.

There were three kinds of funds which could be advanced by banks to merchant capital: money obtained through the discounting of bills; advances on merchandise, valuable papers, or property deposited with the banks; and loans based on personal guarantee. As most commercial transactions were conducted on the basis of postponed payment, when merchants concluded a sale, they did not have cash but other merchants' bills in their hands. These bills were of 30 and 90 days maturity.[111] If the signatures on the bills were reputable, the merchant could discount them at local commercial banks. Most of this discounting operation was carried out in Istanbul, among bigger merchants. Since there was not a bank of re-discount to which commercial banks could apply in order to convert bills again to banknotes, the discounting operation meant that banks had to part with funds which had alternative uses in other kinds of loans. Therefore the rate of discount of commercial bills was high: a minimum of 9%, which increased to at least 12% when various charges were added. A rate of 20% was not unusual.[112] If the Business Bank is taken as a representative commercial bank, its operations should be an indication of the allocation of loanable funds in the banking sector in general. At the end of 1928, for example, discounting of bills represented 8m TL out of a total credit level of 42m TL.[113] In reality, the importance of discounting bills in banking operations was greater than these figures suggest, because the turnover of funds in the case of discounting operations was much faster than in other operations.

Advances on merchandise were the second most important bank operation. This operation entailed the depositing of mostly exportable commodities at the bank's warehouses in order to obtain a certain sum of money – calculated as a ratio of the expected market value of the commodities – as an advance payable when a purchaser was found. Merchants also used banks' warehouses as sales-rooms, exhibiting the merchandise to potential customers. A similar organisation of the import trade was also common. Goods contracted to Turkish merchants would be sent to Istanbul, consigned to a certain bank. This meant that the receiving merchant had to pay the prescribed amount of money – and the interest on this sum if he were late in collecting the goods – to the bank, in order to be able to obtain the bill of lading.[114] It was sometimes the case that the expedited goods were never collected by the Turkish importer. This meant that the bank handling the operation was left stuck with the merchandise and had to sell it on the market. Especially before 1923, Istanbul banks had suffered losses through such defaults. The British commercial attaché wrote in 1924: 'merchants would do well to protect themselves against the possibility of goods not being taken up on arrival'.[115] He recommended that British firms demand 33% cash with order and the remainder against documents delivered through a bank. It seems, however, that difficulties of this sort were not common during the period 1924–29.

It was this type of credit, advanced on merchandise guarantee, which was most likely to find its way to the farmer. The middleman buying from the producer was usually assisted by a bank.[116] He also purchased the crops, and had them delivered against not cash but a promissory note. When the merchant could obtain a money advance from the bank, he was able to make good his promise; and thus the farmer was provided with cash to purchase seed and other requirements of cultivation.

Advances on property were the next in importance.[117] These loans, however, did not resemble ordinary mortgage operations, as they were short-term credits with the mortgaged property only constituting a material guarantee that the loan would be repaid. In effect, these were commercial loans with a mortgage guarantee, and amounted to half as much as credits against the deposit of merchandise; and several times as much as advances on valuable papers.[118] This latter category was also a type of commercial short-term credit advanced against stock and bonds deposited at the banks. But since the practice of purchasing stocks and bonds was not widespread, and because government bonds were not commonly in circulation, the total amount of credit accorded on guarantee of valuable papers remained relatively unimportant.

The third type of loans was for larger sums and was only extended to well-known merchants with a good credit-rating. In the absence of sound information deriving from accounts, the Ottoman Bank and other foreign banks had established offices to inquire into the credit-worthiness of merchants.[119] They lent according to the information thus obtained. These loans were in the form of drawing from a 'debtor's account' kept deposited in the bank.[120] Although the time period for which the sum would be available was fixed, the rights were usually renewed, thus making of this 'debtor's account' a long-term advance. However, the bank always retained the prerogative of reclaiming the deposit with a short notice. Therefore, merchants could only treat the sums advanced as somewhat permanent circulating capital. In 1928, the Agricultural Bank had started debtor's accounts reaching 10m TL and the Business Bank 18m TL.[121]

5.6 Merchant credit

This secondary category of credit, which best illustrates the conjoint operation of merchant and interest-bearing capital, is defined as the credit advanced by merchants to merchants or by merchants to producers. We shall first look at the credit extended by foreign merchant capital to Turkish merchants or producers. This could be divided into two categories: import credit from foreign firms selling to Turkey, which took the form of accepting payment at a later date; and export credit, which consisted of advance payments by foreign purchasers to either Turkish middlemen or direct producers.

The precarious 1920s boom was followed by growing market problems for the producers as the decade advanced. These difficulties were clearly reflected in Turkey's import trade as Turkish importers obtained more favourable credit terms towards the end of the decade. During the occupation period – before 1923 – foreign sellers had run into difficulties with their Turkish debtors who had not fulfilled their contracts. In 1924 both American and British attachés warned that merchandise should not be delivered without exacting a certain proportion of the agreed sum of money in advance.[122] In 1925, one French document described the terms of credit, which had become more strict as they accommodated the warnings.[123] According to this description the credit facility of delayed payments was only granted to well-known Turkish firms. If the reputation of the Turkish firm passed the test, the conditions of credit varied according to the nationality of exporting firms. British and French firms accepted 30 to 60 days of delay in payment, and exceptionally 80 days, but only after half of the payment was collected on delivery. On the other hand, Italian firms gave better conditions, especially on sales of cotton manufactures. We also know that German exporters trying to establish themselves, especially in the tools and machinery market, were more lenient in their offering of credit.

Later in the decade, however, the competition among sellers became more heated, and therefore credit was more readily available. In 1928, the British attaché reported that there were far too many manufacturers' agents in Istanbul trying to sell to Turkish retailers. In order to maintain a footing in the market, they were induced to grant credits up to twelve months 'without sufficient regard to status and financial stability of local clients'.[124] In fact, when the Italian lira unexpectedly appreciated in early 1927, Turkish merchants who had to repay their debts in the foreign currency found themselves in great difficulty. The exchange rate of one-hundred lira which had been about 6.25 TL in the Summer of 1926, had risen to 10.65 TL in the Summer of 1927.[125] Although certain compromises were reached between individual merchants,[126] a considerable number of merchant houses, especially importers of cotton manufactures, declared bankruptcy.[127] Italian firms exporting to Turkey had apparently extended an unorthodox amount of credits on long terms, because the effects of Turkish bankruptcies were felt in Trieste, where Italian manufacturers were also hard hit by the crisis.[128]

Italian cotton manufacturers were not the only exporters expanding their Turkish markets precariously. As has already been mentioned, the year 1926 witnessed a cotton crisis in which producers received unusually low prices and therefore constituted very reluctant customers for importing firms in Istanbul. One consequence was that these firms were unable to fulfil their promises to creditor foreign firms. In May 1927, most exporters to Turkey were felt to be in difficulties because they had not been repaid their advances.[129] A year later, *The Economist* reported that in the cotton textile trade alone the outstanding debt of Istanbul importers amounted to £ 1m or 9m TL.[130] The reporter surmised that losses would fall on Italian, Belgian, and Czech spinners who had granted long-term credits. He added that Manchester manufacturers operated on a cash basis and could therefore weather the storm. It seems from this anecdotal account that although it had become more probable that Turkish importers would default on their promised payments, foreign exporters were ever willing to extend credit in order for sales to take place. Only when the system broke down at its centre did this inflated credit economy in the periphery also have to terminate.

We have concentrated on the provenance of sales credit, and therefore had to pay attention to the connection between foreign sellers and Turkish purchasers. We must now treat the extension of this type of credit into the country. There is unfortunately, not much documentation on this extension; yet we know that, for example, agricultural machinery was sold to the cotton growers in the Adana region under similar advance arrangements.[131] Turkish merchants in Istanbul extended credit to customers in the interior as foreign sellers extended credit to them. In fact, the network extended over the entire economy. Even the village grocer running sort of a general store catering to all of the scant needs in the village extended credit to his customers which was payable after the harvest. Hence most merchants doubled as lenders, the practice approaching usury as the village level was reached. It must not be forgotten that a considerable portion of this mercantile activity consisted of handling imported goods. Even at the village level the grocer sold kerosene, sugar, metal tools, and cotton manufactures, most of them imported merchandise. Therefore, it can be argued that this particular strand of credit, reaching through successive stages, originated in the advance delivery of goods by foreign sellers. The initial credit was granted by a foreign firm exporting to Turkey, and its itinerary reflected the chain of interest-bearing capital which bound the final consumer with intermediary retailers and Istanbul importers. Interest earned at various stages of this network supplemented the mercantile income of intermediaries, wholesale importers, and foreign sellers. From international trade down to the level of local retailing, merchant capital and loans were fused.

Export credit constituted an even more essential element of the system. All of the exportable crops were grown, harvested, and marketed through the utilisation of credit obtained either from banks or from exporting firms and individuals.[132] We have touched upon the limitations of bank credit directed to the agricultural sector; the gap was made up by merchants' credit. Export credit passed through two successive stages in reaching the actual growers of export crops. In the first stage foreign purchasing firms contracted with Turkish merchants and middlemen and paid a sum of money against crops to be delivered during the harvest season. The second stage consisted of these native merchants contracting with the actual producers, and effecting payment several months in advance. This direct contract with the producer, which would be finalised when the crops were collected was termed *à livrer*. The division of labour was such that Turkish merchants dealt in internal trade and brought the merchandise to port cities where it was purchased by agents of foreign firms. The credit advanced by these agents travelled in the reverse direction. Originating in the countries where Turkish exports were received, the credit was advanced to Turkish merchants who employed the money to make *à livrer* contracts with the actual producers. Again, the practice approached usury at the village level, because producers usually would borrow money from merchants at times of need – years of bad harvest when seed had to be purchased – and were therefore at his mercy during the loan negotiation.

The interest rate commanded by export credit increased as the actual producer was approached: the rate obtaining between the foreign agent and the Turkish merchant was similar to bank rates, while producers had to pay usurious rates. High rates of interest in *à livrer* contracts meant that the merchant purchased agricultural crops at preferential prices. In addition to this unequal exchange through which merchant capital obtained its share of profit, producers became bound to the merchant through perpetual indebtedness. Thus merchants – because of their monopoly over credit – could dominate the behaviour of the producer, could control his choices over the nature and volume of production.

Since exporters also had access to bank credit, especially from foreign banks which acted as intermediaries with the receiving firms, the credit advanced to the merchant carried a normal price. In Bursa in 1928 this rate was only 12%.[133] When the interest rate was not specified, it meant that the price had to be negotiated in advance and would incorporate the implicit interest. With this kind of transaction there was always the possibility of default since prices and quantities were negotiated on the basis of past years' trends. In 1929, for example, hazelnuts had been expected to be plentiful, an expectation based on the size of the 1928 harvest and on the area planted. Yet a short time before the harvest was collected, a storm in Giresun and Trabzon destroyed the crop, and farmers were unable to fulfil the *à livrer* contracts they had signed at the beginning of the growing season. When purchasing firms insisted on enforcing the contracts, which stipulated low prices, local chambers of commerce applied to Ankara for governmental intervention. Their pleas, however, were to no avail, and hazelnut growers suffered the consequences.[134]

Although it was usually the case that there was a division of labour between foreign and native merchants, and that the actual producers dealt with Turkish middlemen, the period we are treating witnessed growing attempts by foreign purchasers to come into direct contact with the producers, especially of tobacco and cotton. We have already mentioned the putting-out contracts with which carpet-weavers were bound to foreign trading companies. In a similar vein, American tobacco companies had attempted to purchase tobacco-growing land in the Black Sea region in order to become producing rather than purchasing firms.[135] One method of achieving a permanent status as purchaser and thereby guaranteeing a steady supply of merchandise was through the debt mechanism. In other words, a foreign purchasing firm could eliminate Turkish middlemen, and extend credit directly to producers, against à *livrer* contracts. After a few years of this practice, the relationship often became institutionalised, and the creditor was assured that the producer could not break the debt bondage, especially since alternative sources of credit were forbiddingly expensive.

A spectacular example of such an undertaking was the Italian cotton textile firm SICMAT.[136] A Trieste firm engaged in the trade of cotton yarn and in the manufacture of cotton goods, it established a branch in Adana in 1924. As it was heavily subsidised by the Italian government and had access to credit from the largest Italian banks, it soon became the major purchaser of cotton in the Cilicia region.[137] (The French consul rightly suspected that SICMAT was more than a simple trading company maximising its profits. In fact, the Fascist government in Italy had definite colonialist aims in the south of Turkey. Thus, SICMAT had close associations with the government and all its employees were fascist-approved.)[138] Successfully pushing out competitors from the market (those foreign firms who resisted, like the French company Istiqbal, had in the end to sign contracts of association with SICMAT), the Italian company methodically penetrated Cilician agriculture.[139] It gained the allegiance of local authorities through gifts. In September 1926, the French consul reported: 'it might be presumed that in a short period the cultivation and export of cotton in these provinces will be exclusively handled by Italians'.[140] A growing proportion of the cotton crop was exported to Trieste mills. The most important factor in this penetration had been the credit mechanism. Having access to bank credit and the financial support of the Italian government, the company expanded its operations when other foreign firms found the prospects dubious and hesitated. It was even luckier after the 1926 crisis when growers entered a difficult period and could not repay their debts. Forced to mortgage their lands, they 'eventually became dependent to provide all their cotton to the company'.[141]

This case provides an extreme example of the domination of merchant capital through its credit-extending ability. Merchant's credit provided by an exporting foreign firm to Turkish producers was paradigmatic of peripheral integration. It was merchant capital which dominated the relationship of the periphery with the world economy, but it also made use of money capital; its principal interest lay in developing the export potential of the peripheral economy; its preference was for a dependent body of producers contracting directly with merchant capital; and finally, the division of the mercantile surplus between foreign and native merchants depended on the specificity of the institutional arrangements linking peripheral producers and central markets.

The case of merchant's credit transparently demonstrates the role of the credit system in peripheral structuration. Originating in the core area of the world economy, merchant's credit mobilises the production of exports and the consumption of imports. It serves the crucial role of managing the peripheral economy through a selective promotion of economic activities such that peripheral development is in accord with the requirements of integration into the world economy: credit is only advanced to those producers growing exportable crops. In doing so it creates a structure of dependencies such that the continuation of economic activity in the periphery is threatened when the flow of credit from abroad ceases. Hence merchant's credit ensures the continuing domination of merchant capital in the integration process, and the stability of the structural position of the periphery inside the world economy.

As important, however, is the role that merchant credit plays in creating unequal exchange – the source of profit for merchant capital. The merchant always seeks to purchase goods at below value and sell at above value. Because of the subordinate position of the native merchant, described above, he had not only to buy but also sell – to the foreign merchant – at below value. The use of the credit mechanism provided him with the leverage against the producer where he could purchase the output at much below value and still make a profit despite his subordinate position vis-à-vis the foreign merchant. While the native merchant found the wherewithal of his own profit, the foreign merchant thus enjoyed an even greater unequal exchange. The hierarchy of domination, foreign merchant – native merchant – peasant producer, was parallel to the chain of value extraction: from the producer through unequal exchange aided by usury, and from the native merchant through unequal exchange aided by trade credit.

5.7 Usury

In a situation where the output of the peasant holding was barely sufficient to cover household consumption needs, any downward shift in production, such as in the case of crop failure or inclement weather, forced the peasant to seek material assistance from outside. The banking system could not respond to these needs, not only because of its level of development, but more essentially because the requirements of an institutionalised credit market could not be met by a peasant agriculture barely producing marketable commodities. It was shown above that agricultural credit advanced by banks was only a small proportion of the total credit, and was destined for large-scale farming of export crops. The void was filled by 'the usurer who exercised one of the oldest, most widespread and most profitable professions in Turkey'.[142] Peasant farming, constituting a large majority of agricultural production, required external assistance. In the absence of both traditional support institutions and capitalist credit sources, the transitional form of usury supplied the required assistance.[143]

Usury constituted the crucial link whereby surplus obtained in peasant production was converted into profit for interest-bearing capital. Both money-lending and trade are activities which transfer value and retain a share out of the surplus in the process of this transfer. In the case of Turkey, small-scale peasant farming was the largest category of value-creating activity, and interest-bearing capital obtained most of its profit through the practice of usury. In fact, we may argue that it was this value extracted through usury which ultimately provided all suppliers of credit – usurers, merchants, banks – with their profit. Value was transferred through these institutional levels and allocated according to the interest rate commanded by the various suppliers of loan money. At the same time, since usury provided the direct contact with the most extensive economic activity – peasant agriculture – it constituted the crucial link in peripheral structuration. Historically, entry into the circuit of interest-bearing capital was the preparatory stage in the transition to profit-orientated production for the market. Thus, it was through usury that 'natural economies' underwent destruction by having to produce commodities in order to obtain money.

We mentioned in the preceding section that merchant's credit approached usurious practice at the level of the actual producer. Once again two forms could be distinguished: when the peasant was the seller and when he was the purchaser. The peasant *qua* producer could borrow against the crops he would be harvesting. Since he needed seed and other means of production at the beginning of cultivation, he would contract to receive a cash advance or seed grains which would be repaid with interest after the harvest.[144] When the loan was contracted with a merchant, it would usually be in cash form, and would carry an interest of 5% to 10% per month.[145] In the least marketised areas of the country, the initial loan was in kind and had to be repaid in kind. In such cases the amount repaid was a minimum of one-and-a-half times the initial advance.[146] There were variations on the cash or in kind transactions which involved the conversion of physical amounts to money equivalents through prices. For example, the seed advanced in kind would be evaluated at an elevated price, and the repayment would be in grains accounted at the lowest market price because the peasant would be forced to settle his debt at a time convenient for the creditor.[147] This latter practice often meant that the creditor was also the purchasing merchant. In fact, when the peasant borrowed cash or grains, the contract often involved the obligation to sell his harvest to the creditor. While this type of à *livrer* contract could be considered within the bounds of capitalist transaction in the case of export agriculture – because there was some competition among the buying merchants – for the wheat growing peasant of the interior it often involved an extra-economic coercion mechanism where there was but one purchaser who was also the largest landlord of the area. Of course, the obligation to sell to the creditor, and the price differential thus imposed on the peasant meant that the nominal rate of interest – already usurious – was further augmented to the greater loss of the peasant. It was estimated by the Council of Economics that this rate could reach 25% a month.[148]

When the peasant was the debtor – purchaser, the practice was commonly known as 'harvest credit'.[149] This involved the purchasing of means of production or consumption items from village grocers or from retail merchants in nearby towns. Here the merchandise would be sold to the peasant with the promise of payment during the harvest season.[150] Although the transaction involved a usurious rate of interest, most of the profit resulted from high prices charged by the merchant agreeing to offer credit to the peasant.[151]

Another kind of usurious credit that the peasant could obtain was advanced against mortgaging of his property. Peasants entered into mortgage arrangements when the loan they required was large; this usually meant a sum of money to be used in purchasing land, expensive implements, or in a social event such as a wedding. During the 1920s commodity-producing peasants were motivated to attempt to extend their cultivated lands. This willingness to borrow in order to purchase land or tools was considered by certain commentators to be an important factor contributing to the wide extent of usury.[152] They thought that the economic conditions led peasants to speculate and when there was a crop failure, or a downturn in prices – as in 1926 – peasants could not fulfil their obligations. In fact most of the loans borrowed on mortgaging of property remained unpaid, and the creditors seized peasants' plots of land. Undoubtedly, this was an important mechanism resulting in the concentration of land, since the creditor was usually a large landlord who would take over the peasant's land and accept him as a tenant–sharecropper when he defaulted.[153] Describing this mechanism, the American attaché concluded that 'the prime enemy of agriculture is the usurer'.[154]

In this kind of mortgage-based debt transaction, the peasant would be advanced the sum of money against his property, with the interest already deducted. In addition, the value of his land would be reckoned by the creditor in an unequal relationship which meant that the conditions of borrowing were, in fact, much worse than indicated by the nominal rate of interest of 35% to 40%.[155] The sum of money that the creditor advanced was sometimes obtained in the legal credit market. Because he could show acceptable collateral to banks, the large landlord or the town money-capitalist could borrow at the legal rate of interest, and lend to the peasants at much higher rates.[156] This was apparently a widespread practice in 1927, in the Cilicia region. That conjuncture seems to have been particularly harmful for peasant growers; because even those who could borrow from the Agricultural Bank at normal rates of interest had to default on their payments. The Bank seized their property and auctioned off their animals; only after the government intervened was a reprieve granted to the debtors.[157] A similar conjuncture benefiting usurers seems to have obtained during the hazelnut crisis of 1929 in Trabzon. There too farmers had nowhere to turn to except usurers, and they had to forfeit some of their land.[158]

Usury was closely linked with share-cropping. Some of its forms – for example loans in kind against a portion of the output – were indistinguishable from more formal tenancy arrangements. Yet other forms – notably loans against mortgage – led to share-cropping type arrangements. As Bhaduri has argued persuasively, usury was an essential component of the share-cropping relationship.[159] Without the indebtedness which bound the peasant to the landlord, a share-cropping arrangement in a commodity-producing economy could not guarantee its own continuity: during good harvests and high prices the peasant had the opportunity to accumulate some of this surplus. If this surplus were to be used to purchase new means of production, the rise in productivity might disrupt the relationship between the tenant and the landlord because it would alter the relative shares out of the total product each was entitled to. Thus usury must be considered as an essential element in the stability of share-cropping and not merely an additional feature of that relationship.

More generally, however, usury or the articulation of peasant production and money capital is a major mechanism whereby value is extracted from the peasant sector by the capitalist sector.[160] This value extraction serves two purposes: on the one hand it enables the expansion and development of the capitalist sector; on the other hand it stifles the development potential of peasant agriculture. As was shown in Chapter 2, most of the agricultural sector consisted of subsistence-size holdings while a small minority were landless families. This structure indicates that most peasant families would need to supplement their income in years of bad harvest; in other words they would resort to usurer's capital – an eventuality which allowed for the exploitation of the peasant sector through interest-bearing capital. Ultimately, this interest either reached the capitalist agricultural sector, or it was mobilised by the banking sector to be employed in trade.

5.8 Conclusion

The most widely held opinion about the economic conditions of Turkey in the 1920s was that the shortage of capital constrained would-be entrepreneurs and the credit mechanism could not alleviate the situation.[161] Industrialists complained of the lack of a long-term credit market; small manufacturers had no access to banks which might advance medium-term working capital; farmers were perpetually in search of short-term credits to buy seed, to hire workers to collect the harvest, or to deliver crops to the market. Banks gained importance in this economy, not only because they were the suppliers of credit, but also since they created an accounting money through the credit mechanism. The supply of cash had been fixed and remained stable despite the growing monetisation of the economy and rising income. Banks, therefore, by allocating credits, could decide on the direction of monetisation. The institutional structure of the banking sector was such that those activities associated with foreign trade were favoured. Since these were the activities which yielded the highest rates of profit, it was normal that the banking sector would have a structure favouring them. In fact, peripheralisation is a process of structuration according to the needs of foreign merchant capital. In Turkey the credit market reflected this structuration, and contributed to the growth of merchant capital's domination over the entire economy.

Merchant's credit was more transparent in its intentions than was the banking sector. Here the attempt was to mobilise agricultural production toward export markets. Undoubtedly, merchant's credit also motivated the inception of commodity production in the less marketised areas of the country. This type of credit originated outside Turkey. In both its versions (export and import credit) foreign merchants granted payments facilities to Turkish merchants, who then transferred the extension of credit onto lesser merchants, which eventually reached the actual producer or the final consumer. Since there were profits to be made at each of these stages, we may conclude that it was the value extracted from the actual producer which, in various transformations, was incarnated as profits. If the transaction between foreign merchants and Turkish merchants – at the import or export stage – did not involve the quoting of an interest rate, this was because the prices already reflected and incorporated the interest payment. In other words the share of value extracted from the producer which was transferred abroad was transferred through the price mechanism. This was possible because the prices received by the producers and those formed at the consumption markets diverged grossly.

Usury was both a direct mechanism enabling the extraction of value from the peasant, and a means which created the necessary extra-market environment for merchants to purchase the peasant's product at low prices. Usury also made possible the continuation of the share-cropping relationships through creating debt bondage, thus precluding the transformation of the tenant into peasant proprietor. Money capital, in its manifestation as usury, constituted the most important mode of articulation between traditional peasant farming and the capitalist sector.

In addition to the creation of a peripheral structure, and the extraction of value, the credit mechanism also served to transmit the economic conjuncture in the capitalist centre to the farthest reaches of Turkish agriculture. When there were market problems in the centre, import credit to Turkish purchasers was abundant: when Turkey was expected to export more, credit was extended to producers. Yet when the conjuncture reversed in the centre, this expansion of credit abruptly ceased, leaving producers and merchants unable to recoup their losses. With the breakdown of the system at its centre in 1929, the entire credit mechanism came to a halt.

The credit system appears as a compact network which reflects the structure of the peripheral social formation. It would be wrong, however, to think of this network as an inessential veil concealing the real relations underlying monetary transactions. On the contrary, it is partly through this network that the structuration of the peripheral economy is made possible, the signals for the amount and the nature of commodity production are transmitted, and the control of distant markets over agricultural production is exercised. Money as a universal equivalent is a necessary component of any commodity producing economy; and the credit system an essential facet of a monetary economy. We have found that the analysis of the credit system in Turkey during the stage of its growing peripheralisation provides us with a perspective on the structure of the economy that both traces out its main contours, and focusses on the essential linkages allowing for its cohesion.

6 Conclusion

The specificity of a peripheral transition to capitalism lies in the domination of merchant capital during the process of transition. That the economy in question is integrated into the world economy through trade flows makes it imperative for capital in the centre to have recourse to mercantile activity for the purposes of expanding the scale of accumulation. While, however, merchant capital may be subordinate to the requirements of industrial capital in the centre, it becomes the unique carrier of market relations in the periphery. In that sense, the transformation of the periphery takes place under the direction of merchant capital.

By itself, merchant capital does not necessarily induce the development of capitalist relations as it does the expansion of commodity production. It is only during the internationalisation of productive capital that integration with the world economy directly requires the instigation of wage-labour relations. Merchant capital, however, does create the conditions for the development of capitalist relations by helping dissolve the traditional structure, and by making available to potential producers the means of realisation of their output. Yet this availability is highly partial, and it is in this sense that merchant capital may be said to condition the transition to capitalism in the periphery.

The case study we have undertaken provides an example of peripheral structuration during the domination of merchant capital. With the dissolution of their original social formations, peripheral areas cease to reproduce as isolated units. Components of the peripheral economy come to be orientated to world markets, thus becoming integral parts of the world division of labour. The processes of dissolution and structuration through integration characterise the long duration of peripheral transition to capitalism.

During the period of its domination in the periphery, the process of development of commodity production is shaped and coloured by merchant capital. The priorities and requirements of the valorisation of merchant capital provide an 'ether' in which economic activity finds shape and significance. It was this colouration which we tried to capture through the study of Turkey in the 1920s.

In all historical case studies, there are specificities and conjunctural peculiarities which have to be identified and isolated if a secular trend and a structure are to be discovered. In the case of Turkey in the 1920s there were factors which contributed to the transparency of the structure to be defined. The relative absence of controls on trade, and the lack of restrictions on foreign currency transactions were the principal factors. In addition, Turkey did not have a central bank, and, consequently, the government could not take monetary policy measures which would influence the operations of the banking sector. The world economic conjuncture of the 1920s was another contributory factor, by enabling the actualisation of a trend which had begun with the dissolution of the Ottoman system.

The peripheral state in its ideal form allows the transmission of economic information such that production in the periphery is accommodated into the world division of labour, and the law of value is universalised. In fact, the Turkish state in the 1920s was exemplary in its non-interventionist stance. The two significant economic policy measures taken by the Ankara government were the Law for the Encouragement of Industry and the abolition of the traditional tithe. The latter was a measure which increased the marketable surplus and the potential for marketisation. But, more significantly, this abolition was an indication that the new state had renounced the prerogatives of traditional political authority. The tithe had been the principal mechanism of the collection of surplus by Ottoman political authority, which, through this appropriation, obtained the means of politically establishing an economic order and a redistributive social hierarchy. This abolition, therefore, implied a new relationship between the state and the economy where the political level would no longer dominate the market. An autonomously functioning economy where the law of value reigned had begun to grow in importance ever since external trade became significant. It was in the 1920s that this economy finally emancipated itself from political control and even exercised a short-lived regency over it.

Encouragement of industry did not aim to introduce new parameters into the composition and the structure of the manufacturing sector; its impact was marginally to increase the profitability of one of the existing components of industry. Hence, government policy in the 1920s may not be considered as hindering or even modifying the peripheral integration of the Turkish economy. It is tempting to add that the state was most readily responsive to the demands of the merchants. We have mentioned the interaction between the Chamber of Commerce and the Ankara government, which was the most di-rect evidence of this responsiveness. The manufacturers, on the other hand, continually complained of their inability to voice their demands and griev-ances, and obviously found the Law for the Encouragement of Industry unsatisfactory, especially as they were confronted with a severe shortage of credit. The argument that government policies – whether intentionally or not – served to further the interests of merchant capital, is certainly defensible.

There was one specificity of the Turkish case which requires further discussion. In 1923, Turkey had been the scene of nine years of war, and its richest agricultural areas had been under occupation since 1919. Most of the toll on economic performance had been due to shortages of labour. War deaths and the mass post-war departure of minorities had decreased the labour force by three to four million individuals, mostly men of working age. The departing minorities – Armenians from Cilicia and the interior of Anatolia, and Greeks from Western Anatolia – had also left their properties behind, which represented a significant proportion of the cultivated area. As a result of the shortages of labour and abandonment of land, production in agriculture in 1923 fell below its 1913 level – the last normal year before the war. Thus, at least the period until 1926 could be considered as a period of reconstruction and recovery, when pre-war levels of activity were re-attained. There is no doubt that most of the growth performance in the 1923–29 period may be explained through this recovery. It would, therefore, be misleading to treat the output data, especially in agriculture, as signifying a real expansion of the economic base. What is significant, however, is that the recovery after the war should follow the same lines of integration and dissolution that were shaped in the Ottoman period. In other words, while the structure remained unchanged, a temporary setback was succeeded by the recovery of old economic connections, despite radical changes in the political environment. In this sense, then, both the growth of the output, and the cultivation of the land abandoned by departing populations, allowed for the repeated expression of the previous matrix of economic relations. It is because of the continuing relevance of the peripheral structure that we were able to discuss synchronic relations in a static framework.

The economic performance of the 1920s may be interpreted as the recovery of the secular trend of the Ottoman period, and the beginnings of a further movement along it. This trend came to an end with the world economy falling into a depression in the 1930s. With the depression, the movement of goods and money between Turkey and the world economy slackened; and the Turkish economy became more responsive to the incentives and directions provided by various government policies than to unremunerative world markets. The world conditions of commerce, and new government restrictions on the movement of goods and money, also caused a decline in the share of the surplus appropriated by merchant capital and trade-related interest-bearing capital. Nor was it possible in the 1930s to talk about a peripheral state in Turkey. In this etatist period, the state enjoyed more than a relative autonomy and implemented policies and industrialisation plans, which eventually promoted the interests of productive (industrial) capital. Both in the undertakings by the state and in policies relating to the private sector this prejudice was apparent. In the 1930s, then, the peripheral state and the domination of merchant capital were replaced by an etatism which undermined an already weakened merchant capital and implemented policies favouring industrial capital. The dismantling of the world economy during this period had caused many peripheral countries to resort to similar arrangements. Therefore, we may suggest that the period of peripheralisation lasting from the expansion of trade in the mid-nineteenth century to the Depression of 1929 had constituted a single trend line broken only by conjunctural disturbances. After the depression and the war, the world economy was reconstituted around the priorities of productive capital, where peripheral integration implied different bases of articulation.

In the peripheral formation agriculture plays a paradoxical role. Agricultural production, taken as a whole, remains longer under the domination of a traditional mode of labour organisation and land tenure, while the transformation of the urban economy under the impact of capitalist relations is much more rapid. At the same time, however, it is only through the availability of agricultural surplus that trade with the peripheral economy becomes attractive and profitable to merchant capital. Merchant capital also takes on an active role in furthering this profitability through expanding the reaches of the market. Incentives offered by the market induce the expansion of commodity production, and of the marketable surplus. Hence, while the most tenacious survivals of traditional organisation are found in the agricultural sector, the greatest potential for the expansion of commodity production is also contained there. During the long process of peripheral transition, agriculture will always be characterised by this paradoxical situation where the principal domain of merchant capital will co-exist with the survival of traditional forms. It was the attempt to gauge the respective proportions of commodity and subsistence production which led us to study the importance of marketisation. Commodity production for the market provided the index for the transformation of traditional agriculture under the domination of merchant capital.

In industry, the impact of the world market is felt through two channels. The first, which also enjoys historical priority, is the destruction of crafts, effected by the competition of imports. The second influence is more constructive: a modern manufacturing sector is formed to complement trade relations. In the periphery the composition of this sector is determined by the needs of export processing and by the domestic production of manufactured goods which are either impossible or too costly to trade. In both cases, the modern sector owes its existence to trade relations which create the demand for its output, and supply the technology for the production process. This dual structure of the manufacturing sector is one of the distinguishing traits of the peripheral economy. In the centre of the world economy, industry developed autonomously, and out of a transformation of rural manufactures. A similar transformation was precluded in the periphery because of the competition of imports, and the destruction of traditional manufacturing. Modern industry, on the other hand, was a transplantation which did not threaten the trade relation. Instead, during the period of functioning of the world economy, modern industry in the periphery developed to extend and to complement trade. In our analysis we attempted to assess the relative importances of surviving traditional crafts and newly implanted modern industry. An advantage of our period was that both of these structures could clearly be identified.

In the pre-Depression world economy, the two channels of economic articulation which transmitted the signals orientating the peripheral economy in the world division of labour were trade and banking. Merchant capital provided the markets and the universalisation of price signals. Loan capital, on the other hand, took a more active role in accommodating and encouraging the activities in which the periphery was to engage. In this sense banking was integrally linked to trade. For the Turkish economy in the 1920s, the credit mechanism provided the means for the extension of the monetised sector. It was only through this extension that markets could penetrate the traditional economy. Credit was advanced in large part to merchants and to commercial agriculture, and in both of these situations the expected outcome involved the expansion of the volume of trade. In its interest-bearing capacity, credit also provided a means for the valorisation of money capital within the traditional nexus of agriculture. Thus, both trade and banking were instrumental not only as mechanisms of articulation but also in their capacity as the media of circulation of value. They were the means by which value created in the non-capitalist sector could be introduced into the circuit of capital and thereby contribute to the accumulation of capital.

In our definition of the peripheral economy, the trade relation constituted the key element. In addition to trade, the credit system provided the means whereby market incentives could be followed and translated into production of commodities. These two complementary networks of trade and banking were financed to a large extent by foreign capital. This particular provenance of funds ensured that the Turkish economy as a whole was closely attuned to signals from the world economy. This harmony captures the meaning of a statement which was made earlier: peripheral areas are integrated into the world economy, fulfilling hierarchically determined tasks in the world division of labour. The nature of this subordination and its reflection in the peripheral structure has been the theme of this study.

Notes

Notes to Chapter 1

1 The main theoretical contributions are: Amin's *Unequal Development* (1976); Anderson's two-volume study (1974); Hindess and Hirst (1975); I. Wallerstein's seminal work (1974); Bradby (1975). For a useful survey see Foster-Carter (1976). For an application of the theory to the case of the Ottoman Empire see Islamoglu and Keyder (1977). Most of the empirical research within this paradigm can be found in the following journals: *Critique of Anthropology, Journal of Peasant Studies*, and *Economy and Society*.
2 Cf. R. Luxemburg (1951).
3 Cf. Amin (1974).
4 The discussion on merchant capital follows Kay (1975).
5 Cf. Wallerstein (1974).
6 Cf. Gordon (1978).
7 Cf. Kay (1975). I believe this is also the core of Emmanuel's important work (1972).
8 See Frank (1969).
9 For the text of the 1838 treaty, see Issawi (1966), pp. 38–41.
10 See Shaw (1975).
11 See Kurmus (1974), especially pp. 78–9.
12 See Blaisdell (1929) for a thorough account of this process.
13 See Quataert (1973).
14 Cf. Tezel (1974), and Pamuk (1977).
15 Cf. Keyder (1977).
16 Eldem (1970), Chapter 13.
17 Ibid. pp. 82–4.
18 See Koklu (1947).

Notes to Chapter 2

1 This view found its expression in the 1950s literature discussing alternative development strategies in agriculture vs. industry terms. The radical critique of these discussions pointed to the disadvantages of agricultural exports arguing from the perspective of worsening terms-of-trade for agricultural exporters. See Livingstone (1968) for the first type of discussion, and Singer (1950) for the classic statement of the terms-of-trade thesis.
2 Cf. Wallerstein (1974) where it is argued that bulk trade in non-luxury items is required to participate in the system division of labour. Thus integration presupposes a certain level of transactions, and may not be based simply on profitability.

3 In Barkan (1945). This survey was conducted by a parliamentary commission preparing a land reform act. Thus the figures reported here should reflect the situation in the early 1940s.
4 Ibid. p. 85 and p. 89.
5 Ibid. p. 85.
6 The 1927 Agricultural Census, findings of which can be found in T.C. Basvekalet Istatistik Umum Mudurlugu (1930). (This publication will hereafter be cited as 1930 Statistical Yearbook.) For these figures see p. 165.
7 Koylu (1957) pp. 129–37. This survey was conducted over a representative sample of farms selected from six different regions, and 21 provinces. Its findings relate to the mid-1930s.
8 This survey is reported in Nickoley (1924), p. 296.
9 In Koylu (1957), pp. 138–9.
10 'There are no large exploitations in the Eastern provinces', ibid. p. 139.
11 Kurmus (1974) p. 109.
12 Ibid. pp. 112–19.
13 Ibid. p. 105.
14 Varlik (1977), pp. 50–5.
15 Koylu (1957), p. 136.
16 Calculated from production figures in the Agricultural census, 1930 Statistical Yearbook, p. 173; and from foreign trade figures in T. C. Basvekalet Istatistik Umum Mudurlugu (1928) (hereafter cited as Foreign Trade Statistics 1928), pp. 3–4, 83–84.
17 Ibid. The figure obtained above is divided into the total number of families using appropriate weights. A rural family was composed of 5.2 persons. We use the 1927 Population Census figures in the Statistical Yearbook for 1930, p. 29; and rural population figures in the same source, p. 161.
18 By using the average yield figures in the 1927 Census. See Statistical Yearbook for 1930, p. 176.
19 Cf. OECD (1970) Table 7.
20 This usage and the definition of a 'middle farmer' can be found in my article with F. Birtek. See Birtek and Keyder (1975).
21 This argument is fully developed in Birtek and Keyder (1975).
22 See Koylu (1957), p. 120.
23 Barkan (1945), p. 89.
24 Ibid. The figure Barkan gives is 5.5%.
25 Koylu (1957), p. 139.
26 Statistical Yearbook for 1930, p. 164.
27 On the basis of a 4.5m non-farmer population. Total population in 1927 was 13.6m and farming population 9.1m. See the 1930 Statistical Yearbook, pp. 29 and 161.
28 Cf. Hines et al. (1936), vol. I, p. 242.
29 See Mitchell (1970) who analyses the land use pattern of the Turkish village in terms of Von Thunen's 'isolated estate'. We are arguing here that the Turkish village was not really isolated since there was a degree of commercialisation. See also Tokin (1934), p. 100.
30 Figures in the Agricultural Census. See Statistical Yearbook for 1930, p. 181
31 Mitchell (1970).
32 See Waismann (1928) for a discussion of wool production: pp. 535ff.
33 Ibid. p. 534. Also see Tokin (1934), pp. 45–6 for a discussion on the commercial significance of animal husbandry.

34 Described in Hines et al. (1936), vol. I, p. 261.
35 Foreign Trade Statistics quoted in Hines et al. (1936), vol. 2, p. 560.
36 See Tokin (1934), p. 46.
37 Bulutay, Tezel, Yildirim (1974), Tables 41A and 55A.
38 Tokin (1934), p. 77.
39 'In recent years an average of 20 to 30,000 seasonal labourers came from nearby
    provinces to work in Adana', quoted from a report by the Adana Chamber of
    Agriculture in Tokin (1934), p. 138. Also T. C. Ziraat Vekaleti (1935), p. 37,
    which gives the number as 30,000.
40 See the animal stock statistics in the 1927 Agricultural Census in Statistical
    Yearbook for 1930, pp. 178–81.
41 Tokin (1934) provides a description of this development, pp. 29–45.
42 Cf. Scott (1976) which relates this mode of production control to the particularities
    of the labour market.
43 This is equivalent to the non-revolutionary path described by Marx (1967), p.
    334, where 'the merchant establishes direct sway over production'.
44 See Aricanli (1976), Chapter 2.
45 This is the appropriate formula used by Sussnitzki (1966) to describe the allocation
    of economic activity among different ethnic groups.
46 See Avcioglu (1974), p. 1171; also Timur (1971), p. 96.
47 Childs (1922) in *Encyclopaedia Britannica* 12th edition, vol. XXX, p. 197. The
    article is entitled 'Armenia'.
48 Ibid. p. 202.
49 1930 Statistical Yearbook, pp. 53–4.
50 Pentzopoulos (1962), pp. 29–31.
51 Ladas (1932), p. 442.
52 Ibid. p. 438.
53 Vellay (1920), p. 37.
54 Pentzopoulos (1962), p. 102.
55 Ibid.
56 Pentzopoulos (1962), p. 99.
57 See Ladas (1932), p. 713.
58 Nickoley (1924), p. 296.
59 Calculated from the 1930 Statistical Yearbook, p. 165.
60 Avcioglu (1974), p. 1171.
61 Ladas (1932), p. 706; also pp. 560–1.
62 Tokin (1934), p. 191.
63 This is the argument advanced in Bhaduri (1973).
64 See Milli Iktisat ve Tasarruf Cemiyeti (1931) (hereafter '1931 Agriculture
    Congress'), vol. I, p. 1323, which talks about '2000 tractors which constitute our
    present stock'.
65 See Sarc (1948).
66 Calculated from the 1927 Agricultural Census.
67 See Hatiboglu (1936), p. 15.
68 See our calculations in section 2.8.4.
69 This classification follows the classification we utilised earlier in Birtek and Keyder
    (1975), p. 448.
70 See Eldem (1970), p. 63; and the 1927 Population Census in the 1930 Statistical
    Yearbook, p. 29.
71 Pentzopoulos (1962), p. 151.
72 Ibid. p. 156; and Ladas (1932), p. 662.

73 Pentzopoulos (1962), p. 155.
74 1930 Statistical Yearbook, p. 41.
75 Ladas (1932), p. 714.
76 Ibid. p. 713; Thrace absorbed 38% of the transferred population, and 42% were settled in the Western vilayets.
77 Ibid.
78 Text of the law in Mahoutdji (1937), p. 73, and in A.N.A. 867.50/120, pp. 233–4.
79 Ladas (1932), p. 561.
80 Cavdar (1971), p. 29.
81 See Timur (1971), p. 96. Also FFMA 342/195.
82 These figures are quoted in Hatiboglu (1936), p. 15. There is an ambiguity concerning the lump sum indemnity. Presumably it was granted in order to make up for the loss tractor owners suffered through rising prices of fuel.
83 See Hershlag (1968), pp. 47–51.
84 See Cin (1969) for Ottoman land law as it relates to ownership.
85 For this expansion, see Hirsch and Hirsch (1963), p. 376.
86 Cf. Okcun (1968), pp. 396–7.
87 In fact, the American trade commissioner, Gillespie, thought that improvement of transportation and the agricultural programme both aimed at reducing the import demand of Istanbul. This opinion, however, was ventured in 1924. ANA. 867.50/120, pp. 407–9.
88 Calculated from foreign trade statistics in Statistical Yearbook for 1930, pp. 321–2.
89 Woods (1924), p. 23, and Conker (1935), p. 107.
90 Rivkin (1965), Chapter 3, passim.
91 Kurmus (1974), Chapter 3 deals with the Izmir–Aydin railway, the most important line converging in Izmir.
92 Calculated from Eldem (1970), pp. 86–7.
93 See Earle (1924), passim.
94 See Novichev (1937) for the development of commodity production through the impact of railways.
95 Conker (1935), p. 107; Woods (1930), p. 18.
96 Calculated from the 1927 Agricultural Census, in Statistical Yearbook for 1930, pp. 166–73. all output figures in this section are calculated from this table.
97 Rivkin (1965) gives Ankara's 1920 population as 25,000 (p. 48). 1927 and 1935 figures are from the Population Censuses of the respective years.
98 Eldem (1970), p. 165.
99 Earle (1924).
100 The leading entrepreneurs in this scheme were the Namlizade, tobacco merchants. Woods (1930), p. 21.
101 Conker (1935), p. 108.
102 ANA 867.50/120, p. 233.
103 Conker (1935), p. 120.
104 Ibid.
105 All these figures are from Mahoutdji (1937), p. 48, compiled from German sources.
106 Woods (1924), p. 25.
107 Woods (1928), p. 21.
108 See my article Keyder (1976a) for a discussion of the importance of tithe in the Ottoman system. Also see Islamoglu and Keyder (1977).
109 For the legislative history of the abolition see Aricanli, Bademli, Ugurel (1974).

110 Programme of the government; 14 August 1923. In Arar ed. (1968).
111 Birinci Koy ve Ziraat Kongresi ed. (1938), pp. 62–70.
112 Cf. Birtek and Keyder (1975).
113 Ibid. p. 451.
114 Cumhuriyet Halk Firkasi (1931), speech of the Minister of Finance, p. 197.
115 Statistical Yearbook for 1930, p. 345.
116 Aktan (1950), p. 421; also Aricanli, Bademli, Ugurel (1974), p. 38.
117 Koklu (1947), p. 31.
118 Aktan (1950), p. 421.
119 Hatiboglu (1936), p. 77.
120 1930 Statistical Yearbook, p. 348.
121 Cumhuriyet Halk Firkasi (1931), p. 165; speech by Emin Bey (Sazak) deputy for Eskisehir.
122 1930 Statistical Yearbook, p. 253.
123 This price index of imports is the same as the one which will be used in Chapter 4. It has been prepared from a classification of imports into 30 commodity groups, and unit prices calculated by dividing total values into representative quantities.
124 Hirsch and Hirsch (1966), p. 454.
125 Lerdau (1959), p. 369.
126 Hatiboglu (1936), p. 67.
127 Ibid. p. 60.
128 Ibid. p. 55.
129 Bulutay, Tezel, Yildirim (1974), Table 8.2 C.
130 Ibid.
131 Calculated by Tezel (1975), p. 266.
132 Devlet Istatistik Enstitusu (1969) (hereafter cited as 1927 Industrial Census), p. 28.
133 Discussed in Ilkin and Keyder (forthcoming), section 3.
134 FFMA 424/167, dispatch from Istanbul dated 6 October 1925.
135 Hirsch and Hirsch (1963), p. 376.
136 1930 Statistical Yearbook, pp. 185 and 181; and Cavdar (1971), p. 29 for the number of cattle in 1920.
137 1930 Statistical Yearbook, p. 186.
138 Bulutay, Tezel, Yildirim (1974), Table 1. Cf. League of Nations (1930) which gives 650 kgs/hectare for 1926 (p. 64). In 1928 the world average was 1000 kgs/hectare; ibid.
139 Assuming that the production of Adana region denotes the total trend. 1930 Statistical Yearbook, p. 182.
140 1930 Statistical Yearbook, p. 177.
141 ANA 867.50/114, p. 18.
142 The Economist, 30 October 1926.
143 1930 Statistical Yearbook, p. 182. We assume that the production of the Izmir region represents the total trend.
144 1931 Agriculture Congress, vol. I, pp. 515–19.
145 Output figures in 1930 Statistical Yearbook, p. 183; export figures in 1931 Agricultural Congress, vol. I, p. 516.
146 Ibid. p. 511.
147 ANA 867.50/116, p. 13.
148 1930 Statistical Yearbook, p. 182.
149 Foreign Trade Statistics (1928), Part II, p. 14; and Agricultural Congress, vol. I, p. 612.

150 Foreign Trade Statistics (1928), Part II, p. 13.
151 1930 Statistical Yearbook, p. 182.
152 Ibid.; T. C. Ziraat Vekaleti (1935), p. 35, but see Aktan (1955) for a different set of estimates.
153 *The Economist*, 11 April 1925.
154 *The Economist*, 7 November 1925.
155 *The Economist*, 11 April 1925.
156 Ibid.
157 Agriculture Congress, vol. II, p. 2368.
158 1930 Statistical Yearbook, pp. 329–31.
159 Svennilson (1954).
160 Ibid.
161 1930 Statistical Yearbook, p. 177.
162 Foreign Trade Statistics (1928), pp. 89–90.
163 Agriculture Congress, vol. I, pp. 123–7; and pp. 10–15.
164 Ibid. p. 7.
165 League of Nations (1930), pp. 83–4.
166 *The Economist*, 11 April 1925 and 12 May 1928.
167 Agriculture Congress, vol. I, p. 7.
168 *The Economist*, 12 May 1928.
169 T. C. Basvekalet Istatistik Umum Mudurlugu (1929) (hereafter cited as Foreign Trade Statistics 1929), pp. 89–90.
170 1930 Statistical Yearbook, p. 177.
171 Tokin (1934), pp. 68–70.
172 1930 Statistical Yearbook, p. 177.
173 All output figures from the 1927 Agricultural Census in 1930 Statistical Yearbook, p. 173. All export figures in Foreign Trade Statistics (1928), pp. 83–4.
174 Agriculture Congress, vol. I, p. vi.
175 Agriculture Congress, vol. II, p. 2083.
176 Ibid., pp. 2082–4.
177 Ibid., pp. 2080–1.
178 British prices for wheat, barley, and oats are taken from Mitchell (1963), p. 489. The prices are given for hundred-weight (112 lb); we converted them to kg equivalents. French prices were found in INSEE (1966) *Annuaire Statistique* for 1966, p. 410. Turkish wheat prices in Bulutay, Tezel, Yildirim (1974), p. 229; rye, oats, and barley prices in the 1930 Statistical Yearbook, pp. 211–15. Exchange rates in ibid. pp. 247–8.

Notes to Chapter 3

1 We are arguing here that certain industrial developments should be viewed as resulting out of the integration into the world economy. See the article by Warren (1973) and Emmanuel's comment (1974). Keyder (1976) develops a theory to explain the industrialisation of the periphery.
2 See Saville (1969) and Mendels (1972).
3 Sarc (1940).
4 Cf. Resnick (1970) where a theory is developed explaining the decline of crafts in the periphery. Also see Tilly and Tilly (1971) where it is remarked that 'one of the greatest differences between the industrialisation of Western Europe and the developing countries of today stems from the earlier "proto-industrialisation" of the European countryside', p. 187.

5 For a discussion of rural handicrafts surviving because of high costs of transportation, see Hou (1963); see Hoselitz (1959) for a different approach.
6 Milli Iktisat ve Tasarruf Cemiyeti (1930) (Hereafter 'Industrial Congress'), p. 99.
7 See Cillov (1954) for a discussion of the 1913–15 and the 1927 censuses, and the differences in their coverages.
8 The 1913–15 census has been recently edited by Okcun (1970).
9 This census is reported in Eldem (1973), pp. 43–4; and also in ANA 867.50/120, pp. 348 ff.
10 1927 Industrial Census.
11 Ibid. pp. 7–8.
12 Ibid. p. 15. Cf. Cillov (1954).
13 The most complete compilation is in Hines et al. (1936), vol. 2, passim.
14 We are referring to Okcun (1971).
15 1927 Industrial Census, p. 9.
16 Osman (1935).
17 1927 Industrial Census, p. 56.
18 1930 Statistical Yearbook, pp. 50–1.
19 1927 Industrial Census, pp. 48–53.
20 Eldem (1973), p. 44.
21 1927 Industrial Census, p. 32.
22 Calculated from Eldem (1973), p. 44; and 1927 Industrial Census, pp. 31–45.
23 Eldem (1973), p. 44.
24 Calculated from ibid. and 1927 Industrial Census, p. 32.
25 Agaoglu (1939), p. 110.
26 Eldem (1973), p. 44.
27 Column 1 from 1927 Industrial Census, p. 11; column 2 from ibid. p. 9; column 3 calculated from data in ibid. p. 9.
28 1927 Industrial Census, p. 25.
29 Ibid. pp. 28–9.
30 Ibid. pp. 209–10.
31 ANA 867.50/120, p. 357.
32 In fact, prior to the exchange of populations, Greeks and Armenians owned an important proportion of local firms. For example, in 1915 in Izmir, 75% of the industrial capital was estimated to be furnished by Greeks, Jews, and Armenians. Out of the 3315 manufactories 2425 were Greek-owned; out of 22,000 labourers, 17,000 were Greek. Of course not all of these businesses ceased operation when their owners had to leave. The impact of the Greek departure however must have been considerable. See ANA 867.50/120 p. 349 for the figures.
33 Osman (1935), p. 210.
34 Column 1 calculated from ibid. p. 15; column 3 from ibid. p. 9; columns 2 and 4 calculated from the figures in columns 1 and 3.
35 See Table 3.1.
36 If this figure were 10%, it would give a Hoffmann ratio of 9.0, placing Turkey in the 1920s well behind Hoffmann's stage I. The same ratio for Chile in 1925 was 4.9, for Great Britain 1.5 (1924 figure), and for the U.S. 0.8. See Sutcliffe (1971), p. 35.
37 Hines et al. (1936), vol. II, p. 235.
38 1927 Industrial Census, p. 26.
39 Ibid. p. 27. The export ratio of carpets is calculated from Hines et al. (1936), vol. II, p. 232. Also see 1930 Industrial Congress, p. 108, which gives 70–80% as the ratio of exports.

40 1930 Statistical Yearbook, pp. 315–16.
41 1930 Industrial Congress, p. 39.
42 Ibid. p. 57.
43 Hines et al. (1936), vol. II, p. 221.
44 1927 Industrial Census, p. 26.
45 Hines et al. (1936), vol. II, p. 222.
46 1930 Industrial Congress, p. 62.
47 1927 Industrial Census, p. 27.
48 FFMA 424/190.
49 Pentzopoulos (1962), p. 163.
50 Ibid.
51 1930 Statistical Yearbook, p. 320.
52 FFMA 343/162.
53 1930 Industrial Congress, p. 133.
54 Hines et al. (1936) vol. II, p. 233.
55 1927 Industrial Census, p. 27.
56 FFMA 401/195.
57 Pentzopoulos (1962), p. 164.
58 Ladas (1932), p. 679.
59 Cf. Agaoglu (1939), passim, who deals with the same problem.
60 Okcun (1968), p. 10. The Minister of Economy in February 1923 declared that it
    was a total lie that 'we are against foreign capital'. He gave as evidence the recently
    accepted Chester concession for the government's friendliness toward foreign
    capital; ibid, p. 16. See also pp. 137, 151, 158; and p. 253 for Ataturk's own views:
    'We are ready to grant guarantees to foreign capital as long as it is ready to respect
    our laws.'
61 Ibid. pp. 74–5.
62 Ibid. pp. 426–7.
63 For the text of the law in English see Hershlag (1968), pp. 52–4.
64 1930 Industrial Congress, pp. 24, 25, 157 and 467.
65 Devlet Istatistik Enstitusu (1973), p. 166.
66 Hines et al. (1936), vol. II, p. 260.
67 Ibid. p. 269.
68 1927 Industrial Census, p. 12.
69 Calculated from Hines et al. (1936), vol. II, pp. 259–60.
70 Column 1 calculated from Hines et al. (1936) vol. II, pp. 259–60; column 2 from
    1927 Industrial Census, p. 15.
71 Hines et al. (1936), pp. 260–1.
72 Ibid. pp. 216–32; and p. 208 for the total number of establishments in each
    industry group. 1927 Industrial Census, pp. 9, 27 for 1927 figures.
73 The government constructed two sugar refineries in 1926 in Alpullu and Usak,
    with French aid (FFMA 424/152). Although their production increased to 8140
    tons in 1929, they only supplied 11% of the total domestic consumption, the rest
    being imported. See Hines et al. (1936), p. 235. Also see Sarc (1944).
74 Hines et al. (1936), p. 259.
75 Hershlag (1968), pp. 40–1.
76 See Tezel (1975), pp. 148–50 for a discussion of legislation concerning foreign
    capital.
77 *Turkiye Cumhuriyeti Merkez Bankasi Bulteni* (The bulletin of the Central Bank of
    Turkey), 1935, no. 16, p. 88.
78 Okcun (1971), Table 7, facing p. 126.

79 Ibid. passim.
80 Calculated from ibid. Table 7.
81 The preceding and the following 2 paragraphs constitute interpretations of the figures in Table 7, Okcun (1971).
82 In 1933 it was estimated that 94% of the electricity produced in Turkey originated in foreign companies' plants. See Sevki (1933), p. 40.
83 Okcun (1971), pp. 87–9.
84 Ibid. calculated from Table 7.
85 Ibid. Table 9, facing p. 146.
86 Ibid. p. 87.
87 FFMA 415/84.
88 FFMA 343/122; also see below Chapter 4 for the story of SITMAC, the Italian textile firm established in the Adana region.
89 *The Economist*, 7 July 1930.
90 Woods (1930), p. 27.
91 *The Economist*, 2 January 1926.
92 Okcun (1971), pp. 115–26.
93 Bulutay, Tezel, Yildirim (1974), Table 8.6 A.
94 Snurof (1970) mentions 12 bankruptcies in 1927, and 400 in 1928; p. 37.
95 Tahsin and Saka (1929), p. 107.
96 Ibid. p. 55.
97 Tahsin and Saka (1930), p. 122.
98 Ibid. p. 125.
99 Kurmus (1978).
100 Ibid.
101 Tahsin and Saka (1929), p. 48.
102 Tahsin and Saka (1930). pp. 126–7.
103 Tahsin and Saka (1929), p. 53.
104 Ibid. p. 52.
105 1930 Industrial Congress; reports on textiles, leather, chemical, and metal industries, passim.
106 1927 Industrial Census; calculated from p. 15.
107. Agaoglu (1939), pp. 105–6.
108. Ibid. p. 111.
109. Ibid. p. 122.
110. According to Tezel's (1975) Chapter 3 calculation, the 1927 urban population was below the urban population of the 1880s. The 1927 population census showed that Istanbul and Izmir's populations had declined by 40% between 1913 and 1927. There were rumours in 1927 that the census takers deliberately understated Istanbul's population because the Ankara authorities did not want too many deputies from the old capital. See ANA 867.50/133 dispatch from Grew.
111 Snurof (1970), pp. 57–8.
112 For a history of labour legislation in the 1920s, see Nedjide (1928), pp. 235–43.
113 Snurof (1970), pp. 59–69.
114 Calculated from 1927 Industrial Census, p. 15 and Foreign Trade Statistics (1928), Part I, 'Imports'.
115 Ibid. calculated as a proportion of total imports.
116 1927 population census figures, in 1930 Statistical Yearbook, p. 51.
117 Ibid. p. 189; and 1927 Industrial Census, p. 12.

Notes to Chapter 4

1 Calculated from national income estimates in Bulutay, Tezel, Yildirim (1974), Table 8.2 A: G.N.P. in current prices; and from trade figures in 1930 Statistical Yearbook, p. 310.
2 According to Eldem's (1970) estimates, the ratio of imports to national income between 1911 and 1914 was around 17%. See pp. 193 and 302. In 1934, the ratio had declined to 7%. See Ekonomi Bakanligi (1935), p. 46; and Bulutay, Tezel, Yildirim (1974), Table 8.2 A.
3 Yugoslavia's population was similar to Turkey's (13.9m in 1931 vs 13.6m in 1927), and her imports amounted to 7632 dinars or 305.3m TL in 1926. Turkey's imports were 234.7m TL. Bulgaria with a population of 5.5m imported 90.1m TL of goods. Brazil with a population of 41m (1931) imported 743.2m TL. All these figures are calculated from League of Nations (1932), pp. 16, 20–3, 195–9.
4 See Kindleberger (1973), Chapter 3. As Kindleberger says: the boom 'was neither general, uninterrupted nor extensive' (p. 58). Nevertheless most indicators showed signs of growth until 1929.
5 League of Nations (1931), p. 19.
6 Ekonomi Bakanligi (1935), p. 43.
7 Hines et al. (1936), p. 544.
8 Mears ed. (1924), p. 340.
9 Hines et al. (1936), p. 544.
10 See Tezel (1975), Chapter 6.
11 Koklu (1947), p. 24.
12 Tezel (1975), p. 117.
13 Calculated from 1930 Statistical Yearbook, p. 338.
14 Koklu (1947), pp. 24 and 31.
15 Tezel (1975), p. 119.
16 Column 1 from 1930 Statistical Yearbook, pp. 315–16. Column 2 from calculations by Kurmus (1978) which he kindly allowed us to see before publication.
17 See, for example, Istanbul Milli Sanayi Birligi (1928), and Istanbul Ticaret ve Sanayi Odasi (1928).
18 These rates of protection were calculated by Kurmus (1978).
19 Calculated from 1928 Foreign Trade Statistics, pp. 1–79.
20 Ibid. The output figure is the estimate offered by Bulutay, Tezel, Yildirim (1974), Table 5.2. Eldem estimates one third for 1927, see Eldem (1946), p. 70.
21 See section 3.4.
22 Calculated by Tezel (1975), p. 224.
23 Ibid.
24 1930 Statistical Yearbook, p. 315.
25 See Bulutay, Tezel, Yildirim (1974), Table 2.5.
26 1930 Statistical Yearbook, pp. 323–31.
27 See Houille (1937), pp. 51–3, for the causes of the trade deficit in 1929.
28 1930 Statistical Yearbook, pp. 322–34.
29 Ibid. p. 316.
30 Ibid.
31 Ibid. pp. 323–33.
32 In Turkey's case the index of unit import prices of cotton goods was 105 in 1925; 98 in 1926; and 86 in 1927 (1924 = 100). Calculated from ibid. pp. 325–31.

33 Tezel (1975), p. 218; 1930 Statistical Yearbook, pp. 314 and 316.
34 Hines et al. (1936), vol. 2, pp. 233, and 248, 249.
35 All figures in this table from 1930 Statistical Yearbook, pp. 319–20.
36 Ibid.
37 Foreign Trade Statistics (1928) and (1929). Tables under the heading: 'Imports and exports according to buying and selling countries.'
38 See the report by the Turkish Commercial attache in Trieste in 1931 Agricultural Congress, vol. 2, pp. 2294–2319.
39 Foreign Trade Statistics (1928), Part II, p. 123.
40 ANA 867.50/120, p. 386.
41 Woods (1928), p. 14.
42 ANA 867.50/117.
43 See Frank (1976). Using 1928 figures he finds that 'underdeveloped' regions exported $1490m more merchandise than they imported (p. 412).
44 This table is compiled from the figures in Foreign Trade Statistics, which are also reported in the 1930 Statistical Yearbook, p. 310.
45 Zihni (1932), p. 19; and Ali Iktisat Meclisi (Supreme Council of Economics) (1929), p. 8.
46 This was an advisory body of 24 members, half appointed by the government and half elected by various economic institutions such as chambers of commerce. Its composition indicates the dominance of members with commercial interest, usually connected with foreign capital and foreign trade. See ANA. 867.50/131 for details of institution and 867.50/137 for the composition of the first council.
47 Ali Iktisat Meclisi (1929), Ali Iktisat Meclisi (1930), *Turkiye Cumhuriyeti Merkez Bankasi Bulteni*, 1935, no. 16, pp. 86–9.
48 Hines et al. (1936), vol. II, p. 590. The exchange rate we are using in the calculation is the open market rate reported in 1930 Statistical Yearbook, p. 247.
49 See Ali Iktisat Meclisi (1930), p. 5; Zihni (1932), p. 18. Cf. FFMA 343/19, p. 11 for the effects of this new tax on foreign merchants.
50 Ali Iktisat Meclisi (1930), p. 6.
51 Zihni (1932), p. 19.
52 Column 2 is taken from 'value corrections' of the balance-of-payments tables prepared by the Supreme Council of Economics. See *Turkiye Cumhuriyeti Merkez Bankasi Bulteni*, 1935, p. 86. Column 3 is calculated by adding these corrections to the f.o.b. value of exports; column 4 gives the new figures for deficit based on revised export figures.
53 See for example Nahid (1931). Houille (1937), Zihni (1932) all of whom argue the monetarist thesis of a direct relationship between the depreciation of the currency and balance-of-payments difficulties. Also see Aydemir (1931), pp. 128 ff; and Geveci (1933) which started a polemic between monetarists and proto-Keynesians: cf. Tokin (1933).
54 1930 Statistical Yearbook, p. 336.
55 Foreign Trade Statistics (1928), part II, pp. 201, 210, 212.
56 Calculated from 1930 Statistical Yearbook, p. 336.
57 See Diaz (1970), pp. 290–91.
58 Calculated from GNP figures in Bulutay, Tezel, Yildirim (1974), table 8.2 A.
59 Calculated from *Turkiye Cumhuriyeti Merkez Bankasi Bulteni* (1935) no. 16, pp. 86–9.
60 For the treatment of the Ottoman Public Debt in Lausanne and later in the Paris convention, see Sitki (1935).
61 See Ali Iktisat Meclisi (1930), p. 5.
62 Ibid., Table facing page 8.

63 See Chapter 5 infra for a discussion of these topics.
64 *Turkiye Cumhuriyeti Merkez Bankasi Bulteni* (1934), no. 11, p. 103.
65 'The amount making up private hoards [of gold] is indefinitely described as enormous.' See Ravndal's dispatch in 1924, ANA 867.50/120, p. 442.
66 FFMA 342/195, report by Banque Nationale Française du Commerce Exterieur, dated 31 October 1925.
67 Unit prices for each of the 30 categories in foreign trade statistics were calculated, and indexes prepared for each of the 30 categories. Then using 1926 and 1928 value weights, we calculated a composite price index for exports and imports, taking 1926 and 1928 as 100. (When quantities are given in more than one unit—e.g. in the group 'vehicles and ships', tons are given as well as numbers – we utilised the same rate of conversion for all the years.) The data are to be found in 1930 Statistical Yearbook, pp. 321–34, for the years 1923–28, and in Foreign Trade Statistics (1929), pp. 1–159 for the year 1929.
68 League of Nations (1931), p. 125.
69 League of Nations (1945), p. 85.
70 See Table 4.10 for sources.
71 See Emmanuel (1972) for a convincing theory arguing the inequality of exchange due to differing remunerations of labour.
72 See Foreign Trade Statistics (1928), p. 228. In 1928, during those four months, exports were on the average 18.5m TL, as opposed to the 14.5 monthly average for the year. In 1927, the figures were 16m and 13m TL, respectively.
73 Ali Iktisat Meclisi (1928), pp. 100–1.
74 1930 Statistical Yearbook, p. 247.
75 867.5151/12 dispatch by Bristol, dated 16 March 1927. The law was published on 1 March 1927.
76 1930 Statistical Yearbook, p. 247; annual depreciation calculated by us.
77 ANA 867.50/120, p. 424.
78 See Houille (1937), p. 45 for a discussion of this crisis.
79 See Ilkin (1973) for the history of the negotiations and legislation leading to the formation of the Central Bank.
80 See 1930 Statistical Yearbook, p. 253.
81 Hines et al. (1936), vol. 2, p. 540.
82 Ibid.
83 Tahsin and Saka (1929), p. 76.
84 Okcun (1971), p. 148.
85 Ibid.
86 Ilkin (1971), contains a full history of this company.
87 See, for example, the report by the American vice-consul, Edwin A. Plitt, 'Selling to the Turk', in ANA 867.50/120, pp. 412 ff. Also *The Economist*, 2 January 1926, where English manufacturers of automobiles are asked to enter the Turkish market of medium priced cars.
88 Ali Iktisat Meclisi (1928), p. 70.
89 Ibid.
90 Ibid. p. 61, Also see Chapter 5, below.
91 Hines et al. (1936), vol. 2, p. 539.
92 Ibid.
93 Tahsin and Saka (1930), p. 139.
94 Hershlag (1968), p. 40.
95 Okcun (1971), p. 93.
96 Woods (1930), pp. 29–30.

97   Okcun (1971), p. 93.
98   1931 Agricultural Congress, vol. II, p. 2290.
99   Tahsin and Saka (1930), pp. 136–7. See also FFMA 342/229, for the distribution of foreign insurance companies: 12 were French, 11 German, and 9 British.
100 Okcun (1971), p. 146.
101 Ali Iktisat Meclisi (1928), p. 73.
102 Hines et al. (1936) vol. 2, p. 324.
103 1931 Agricultural Congress, vol. 2, p. 2291.
104 *The Economist*, 26 June 1926. The most lucrative line for Turkish ship-owners was Istanbul–Mersin, yet they were unable to provide a dependable connection. See FFMA 343/19, p. 45.
105 Zihni (1932), p. 120.
106 Hines et al. (1936), pp. 322–4.
107 Calculated from Hines et al. (1936), pp. 325–7.
108 See, for example, Woods (1928), p. 14 where it is reported that at least five sixths of the tobacco exported to Trieste was processed there and re-exported. For hazelnuts, and how Turkish produce was mixed with inferior quality Italian produce, see 1931 Agricultural Congress, vol. 1, p. 514.
109 1931 Agricultural Congress, vol. 2, p. 2296.
110 See Vellay (1920), p. 44.
111 See *The Economist*, 26 June 1926; and 7 August 1926.
112 Pentzopoulos (1962), p. 210.
113 *The Economist*, 26 June 1926.
114 Ahmet Serif, who in the etatist period became an important official, in 1931 Agricultural Congress, vol. 2, p. 2291.
115 Ibid. pp. 2291–2.
116 Hines et al. (1936), vol. 2, pp. 344–97.
117 1931 Agricultural congress, vol. 2, p. 2289.
118 It seems that Turkish shippers had accumulated considerable profits during the war of liberation, through arms contrabandage. A German ex-officer reported in 1923 that Turkish shippers who had enjoyed high profits carrying munitions did not wish to give up their sources of income; and therefore applied to the government for support against foreign competition. It was as a result of this application that the government granted Turkish shippers 500,000 TL of credit to purchase new ships in England, which in turn attracted new entrepreneurs to the field. Report translated in ANA 867.50/123.
119 Ali Iktisat Meclisi (1928), p. 73.
120 Hines et al. (1936), vol. 2, pp. 325–6.
121 A. H. Basar cited in Avcioglu (1968) pp. 195–6.
122 Hines et al. (1936), vol. 2, p. 363.
123 Ali Iktisat Meclisi (1928), Hines (1936), vol. 2, Basar (1929), Ethem (1929), passim.
124 Ali Iktisat Meclisi (1932), pp. 38–42.
125 Ali Iktisat Meclisi (1932), p. 9.
126 Ibid. p. 30.
127 Ali Iktisat Meclisi (1928), p. 75.
128 Ibid. See also *The Economist*, 13 March 1926.
129 Ali Iktisat Meclisi (1932), p. 9.
130 *The Economist*, 30 October 1926.
131 Yet, as early as September 1923, the American attaché Ravndal reported to Washington: 'It is believed that the government would consider an application on

the part of a bona fide foreign concern for a concession for a free port in Constantinople.' ANA 867.50/111.
132 *The Economist*, 30 October 1926.
133 Ali Iktisat Meclisi (1932), p. 49.
134 See Woods (1928), pp. 20–1; also FFMA 343/7.
135 *The Economist*, 30 October 1926.
136 Nezihi (1932), p. 230.
137 Hines et al. (1936), vol. 2, p. 536.
138 Nezihi (1932), p. 16.
139 Sanda ed. (1935), p. 39.
140 *The Economist*, 18 September 1926.
141 Sanda ed. (1935), pp. 346–7.
142 Nezihi (1932), p. 282.
143 Sanda ed. (1935), p. 587.
144 Ibid. pp. 139 and 601.
145 Ibid. p. 40.
146 Ibid. pp. 639 ff.
147 Ibid. pp. 640 and 647. See also FFMA 343/7.
148 Nezihi (1932), p. 276.
149 Sanda ed. (1935), p. 409.
150 1931 Agricultural Congress, vol. 2, pp. 2077–9.
151 FFMA 343/19, Rapport sur la situation économique et financière de la Turquie, p. 9.
152 Ibid. p. 7.
153 Okcun ed. (1968), pp. 90–4 contain a report prepared for the National Association of Turkish trade, an unofficial organisation of merchants, on the Regie. Also see ibid. pp. 359–62 for a contemporary journal article advocating the abolition of the Regie. Cf. *The Economist*, 11 April 1925.
154 FFMA 343/19, p. 38.
155 FFMA 343/213; October 1929 report from the consul at Trabzon.
156 In this connection, cf. the report by Banque Nationale Française du Commerce Exterieur in October 1925: 'Hier, les questions du commerce maritime. . . semblaient être abandonnées a l'initiative étrangère. Aujourd'hui le Ture entend s'employer dans ce domaine, prendre une part plus active dans la mise en valeur de son pays.' See FFMA 342/185.

Notes to Chapter 5

1 Cf. de Brunhoff (1973), Chapter 2.
2 See Eldem (1970), p. 228; and Koklu (1947), p. 8.
3 Ibid.
4 See Kitapci (1939), Chapter 1; and Koklu (1947), pp. 8–10.
5 Koklu (1947), pp. 11–17.
6 Ibid. p. 24.
7 ANA 867.50/120, p. 442.
8 ANA 867.50/112; and FFMA 342/185.
9 ANA 867.50/120, p. 442; in 1929, coins amounted to 8.5m TL, see Koklu (1947), p. 29.
10 Ilkin (1973), pp. 19–21.
11 See Woods (1928), p. 7; and *The Economist*, 11 February 1928.
12 See the Annual Report by Sir Herbert Lawrence in *The Economist*, 30 June 1928.

13 Hines et al. (1936), vol. 3, p. 141.
14 Hines et al. (1936), vol. 3, p. 52.
15 Column 1 from Bayar (1939), p. 83; Column 2 from Hines et al. (1936), vol. 3, p. 48; and Tahsin and Saka (1929), p. 94.
16 Tahsin and Saka (1930), pp. 64, and 94.
17 Column 1 from Bayar (1939), p. 91; Column 2 figures are estimates as explained in the text; Column 3 equals total deposits minus savings deposits.
18 If demand deposits are considered to consist entirely of commercial accounts; then Column 1 accords with the traditional definition of money supply. Column 2 was calculated using the figures in Table 5.2
19 Bulutay, Tezel, Yildirim (1974), Table 8.2.A.
20 Bayar (1939), pp. 23–4.
21 Colocotronis (1934), pp. 39–41.
22 For the history of this bank, see T. C. Ziraat Bankasi (1938), and T. C. Ziraat Bankasi (1964); for its foundation see Quataert (1973).
23 See Biliotti (1909); Delaygue (1911).
24 See Okcun (1973), pp. 6–60.
25 Ibid. pp. 158–65.
26 Ibid. p. 18.
27 Colocotronis (1934), pp. 51–2; and Bayar (1939), p. 41.
28 ANA 667.50/120, p. 470.
29 Okcun (1973), p. 6.
30 ANA 867.50/120, p. 471.
31 FFMA 400/36, 400/39, 400/40.
32 FFMA 400/111, dispatch from the French Embassy in Istanbul to Paris.
33 ANA 867.50/126, from the consul in Izmir to the Embassy dated 10 July 1925.
34 FFMA 400/114, dated 19 January 1925.
35 Hines et al. (1936), vol. 3, p. 45.
36 Ilkin (1973); FFMA 401/133, 135, 136, 139, 143; all dispatches – dated 1927 and 1928 – dealing with Turkish government's endeavours to finance a central bank.
37 See Colocotronis (1934), p. 30.
38 FFMA 401/173, dispatch from the French consul in Adana, dated 7 January 1929.
39 Okcun (1973), pp. 82–156.
40 Calculated from 1930 Statistical Yearbook, pp. 278–306.
41 Okcun (1975), p. 474.
42 ANA 867.50/119.
43 Bayar (1939), pp. 79, 81, 84, 101.
44 FFMA 401/121, dispatch from the ambassador, dated 11 May 1927.
45 FFMA 401/158, from the consul in Samsun, dated 13 October 1928.
46 FFMA 401/131, dated 26 November 1927.
47 Silier (1975), p. 493.
48 Calculated from 1930 Statistical Yearbook, p. 264. For its activity see Okcun (1973), p. 81.
49 Reported by the French Embassy, 2 February 1926 and 26 March 1926; FFMA 401/49 and 401/55.
50 *Journal d'Orient*, 26 March 1926; reported in FFMA 401/62.
51 ANA 867.51/383, 384, 390, 392.
52 FFMA 401/174.
53 Suvla (1933), p. 39.
54 Calculated from section 5.2.
55 FFMA 401/161, dated 17 October 1928.

56 ANA 867.50/120, p. 480.
57 Report from the American commercial attaché' George Bie Ravndal; ANA 867.50/120, pp. 480–1.
58 Okcun (1973), pp. 74–5.
59 See Table 5.2; Bayar (1939), pp. 91–2.
60 Hines et al. (1936), vol. 3, p. 51.
61 ANA 867.50/120, p. 477.
62 Ibid.
63 FFMA 342/185, Banque Nationale Française du Commerce Extérieur, Bulletin Hebdomadaire du 24 October 1925: 'L'aspect économique du nouveau régime en Turquie.'
64 Ibid.
65 Hines et al. (1936), p. 55.
66 ANA 867.50/120, p. 478.
67 FFMA 400/153, report dated 23 April 1925.
68 FFMA 400/114, report dated 19 January 1925.
69 FFMA 401/158, dispatch from the consul in Samsun, dated 13 October 1928.
70 ANA 867.50/126, dispatch from the consul in Izmir, dated 10 July 1925, p. 39.
71 FFMA 401/158, 13 October 1928.
72 FFMA 343/199.
73 *The Economist*, 14 July 1928.
74 FFMA 342/214.
75 FFMA 415/56.
76 Ibid. See also 401/158, dispatch from the consul in Samsun, dated 13 October 1928.
77 FFMA 415/56, dispatch from the consul in Adana, dated 17 March 1927.
78 Calculated from the following sources: Hines et al. (1936), p. 48, for the credits of the Ottoman bank; Ibid. p. 50, for the credits of the Bank of Salonica. All other foreign banks are assumed to have extended a volume of credit equal to that of Bank of Salonica. Total credit advanced by foreign banks thus adds up to approximately 185m TL. To this we add the credits extended by Turkish banks, of which 70% was extended by the Agricultural and the Business Banks, see Bayar (1939), p. 140.
79 1930 Statistical Yearbook, pp. 262 and 271.
80 Hines et al. (1936), vol. 3, p. 48.
81 1930 Industry Congress, p. 164.
82 Ibid. p. 288.
83 Ibid. p. 69.
84 Ibid. pp. 71, 152.
85 Ibid. p. 23.
86 Ibid. p. 69.
87 Our information on the credit mechanisms of the Agricultural Bank is derived from Atasagun (1939) and (1943).
88 Cf. ANA 867.50/120, p. 468.
89 Atasagun (1943), p. 125.
90 Atasagun (1939), p. 230.
91 Ibid. p. 277.
92 Ibid. pp. 245, 349.
93 Ibid. p. 235.
94 Ibid. p. 240.
95 Atasagun (1943), p. 125.
96 Atasagun (1939), p. 349.

97 Atasagun (1943), p. 130.
98 Atasagun (1939), p. 251.
99 Ibid. pp. 256–7.
100 Atasagun (1943), p. 130.
101 Atasagun (1939), p. 126; Atasagun (1943), p. 368.
102 Atasagun (1943), pp. 369, 371.
103 Ibid. p. 324.
104 Atasagun (1939), p. 219.
105 Atasagun (1943), p. 264.
106 Atasagun (1939), p. 286.
107 Ibid. p. 287.
108 Okcun (1973), p. 37.
109 Atasagun (1943), pp. 136–7.
110 ANA 867.50/120, p. 480.
111 Hines et al. (1936), p. 53.
112 Bayar (1939), p. 115; Hines et al. (1936), p. 59. ANA 867.50/120, p. 480.
113 1930 Statistical Yearbook, p. 271.
114 ANA 867.50/120, p. 424.
115 Woods (1924), p. 34.
116 ANA 867.50/120, p. 479.
117 Bayar (1939), p. 134. We are still following the example of the Business Bank.
118 Bayar (1939), pp. 129–30.
119 Hines et al. (1936), vol. 3, p. 55.
120 Bayar (1939), pp. 136–7.
121 1930 Statistical Yearbook, pp. 262, 271.
122 Woods (1924), p. 34; ANA 867.50/120, p. 478.
123 FFMA 342/195, Report by Banque Nationale Française du Commerce Extérieure, dated 31 October 1925.
124 Woods (1928), p. 16.
125 1930 Statistical Yearbook, p. 248.
126 *The Economist*, 12 May 1928.
127 Effimiadis (1936), vol. II, p. 176.
128 Woods (1928), p. 16.
129 Ibid. pp. 35–41.
130 *The Economist*, 14 July 1928.
131 FFMA 342/214, dispatch from the French consul in Adana, dated 4 November 1926.
132 Ali Iktisat Meclisi (1928), p. 61.
133 FFMA 343/158, dispatch from the French consul in Bursa describing a deal between an exporting merchant and local weavers.
134 FFMA 343/199, dispatch from the French consul at Trabzon.
135 ANA 867.5211/32, letter from Ligget and Myers Inc. to the US Secretary of State, dated 18 June 1925.
136 FFMA 417/146, dispatch from the French consul in Adana, dated 1 September 1926.
137 *The Economist*, 8 August 1925.
138 FFMA 424/203, dispatch from the French consul in Adana, dated 10 December 1926.
139 FFMA 417/146.
140 Ibid.
141 Ibid.

142 ANA 867.50/120, p. 481.
143 Usury is termed transitional because it denotes the articulation of money capital with a pre-capitalist formation, and contributes to the dissolution of the pre-capitalist system.
144 1931 Agriculture Congress, vol. 2, p. 2463; and Tokin (1932), p. 31.
145 Ibid. p. 2464; Ali Iktisat Meclisi (1928), p. 60.
146 1931 Agriculture Congress, vol. 2, p. 2450.
147 FFMA 342/185.
148 Ali Iktisat Meclisi (1928), p. 61.
149 1931 Agriculture congress, vol. 2, p. 2464.
150 Ibid. p. 2452.
151 Ibid. p. 2453.
152 Ibid. p. 2464.
153 Tokin (1932), p. 32.
154 ANA 867.50/120, p. 238.
155 Ibid, and 1931 Agricultural Congress, vol. 2, p. 2453.
156 FFMA 415/56.
157 Ibid.
158 FFMA 343/199.
159 Bhaduri (1973).
160 See Gutelman (1974), pp. 53–66, the chapter entitled 'Le mode de production parcellaire.'
161 Cf. *The Economist*, 13 March 1926: 'with a little more capital there is no doubt that many industries would spring up'. Also see FFMA 342/185: 'La question des capitaux et de l'organisation de credit est une des principales préoccupations actuelles en Turquie ... L'insuffisance de capitaux de roulement se fait ... sentir', from a report by Banque Nationale Française du Commerce Extérieur, dated 24 October 1925.

References

Documentary sources

ANA American National Archives. Documents concerning economic conditions in Turkey, 1919–29, are contained in volume 353, rolls 56–71, but especially 56 and 60. These were consulted in microfilm form.

FFMA French Foreign Ministry Archives. Original documents at Quai d'Orsay. The relevant files are 342–343 (Situation économique, dossier general); 349–350 (Finances, dossier general); 400–401 (Etablissement financiers, dossier general); 415 (Agriculture); 417 (Commerce) 424 (Industrie).

Printed material

Agaoglu, S. (1939), *Kucuk Sanat Meseleleri Turkiyede ve Baska Yerlerde* (Problems of artisanal production in Turkey and other places), Istanbul.

Aktan, R. M. (1950), 'Agricultural Policy of Turkey, with Special Emphasis on Land Tenure', UC Berkeley PhD thesis in Agricultural Economics.

 (1955), *Turkiyede Ziraat Mahsulleri Fiyatlari* (Prices of agricultural products in Turkey), Ankara.

Ali Iktisat Meclisi (1928), *Hayat Pahaliligi* (The high cost of living), Publication A-2, Ankara.

 (1929), *Turkiyenin Tediye Muvazenesi, 1926* (Turkey's balance of payments, 1926), Publication A-3, Ankara.

 (1930), *Turkiyenin Tediye Muvazenesi, 1927* (Turkey's balance of payments, 1926), Publication A-4, Ankara.

 (1932), *Turkiyenin Liman Hizmetleri ve Limanlarimizin Inkisafini Temin Edecek Tedbirlere dair Teklifler* (Port facilities in Turkey and proposals concerning the improvement of our ports), Publication A-9, Ankara.

Amin, S. (1974), *Accumulation on a World Scale*, New York.

 (1976), *Unequal Development*, New York.

Anderson, P. (1974), *Passages from Antiquity to Feudalism*, London.

 (1974), *Lineages of the Absolutist State*, London.

Arar, I. (1968) ed., *Hukumet Programlari, 1920–1965* (Government programmes, 1920–65), Istanbul.

Aricanli, A. T. (1976), 'The Role of the State in Social and Economic Transformation of the Ottoman Empire, 1807–1918', Harvard University PhD thesis in Economics.

Aricanli, T. R. Bademli, I. Ugurel (1974), 'The Abolition of Asar', mimeographed, Cambridge, Massachusetts.

Atasagun, Y. S. (1939), *Turkiye Cumhuriyeti Ziraat Bankasi, 1888–1939* (The Agricultural Bank of the Turkish Republic, 1888–1939), Istanbul.

(1943), *Turkiye'de Zirai Borclanma ve Zirai Kredi Politikasi* (Agricultural borrowing and agricultural credit policy in Turkey), Istanbul.

Avcioglu, D. (1968), *Turkiye'nin Duzeni* (The order of Turkey), Ankara.

(1974), *Milli Kurtulus Tarihi, c. 3* (The history of national liberation, vol. 3), Istanbul.

Aydemir, S. S. (1931), *Cihan Iktisadiyatinda Turkiye* (Turkey in the world economy), Ankara.

Barkan, O. L. (1945), 'Ciftciyi Topraklandirma Kanunu ve Turkiye'de Zirai Bir Reformun Ana Meseleleri' (Law for the Endowment of the Farmer with Land and Fundamental Problems of an Agricultural Reform in Turkey), in *Istanbul Universitesi Iktisat Fakultesi Mecmuasi*, vol. 5. nos. 1–2.

(Basar), A. Hamdi (1929), *Istanbul Limani*, Istanbul.

Bayar, T. (1939), *La Turkiye Is Bankasi*, Montreux.

Bhaduri, A. (1973), 'A Study in Agricultural Backwardness under Semi-Feudalism', in *Economic Journal*, vol. LXXIII, no. 329.

Biliotti, A. (1909), *La Banque Impériale Ottomane*, Thèse, Paris.

Birinci Koy ve Ziraat Kalkinma Kongresi (1938) ed., *Turk Ziraat Tarihine Bir Bakis* (A glance at Turkish agricultural history), Istanbul.

Birtek, F. and C. Keyder (1975), 'Agriculture and the State: An Inquiry into Agricultural Differentiation and Political Alliances, the Case of Turkey', in *Journal of Peasant Studies*, vol. 2, no. 4.

Blaisdell, D. C. (1929), *European Financial Control in the Ottoman Empire: A Study of the Establishment, Activities, and Significance of the Administration of the Ottoman Public Debt*, New York.

Bradby, B. (1975), 'The Destruction of Natural Economy', in *Economy and Society*, vol. IV, no. 2.

Brunhoff, S. de (1973), *La Politique Monétaire: Un essai d'interprétation marxiste*, Paris.

Bulutay, T., Y. S. Tezel and N. Yildirim (1974), *Turkiye Milli Geliri, 1923–1948* (National income of Turkey, 1923–48), Ankara.

Cavdar, T. (1971), *Milli Mucadele Baslarken Sayilarla Vaziyet ve Manzarai Unumiye* (The overall situation in numbers on the eve of the national struggle), Istanbul.

Childs, W. J. (1922), 'Armenia', in *Encyclopedia Britannica*, 12th edition, vol, XXX, London.

Cillov, H. (1954), 'Turkiye'de Sanayi Istatistikleri' (Industrial statistics in Turkey), in *Istanbul Universitesi Iktisat Fakultesi Mecmuasi*, vol. 16, nos. 1–4.

Cin, H. (1969), *Miri Arazi ve Bu Arazinin Mulk Haline Donusmesi* (Crown land and its transformation into private property) (Ankara: Ankara Universitesi yayini).

Colocotronis, C. V. (1934), *L'organisation bancaire des pays balkaniques et les capitaux etrangers*, thèse, Paris.

Conker, O. (1935), *Les Chemins de Fer en Turquie et la Politique Ferroviare Turque*, Paris.

Cumhuriyet Halk Firkasi (1931), *Ucuncu Buyuk Kongre Zabitlari* (Proceedings of the Third Great Convention), Istanbul.

Delaygue, L. (1911), *Essai sur les Finances Ottomanes*, Thèse, Paris.

Devlet Istatistik Enstitusu (1969), *Sanayi Sayimi 1927* (Industrial Census 1927), Ankara.

(1973), *Fifty Years of Social and Economic Development in Turkey*, Ankara.

Diaz Alejandro, C. (1970), *Essays on the Economic History of the Argentine Republic*, New Haven.

Earle, E. M. (1924), *Turkey, the Great Powers and the Bagdad Railway: A Study in Imperialism*, New York.

Effimiadis, Y. (1936), *Cihan Iktisadi Buhrani Onunde Turkiye, c. 2* (Turkey in front of the world economic crisis), Istanbul.

Ekonomi Bakanligi (1935), *Dis Tecim* (Foreign trade), Ankara.

Eldem, V. (1946), 'Les progrès de l'industrialisation en Turquie', in *Revue de la Faculté des Sciences Economiques de l'Université d'Istanbul*, vol. 8, nos. 1–4.
  (1970), *Osmanli Imparatorlugunun Iktisadi Sartlari Hakkinda Bir Tetkik* (Research on the economic conditions of the Ottoman Empire), Ankara.
  (1973), 'Mutareke ve Milli Mucadele Yillarinda Osmanli Imparatorlugunun Ekonomisi' (The economy of the Ottoman Empire during the armistice and the national struggle), paper presented to the seminar on the Economic History of Turkey at Hacettepe Universitesi, June 1973.
Emmanuel, A. (1972), *Unequal Exchange: A Study in the Imperialism of Trade*, London.
  (1974), 'Myths of Development versus Myths of Underdevelopment', in *New Left Review*, 85.
Ethem, M. (1929), *Der Hafen von Stambul und Seine Organisation*, Leipzig.
Foster-Carter, A. (1976), 'From Rostow to Gunder Frank: Conflicting Paradigms in the Analysis of Underdevelopment', in *World Development*, vol. IV, no. 3.
Frank, A. G. (1969), *Capitalism and Underdevelopment in Latin America: Historical Studies of Chile and Brazil*, New York.
  (1976), 'Multilateral Merchandise Trade Imbalances and Uneven Economic Development', in *Journal of European Economic History*, vol. 5, no. 2.
Geveci, T. (1933), *Para Dusmesi Tediye Muvazenesi Bozuklugunun Sebebi midir Neticesi midir?* (Is the depreciation of money cause or effect of the balance-of-payments deficit?), Istanbul.
Gordon, D. M. (1978), 'Up and Down the Long Roller Coaster', in *U.S. Capitalism in Crisis*. Published by the Union of Radical Political Economics, New York.
Gutelman, M. (1974), *Structures et Réformes Agraires, Instruments pour l'Analyse*, Paris.
Hatiboglu, S. R. (1936), *Turkiye'de Zirai Buhran* (Agricultural crisis in Turkey), Ankara.
Hershlag, Z. Y. (1968), *Turkey, The Challenge of Growth*, Leiden.
Hindess, B. and P. Hirst (1975), *Pre-capitalist Modes of Production*, London.
Hines, W. D. et al. (1936), *Turkiye'nin Iktisadi Bakimdan Umumi Bir Tetkiki 1933–1934, c.1, c.2, c.3* (A general economic survey of Turkey, 1933–34, vols. 1–3), Ankara.
Hirsch, E. and A. Hirsch (1963), 'Changes in Agricultural Output Per Capita of Rural Population in Turkey, 1927–1960', in *Economic Development and Cultural Change*, vol. 11, no. 4.
  (1966), 'Changes in Terms of Trade of Farmers and their Effect on Real Farm Income Per Capita of Rural Population in Turkey, 1927–1960', in *Economic Development and Cultural Change*, vol. 14, no. 4.
Hoselitz, B. F. (1959), 'Small Industry in Underdeveloped Countries', in *Journal of Economic History*, vol. XIX, no. 4.
Hou, C.-M. (1963), 'Economic Dualism: The Case of China 1840–1937', in *Journal of Economic History*, vol. XXIII, no. 3.
Houille, R. (1937), *La Politique Monetaire de la Turquie*, Paris.
INSEE (1966), *Annuaire Statistique* for 1966, Paris.
Ilkin, S. (1971), 'Turkiye Milli Ithalat ve Ihracat Anonim Sirketi' (Turkish National Import and Export Company), in *M.E.T.U. Studies in Development*, vol. 1, no. 2.
  (1973), 'Turkiye Cumhuriyeti Merkez Bankasinin Kurulusu' (The Foundation of the Turkish Central Bank). Paper presented at the Seminar on the Economic History of Turkey, June 1973.
  (1978) ed., *Turkiye Iktisat Tarihi Uzerine Arastirmalar* (Research on Turkish economic history), Ankara.
Ilkin, S. and C. Keyder (forthcoming), *The Chester Concession*, Ankara.
Islamoglu, H. and C. Keyder (1977), 'Agenda for Ottoman History', in *Review*, vol. 1, no. 1.
Issawi, C. (1966) ed., *The Economic History of the Middle East 1800–1914*, Chicago.

Istanbul Milli Sanayi Birligi (1928), *Milli Sanayimizin Himayesi* (The protection of our national industry), Istanbul.
Istanbul Ticaret ve Sanayi Odasi (1928), *Yeni Gumruk Tarifesi Hakkinda Istanbul Ticaret ve Sanayi Odasinin Tetkikati* (Investigations of the Istanbul Chamber of Commerce and Industry on the new customs tariff), Istanbul.
Kay, G. (1975), *Development and Underdevelopment: A Marxist Analysis*, London.
Keyder, C. (1976a), 'The Dissolution of the Asiatic Mode of Production', in *Economy and Society*, vol. 5, no. 2.
  (1976b), *Azgelismislik, Emperyalizm, Turkiye* (Underdevelopment, imperialism, Turkey), Istanbul.
  (1977), 'Ottoman Finance and Economy, 1881–1914', paper delivered at the Hacettepe Conference on the Economic History of Turkey, June 1977.
Kindleberger, C. P. (1973), *The World in Depression, 1929–1939*, Berkeley.
Kitapci, T. (1939), *L'Histoire Monétaire de la Turquie*, Thèse, Dijon.
Koklu, A. (1947), *Turkiye'de Para Meseleleri* (Issues of money in Turkey), Ankara.
Koylu, K. (1957), *Ziraat Iktisadi: Zirai Isletmecilik, c.1* (Agricultural economics: agricultural management, vol. 1) Ankara.
Kurmus, O. (1974), *Emperyalizmin Turkiye'ye Girisi* (Penetration of imperialism into Turkey), Istanbul.
  (1978), '1916 ve 1929 Gumruk Tarifeleri uzerine Bazi Gozlemler.' (Some observations on 1916 and 1929 tariff systems), in Ilkin (1978).
Ladas, Stephen P. (1932), *The Exchange of Minorities: Bulgaria, Greece and Turkey*, New York.
League of Nations (1930), *International Statistical Year-Book, 1929*, Geneva.
  (1931), *The Course and Phases of the World Economic Depression*, Geneva.
  (1932), *Statistical Yearbook of the League of Nations 1931/32*, Geneva.
  (1945), *Economic Stability in the Post-War World*, Geneva.
Lerdau, E. (1959), 'Stabilization and the Terms of Trade', in *Kyklos*, vol. XII, fasc. 3.
Livingstone, I. (1968), 'Agriculture vs Industry in Economic Development', in *Journal of Modern African Studies*, vol. 6, no. 3.
Luxemburg, R. (1951), *The Accumulation of Capital*, London.
Mahoutdji, A. E. (1937), *Die Turkische Agrar- und Industriepolitik nach dem Kriege*, Leipzig.
Marx, K. (1967), *Capital*, vol. 3, New York.
Mears, E. G. (1924) ed., *Modern Turkey: A Politico-Economic Interpretation, 1908–1923*, New York.
Mendels, F. (1972), 'Proto-industrialization: The First Phase of the Industrialization Process', in *Journal of Economic History*, vol. XXXII, no. 2.
Milli Iktisat ve Tasarruf Cemiyeti ed. (1930), *Sanayi Kongresi 1930* (Industrial Congress 1930), Ankara.
  (1931), *1931 Birinci Ziraat Kongresi* (1931 First Agricultural Congress), Ankara.
Mitchell, B. R. (1963), *Abstract of British Historical Statistics*, Cambridge.
Mitchell, W. A. (1970), 'Turkish Villages in Interior Anatolia and Von Thunen's Isolated State: A Comparative Analysis', in *The Middle East Journal*.
Nahid, H. (1931), *Les Symptomes de la Crise Turque et son Remède*, Paris.
Nedjide Hanum (1928), 'La Législation Ouvrière de la Turquie Contemporaine', in *Revue des Etudes Islamiques*, vol. I, no. 2.
Nezihi, H. (1932), *50 Yillik Oda Hayati* (50 Years of the Chamber), Istanbul.
Nickoley, E. F. (1924), 'Agriculture', in Mears ed., *Modern Turkey* (1924).
Novichev, A. D. (1937), 'The Development of Commodity-Money and Capitalistic Relations in Turkish Agriculture', in Issawi ed., *The Economic History of the Middle East 1800–1914* (1966).

OECD (1970), *Capital and Finance in Agriculture*, Paris.

Okcun, G. (1968) ed., *Turkiye Iktisat Kongresi, 1923-Izmir: Haberler, Belgeler, Yorumlar* (Economic congress of Turkey, 1923 – Izmir: News, documents and commentaries), Ankara.

ed. (1970), *Osmanli Sanayii; 1913, 1915 Yillari Sanayi Istatistiki* (Ottoman industry; industrial statistics of 1913 and 1915), Ankara.

(1971), *1920–1930 Yillari Arasinda Kurulan Turk Anonim Sirketlerinde Yabanci Sermaye Sorunu* (The issue of foreign capital in the Turkish incorporated companies established in the 1920–30 period), Ankara.

(1973), '1909–1930 Yillari Arasinda Turkiye'de Bankacilik Alaninda Kurulan Anonim Sirketler' (Incorporated companies founded in Turkey in the field of banking in 1909–30) paper presented to the seminar on the Economic History of Turkey at the Hacettepe University, June 1973.

(1975), '1909–1930 Yillari Arasinda Turkiye'de Bankacilik Alaninda Kurulan Anonim Sirketler' (Banking corporations established in Turkey, 1909–30), in *Turkiye Iktisat Tarihi Semineri*, ed. O. Okyar.

Okyar, O. ed. (1975), *Turkiye Iktisat Tarihi Semineri* (Seminar on Economic History), Ankara.

Osman, M. (1935), 'L'Artisanat en Turquie', in *Revue International du Travail*, Geneve.

Pamuk, S. (1977), 'Osmanli Imparotorlugunda Yabanci Sermaye' (Foreign capital in the Ottoman Empire). Paper delivered at the Hacettepe Conference on the Economic History of Turkey, June 1977.

Pentzopoulos, D. (1962), *The Balkan Exchange of Minorities and its Impact upon Greece*, Paris.

Quataert, D. (1973), '*Ottoman Reform and Agriculture in Anatolia 1876–1908*'. Unpublished PhD dissertation University of California, Los Angeles.

Resnick, S. A. (1970). 'The Decline of Rural Industry under Export Expansion: A Comparison among Burma, Phillippines, and Thailand, 1870–1938', in *Journal of Economic History*, vol. XXX, no. 1.

Rivkin, M. D. (1965), *Area Development for National Growth: The Turkish Precedent*, New York.

(Sanda) Avni, H. ed. (1935), *Istanbul Ticaret ve Sanayi Odasi, 1926–1927–1928 Seneleri Faaliyet ve Muamelatina ait Umumi Rapor* (General Report on the 1926–28 activity of the Istanbul Chamber of Commerce and Industry), Istanbul.

Sarc, O. C. (1940), 'Tanzimat ve Sanayiimiz' (Reformation of 1839 and our industry), in *Tanzimat*, vol. 1.

(1944), 'The Demand for Sugar in Turkey', in *Revue de la Faculté des Sciences Economiques de l'Université d'Istanbul*, vol. 5, no. 3–4.

(1948), 'Changes in the Rural–Urban Distribution of the Turkish Population', in *Revue de la Faculté des Sciences Economiques de l' Université d'Istanbul*, vol. 9, nos. 1–2.

Saville, J. (1969), 'Primitive Accumulation and Early Industrialization in Britain', in *Socialist Register 1969*.

Scott, C. D. (1976), 'Peasant Proletarianization and the Articulation of Modes of Production: The Case of Sugar Cane Cutters in Northern Peru, 1940–69', in *Journal of Peasant Studies*, vol. 4. no. 2.

Sevki, M. (1933), 'Elektrikli Turkiye' (Turkey with electricity), in *Kadro*, no. 13.

Shaw, S. (1975), 'The Nineteenth Century Ottoman Tax Reforms and Revenue System', in *International Journal of Middle East Studies*, vol. VI, no. 1.

Silier, O. (1975), '1920'lerde Turkiye'de Milli Bankaciligin Genel Gorunumu' (The overall appearance of national banking in Turkey in the 1920s), in *Turkiye Iktisat Tarihi Semineri*, ed. O. Okyar.

Singer, H. W. (1950), 'The Distribution of Gains Between Investing and Borrowing Countries', in *American Economic Review Proceedings*, vol. 40.

Sitki, I. (1935), *La Répartition de la Dette Publique Ottomane par les Traités de Paix*, Paris.

Snurof, A. (1970), *Kemalist Devrim ve Turkiye Proletaryasi* (Kemalist Revolution and Turkish Proletariat), Istanbul.

Sussnitzki, A. J. (1966), 'Ethnic Division of Labour in the Ottoman Empire', in Issawi ed., (1966).

Sutcliffe, R. B. (1971), *Industry and Underdevelopment*, London.

Suvla, R. A. (1933), *La Banque Centrale de la République Turque*, Lausanne dissertation, Istanbul.

Svennilson, I. (1954), *Growth and Stagnation in the European Economy*, Geneva.

Tahsin, H. and R. Saka (1929), *Sermayenin Sirketlerdeki Hareketi* (The movement of capital in firms), Istanbul.

(1930), *Sermaye Hareketi* (The movement of capital), Istanbul.

Tezel, Y. S. (1974), 'Notes on the Consolidated Foreign Debt of the Ottoman Empire', in the *Turkish Yearbook of International Relations 1972*.

(1975), 'Turkish Economic Development, Policy and Achievements', PhD thesis, Cambridge University.

Tilly, C. and R. Tilly (1971), 'Agenda for European Economic History in the 1970's', in *Journal of Economic History*, vol. XXXI, no. 1.

Timur, T. (1971), *Turk Devrimi ve Sonrasi 1919–1946* (Turkish revolution and its aftermath 1919–46), Ankara.

Tokin, I. H. (1932), 'Turkiye Koy Iktisadiyatinda Borclanma Sekilleri' (Forms of borrowing in Turkish village economy), in *Kadro*, no. 3.

(1933), 'Turk Parasinin Kiymeti ve Kemmiyetciler' (The value of Turkish currency and the quantity theorists), in *Kadro*, nos. 16–17.

(1934), *Turkiye Koy Iktisadiyati* (Village economics of Turkey), Ankara.

T. C. Basvekalet Istatistik Umum Mudurlugu (1928), *Dis Ticaret Istatistikleri 1928* (Foreign Trade Statistics 1928), Ankara.

(1929), *Dis Ticaret Istatistikleri 1929* (Foreign Trade Statistics 1929), Ankara.

(1930), *1930 Istatistik Yilligi* (Statistical Yearbook, 1930), Ankara.

T. C. Ziraat Bankasi (1938), *Ziraat Bankasinin Elli Senelik Hayati ve Faaliyeti* (Fifty years in the life and activities of the Agricultural Bank), Ankara.

(1964), *Yuz Yillik Teskilatli Zirai Kredi* (A hundred years of organised agricultural credit), Ankara.

T. C. Ziraat Vekaleti (1935), *Pamuk ve Pamukculuk Hakkinda Raporlar* (Reports on cotton and cotton-growing), Ankara.

Varlik, B. (1977), *Emperyalizmin Cukurova'ya Girisi* (Penetration of imperialism into Cilicia), Ankara.

Vellay, C. (1920), 'Smyrna, A Greek City', in *Hellas and Unredeemed Hellenism*, American Hellenic Society Publications, New York.

Waismann, I. A. (1928), 'L'économie rurale de la Turquie', in *Revue des Etudes Islamiques*, vol. IV.

Wallerstein, I. (1974), *The Modern World-System*, New York.

Warren, B. (1973), 'Imperialism and Capitalist Industrialization', in *New Left Review*, 81.

Woods, H. (1924), *Report on the Economic and Commercial Conditions in Turkey, April 1924*, London.

(1928), *Report on the Economic and Commercial Conditions in Turkey, May 1928*, London.

(1930), *Economic Conditions in Turkey*, London.

Zihni, B. (1932), *La Balance des Comptes de la République Turque*, Paris.

Index